Flashes of Merriment

Flashes of Merriment

A Life Remembered

by

Bob Scott

ISBN 0-9647066-5-2

Printed in the United States of America

Published by Wellstone Press
295 East Main, Ashland, Oregon 97520

Edited by Jonah Bornstein

Cover painting from Louis Leopold Boilly's "Thirty-Six Faces of Expression" courtesy of Paris/SuperStock. Cover design by Jonah Bornstein. Back cover photo by Jim Craven of the Medford Mail Tribune. Title page illustration by Campbell Grant from *Twisted Tales from Shakespeare*.

ACKNOWLEDGEMENTS

I want to acknowledge the following spiritual teachers and astrologers, some of whom I have been blessed to know personally, and without whom my stay on this planet would have been infinitely less rewarding: Paramahansa Yogananda, Edgar Cayce, Marcus Bach, Ram Dass, Philip Wheelwright, and Rev. Doctor Tom Costa—the principal formulators of my thoughts and psyche. My personal teachers: George Silva, Renée Hatfield, Bob Hoffman, Charles Montgomery, Mary B. Buckner, Elizabeth Long, Maxine Asher and Bill McGarey. Lastly, the great cosmic connections: Jeff Mayo, Sidney Omarr, Lynn Palmer, Katherine de Jersey, Robert Hand, Doris Chase Doane, Robert Chaffee and Diane Ronngren. And all my clients, who have taught me humility, compassion and love.

I give my sincere gratitude to those without whom this book would not be: my impeccably intuitive editor and publisher, Jonah Bornstein and his editorial assistant Darrah Danielle; my patient, professional assistant, Sharon Spalding. And to my caregivers *extraordinaire*, Jennifer Moon, Sharon Spalding, Toni Wyndearo, Janell Donalson, Twylaa Jacobson, Mary Mahoney Henie, and Cylone Moore. Finally, I thank my neighbor and great friend Terttu Harker for all her love and care.

All chapter epigrams from the works of William Shakespeare.

Contents

Foreword

Everyone has a story. I am telling mine.

My life has not been extraordinary in any usual respect. I have not taken great physical risks, such as climbing Mt Everest, nor have I achieved fame. But there are points that have a unique quality which may prove exemplary of the way a person can use his talents and abilities—so that at the end of one's life he might look back and say, "This was satisfactory."

My goal in this book is to describe my life in a mixture of specific events and broad strokes that capture the essence of how I have lived. I do not recall everything vividly enough to claim that the events are absolutely correct. Time and space render much of life indistinct and sometimes confused. But what I describe is basically the way it was.

Stories, even of a life, sometimes take on a life of their own. They tell us who we are and what we have done. An autobiography reflects the truth of experience. If I have embellished and exaggerated, it has been in the interest of underlining the truth of the experience—not to pretend something was that was not.

Background

You will learn in some detail about my experiences as an infant and child actor. The period after the films reveals the reactions of a young man growing up and coming to the realization that his talents and desires were not geared toward acting.

In high school, I determined that I wanted to pursue an academic life. This was to be a short-lived desire, for I gave academia up when I found I could not relate well enough to the academic society of the university to become comfortable as a teacher. Instead of spending my life in front of classrooms and at faculty meetings, I became a professional librarian.

After 16 years in the profession, I became oriented to the metaphysical and spiritual worlds. This was not to negate academic pursuits. It simply resonated with my own being and what I knew I had to do. This new approach to living rewarded me many times over for the rest of my life. My outlook on reality was completely altered, and I became an astrological counselor.

Looking back, I see that my search for meaning in the universe began in high school as it does for so many adolescents. I wanted to find out the "why" of how life worked and thought science might provide the answer. However, neither physics nor chemistry seemed able to answer the most basic questions of existence.

In my late twenties, I again began to seek an answer to this question and came to realize that only in metaphysics do we get into the ultimate answers of why creation operates as it does. Everything else seems to fall short. The spiritual explains the hows and whys of the universe much more satisfactorily than the pursuit of knowledge of the world.

I believe this search for meaning in existence underlies all aspects of the story of my life. The many paths I have walked, from childhood through adulthood, have led me to where I am now.

Cerebellar Ataxia

Few easily escape trauma and illness. When we scan our lives we see what role these experiences play on the course of our lives. At the age of 18, my body began to shake. These tremors, much later diagnosed as Cerebellar Ataxia, played a major part in my life's direction. As a young man, the tremors slowed down my physical reactions. My frustration was no small thing. Intellectually, I knew I should have more ability to do things like typing and sports. However, over a relatively short period of time, I overcame this handicap. It did not prevent me from leading a full life, that is, until it hit me hard at age 60.

For most of my life, the doctors, unable to find a physical cause for the tremors, determined that my symptoms were the result of a neurotic condition. I underwent twenty years of psychotherapy, hoping to alleviate the undetermined neurosis that caused my symptoms. I was no more neurotic than the next guy. I am sure, if neurosis made neurotics shake, we'd have a nation of shaking people. In fact, due to this misdiagnosis, I spent forty-three years believing I was neurotic, blaming myself for my shortcomings. Only now do I know that no one is to blame at all.

My spiritual orientation to existence has proved a blessing. I am sure everything in the universe happens for a reason. I've been led to different people and disciplines in my life that would prepare me for the crisis that I now face. I understand that some people would be shocked when faced with a debilitating disease. But spiritual experiences have taught me to accept what is happening and to glory in what I've experienced in life. This attitude has served me well. I believe I am less frustrated by this disease than I would have been if I had been oriented to the mundane.

This does not mean I am entirely happy with all other aspects of my life. It does not mean that certain events don't cause me pain. If given the opportunity and foresight I have now, I certainly would have approached love and friendship differently. As you will learn, I didn't grow up with the tools to create or be open to intimacy. I was married for eight years. I've had a few other intimate relationships with women, but none lasting longer than the eight years of my marriage. My one regret is that I did not have a more sustaining relationship.

Still, I know I've accomplished a great deal. I know there has been meaning to my life. If not, I would not have had the peak spiritual experiences which you will read about in this book. I believe I have lived for a specific purpose, and I want to share this.

When asked, "What is your reaction to the statement that *life is a joyous experience*"? I believe that if *you* believe you are on the right path, you will be joyous. Some say life is not a joyous experience. They are discouraged, defeated by the movement of their lives. They say, "Life is so painful, I can't wait to get off the wheel." These people have a lot of evolving to do. My reply is that they'd better rethink that belief, because they'll never get off the wheel with that attitude.

As of this writing, I am 62, and a new disease has been diagnosed. It attacks the body's muscles and lays them to waste. It is ALS (amyotrophic lateral sclerosis), also known as Lou Gehrig's Disease. Each disease feeds off the other. The ataxia is located in the cerebellum, which is the CPU of the body, coordinating, among other things, muscular motion. In my case, it's like a radio station that keeps fading in and out. Through decimation, the ALS creates a situation where even when the radio station is coming in strong, there are no muscles to receive the signal. The body cannot respond.

It is my firm belief that what I am is not my body, nor is my life the secular and judgmental summation of the society in which I have lived. I am the spiritual summation of the experiences described in this book—the people, places and things that make up a life.

Bob Scott
Spring, 1999

Success is to be measured not so much by the position that one has reached in life, as by the obstacles he has overcome while trying to succeed.
—Booker T. Washington

Chapter I

THE BOY WHO DID NOT CRAWL

At my nativity
The front of heaven was full of fiery shapes
Of burning cressets, and at my birth
The frame and huge foundation of the earth
Shak'd like a coward.
　　　—*Henry IV, Part I*

Reports of the events and subsequent consequences surrounding my delivery into this Planet have never been defended, and they will not be so now, as I only intend to describe them to the best of my knowledge. A life is not to be defended but to know. We can only do so in accordance with the vagaries of our memories.

Now God the Father may be of the opinion that a baby is a sign that the world should go on, but I'm not at all sure that my father shared that opinion. More than once I have been told that, but for a full moon, I would not be here. I have it on some authority that I was born on an exact full moon—think what the consequences of that are for you, dear reader! It happened one Thursday night in October of 1936 at 9:57 p.m. in California's Hollywood Hospital. It was two days before Halloween. According to my mother's baby book, it was trick or treat. I never got treated, and I never crawled, which was quite a trick, because this is a necessary stage in an infant's development. It could have been an early sign of Cerebellar Ataxia, the condition that particularly defines my existence today.

I believe my grandmother De Kay was the first to know of my arrival. As I have two half-sisters, Patricia Marilyn and Harriet Ann (my father's), it sort of follows that everyone was rooting for a boy. I know my mother was. Throughout gestation, she meditated on an image of a baby boy whom I mysteriously came to resemble! The power of the mind is truly incredible! My grandparents were probably shocked that their eldest daughter would have any child by my father; he was not their favorite son-in-law. This may have had some bearing on my being my mother's only child.

My entrance into this world was supervised by Doctors Glen English and E.J. Krahulik. Two doctors attended her because my mother was over forty. This proved to be good medical foresight, as it was a Caesarian delivery. My mother had taught ballet while carrying me. Pre-natal astrological work that I had done in my forties suggested activity-induced complications during her first three months of pregnancy. Who knows whether this may be the origin of motor problems in my later life? It was later discovered that I was born with a small cerebellum, the seat of coordination. At any rate, with two doctors on the job, I arrived safely—at least from a medical point of view. I wonder if any baby truly arrives safely, either through the birth canal or by Caesarian section.

I was named Robert Edward after my cousin, Bob Stauff, and my mother's eldest brother, Bob de Kay. The Edward was after her father, Richard Edward de Kay. It was a good choice, I suppose, for Robert means "famous" and Edward "one who guards his own prosperity or fortune."

Some fortune! These were the latter years of the Depression. My father was a Reemployment Representative for the Southern California WPA—a noble if not lucrative or secure position, despite the policies of FDR. I have mentioned that my mother taught ballet in Hollywood. Not too lucrative a profession at a time when eating and dancing were in conflict. Robert Edward was about to change material fortune and prosperity for both, not dramatically, perhaps, but certainly sufficiently enough to allow him to appreciate, in later years, the abundance of ethical, moral and spiritual fortune and prosperity he inherited from those two very admirable souls—his parents.

My mother, Loys Euniece de Kay, was strikingly beautiful. As a child I reveled in her long auburn hair. Born in Willow Creek, Montana in 1897 to a daughter of pioneers who had crossed the Great Salt Lake, and a father of French descent, she was the eldest of seven children. Before she met my father, she had married twice, the last to a pianist and opera singer she had known in her silent film days. She had become a ballerina through dancing which she had undertaken at a young age to help overcome spinal meningitis, a terrible disease she contracted at age 11; she danced professionally, but eventually found teaching dance more compatible with her personality. By the time she married my father in 1932, a film career had been abandoned and she had founded the *Screen Artist* casting directory, which later became the *Players*.

My father, George Harrison Scott, was a handsome, silver-haired insurance broker. Born in Beef Slough, Wisconsin in 1888 to a Scottish mother who died shortly thereafter and a father of Welsh descent. He was one of three children and was raised by an aunt and uncle in the mining country of Minnesota. A succession of jobs had finally brought him to Southern California in the early part of the century. It was there that he encountered my mother, working in the same building on Hollywood Boulevard. They met one afternoon on the stairs, became acquainted and fell in love, or a reasonable facsimile thereof, and six years later....

I was born into an uncaring, but well intended household, where no one had any idea of what parenting meant. My mother was so excited about having a child after two childless marriages that she tried to make up for her lack

of parenting skills by overindulging and completely ignoring the reality of my being and my needs as a child.
My father was so unconsciously angry at having another
child that what parenting skills he had developed with
my sisters were totally subverted.

Chapter 2

A MIXED BAG

Confusion now hath made his masterpiece.
—*Macbeth*

I guess anyone's childhood is a mixed bag, but details of what goes into the mix of each bag differ. Something extraordinary marks each one, and that is why I am going to tell you about my first relatively innocent experiences in this world.

It was a nurturing place and time to begin my journey. I have fond recollections of Hollywoodland and our sumptuous home at 2910 North Beachwood Drive. It was an imposing old stone and wood house, well built, roomy and palatial. There were eight rooms plus a huge vaulted living room with a too-seldom used fireplace (my father did not like to empty the ashes). And that was upstairs! Down the inside stairwell off the kitchen hall was a four-room apartment with an outside entrance which my parents rented out. Adjacent to that was what became my secret place, a labyrinthine basement built to accommodate termites. In prohibition days, there were tales of bathtub gin. In my early school days it was occupied by curious and hookey-playing youths who wanted to play ghosts. In later years we played strip poker, and held clandestine and direful-for-adults meetings in the round and spooky stone wine cellar where "No Grownups Allowed" was posted on the door.

*My sister Harriet,
happy with her
troubled little
brother.*

Many are the hours I spent playing on the ivy covered hillside that was our spacious backyard. Pirates and cowboys and injuns would ride or walk through the loam and leaves in pursuit of freedom and dreams, down the paths on the hill to the little duckpond (that never worked like a waterfall as it should have), and the giant stone steps that dropped into the reality and security of the patio. I loved that duckpond, and when I became able, would wade in it frequently, avoiding the yucca and the sawgrass that grew on the hill around it. Because I liked this pond someone gave me a duck. It occupied the pond during the day but at night waddled in through the front door and into our large fireplace—its nightly boudoir. I named the duck Scorchy Burns, and this loud, white quack was with us from my fourth birthday until I started school.

My father rented our house from an old actor named George Irving, for the reasonable sum of $75 a month. It was situated in a real estate development called Hollywoodland, almost directly beneath and three or four miles from the big letter sign that now reads "HOLLY-WOOD" (the "land" was removed from the sign in the '60s). The north end of Beachwood Drive is located near the hill on which this sign stands, and was just dirt at the time. Here there were riding stables where we rented horses, cantered around or even shot home movies. About a mile south of the stables the road became paved. This juncture was marked by a park and a tennis court, where games of all sorts were played, square dances were held, and reluctant fathers tried to teach their sons to play ball, while remaining perfectly still—their enthusiasm as flexible as a dried stick.

The neighborhood was a paradise for raising kids, and a cultural haven for adults—especially if you were involved in the arts or connected to the movie colony. Next door lived Marie Wilson, in whose yard I often frolicked when a toddler; a director named Gill lived in the large white house on the other side of us. Up Beachwood Drive lived Miklos Rosza and other musicians and artists of note; on a street to the south of us leading up toward Mulholland Drive, James M. Cain wrote *The Postman Always Rings Twice*, and advised my mother on a novel that she was writing. The place was filled with creative energy and a refined lifestyle—an energy that presented unique opportunities to any kid lucky enough to be born into it.

My most intense memories of early childhood are not of the other kids in the neighborhood, whom I knew well later, but of the house, my sisters, my mother's parents, my Uncle Bob—and the movie studios.

I did not have my own room in that giant house until later, when my sisters moved out. I had to sleep in my mother's room, which is logical for a very young child, but this went on until I was over eleven years old. I'm sure that even then I wondered why Mommy and Daddy didn't have the same bedroom. At that time my father (or Grumpus Grouch, as I dubbed him at age four) had the third bedroom, and my sisters the second. Until I was eight or so, I didn't mind not having my own space. I had croup a couple of times before I was six, as well as measles and chicken pox, and to be there in my mother's big bedroom where I could be easily cared for was a comfort. I can remember creating my little corner of that bedroom, with photos of the Winchester Mystery House on the wall (my cousin Bob Stauff had taken us there one summer); and my own desk with my stamp collection on it (later there was a pin-up of Virginia Mayo on the wall). By this time, my mother got the hint, so when Harriet moved out and left the bedroom off the patio free, I took it over.

My mother taught ballet during most of my childhood, until I was fifteen or so. She did her very best during my school years to see that I was well cared for, either by Harriet or Patricia, a friend or a welfare worker when I had to be at a studio, or, for a brief time, my Aunt Jean (Bob Stauff's mother). Jean was very good to me, and taught me how to clean up after myself.

My sisters were very kind. They were teenagers by the time I was born. Pat was thirteen or fourteen and left home a few years after I arrived, first to Long Beach City College and later to work on the Manhattan Project in Oakridge, Tennesee. My strongest memory of her is when I was about three or four—a tall, graceful dark haired girl, who was never home, except for the nightly skirmish at the dining room table. These repressed food fights were probably all the being at home she could stand. Fortunately, I was young enough that her wrath and indignation did not fall on me. I do remember her reading the Old Testament to me one summer evening, and commenting that it was just a bunch of stories and saying, "You don't really believe this, do you?" I sometimes wonder if that is the person to whom I owe the genesis of my later inquiry into comparative religion!

Harriet would read to me at times, too. I remember one cold wintry afternoon when I was four she was holding me on the couch in the living room and reading. We saw smoke coming out of the furnace duct in the wall, just at the upper right corner. She called the fire department and carried me out when the firemen came. The fire was put out quickly; and the kitchen and the Frigidaire on the other side of the wall were badly damaged. This left me with a lasting impression of the powerful potential of fire.

My father always behaved in a very silly manner around Harriet, and I always felt bad because I couldn't understand why he seemed to favor her over my mother. Many times, especially at the table, my parents had fights because my father wanted to let Harriet do something and my mother didn't. He'd end up on the living room couch with his head buried in a newspaper and mother would end up sniffling behind the closed kitchen door.

The dinner scene was always spectacular, an adult ritual I was to observe and not partake in. One lovely summer evening , sitting around the dining room table before the open French windows which let in a balmy breeze, Robert Edward decided he'd had enough of this being ignored, and from the day-bed in the corner where he had fled to avoid flying monosyllabic missiles, let fly from his pudgy, little fist a huge pillow. The pillow knocked over at least a pitcher of iced tea with mint from our garden, and landed squarely on the butter dish. This diplomatic action not only ended the squabble, but may have endeared me to my sisters forever. Pat saw in me a kindred soul, a fellow rebel; Harriet knew she had someone who could, when necessary, distract and redirect the attention of that fulminating beast, our father. This is the only time I can remember him taking a razor strop to my behind. Another spanking I received was from a neighborhood mother named Boyes, after her son and I shredded four Hawaiian leis on his bedroom floor.

Harriet was the more beautiful sister, and she had a lovely singing voice which I heard a lot of around the house—whether I liked it or not. She took lessons from a Madame Coshetts down the street. She could also dance, and my mother gave her instruction. Later, she was in the ensemble of many MGM musicals. However, she did more than that for show biz. More often than not, she had to escort little brother to work on the movie sets. And thereby hangs a tale....

Chapter 3

THERE'S NO BUSINESS LIKE MOVIE BUSINESS

Am I in earth, in heaven, or in hell?
Sleeping or waking, mad or well-advised?
— The Comedy of Errors

Signing your baby up to work in films was just another way to make money for parents who had the option in a time of economic hardship and depression. No doubt, this is what drove my mother to sign me up when I was seven months old. Fifty-five dollars a day was my usual wage as an extra, which was the bulk of my work. It helped to feed and clothe the family when money was short. My mother never ceased telling me that my first check went to buy my sisters new shoes—after she had saved in a scrap book the first dollar I had earned. As I got older, I entered the realm of the bit player at a hundred dollars a day, and once even had a starring role at five hundred dollars a week. Work was sporadic, especially after the age of eleven, when I rebelled against not being able to live the life of a normal boy. I was not "in the movies" with all that that implies; I worked in films, and the experience had, at best, a questionable effect on my later life, necessitating uncommon therapy.

As I've said, my mother had been an actress and dancer in the silent films. She had even danced with Valentino, so it probably seemed natural to her that her son should also serve in that capacity (although I never could dance well). Her sister, Frances, was a talent agent for such stars as Jane Withers and Shirley Temple, Kenny Baker and Dana Andrews.

At the tender age of seven months, I was processed by Central Casting in Hollywood. Whenever someone mentions this, I get a distinct memory of being laid upon a cold, greenish counter in a long room, shivering with fear as the lights shone down on me (I also have a memory of being circumcised in a similar setting at about this age. Which memory informed the other, I will never know).

I must have pleased those in charge, for my first job came shortly after. My social security card was issued on May 19, 1937, before I was one year old. The name of the picture was *Baby Sandy*, and I think I was a stand-in for the star named Baby Sandy. It was filmed on a sound stage at Universal Studios. My only memory of this is being carried by Miss Spring Byington into an elevator with very bright lights all around. Years later, this memory was confirmed by Spring, who became a neighbor of ours in Hollywoodland. I must have been fairly large as a baby, for I am also told that Claudette Colbert refused to have me in *Drums Along the Mohawk* not too long after, as I was too heavy for her to carry! At least Spring could support me; I think that Colbert could have too—she was just being a movie star. It is note-worthy that the baby she finally agreed to carry, June Hedin, became my first crush years later when we were teenagers.

A year or so later, sister Pat took care of me on the set of *In Old Chicago*, which starred Tyrone Power, Jr. and Alice Faye. I was carried by Miss Faye in a carriage on a blazing street during the "Great Chicago Fire of 1917." A baby cannot distinguish between a staged illu-sion and the real thing. I was fairly frightened, and at times, even today, I am very uncomfortable and cautious around the friendliest of fires. I am sure the incident of the fire in the kitchen added to my reaction on the set. Early childhood experiences have long ranging consequences.

I have no idea how much I actually worked as a baby and toddler. Judging from the number of professional baby photos that survive, I must certainly have done the round of the studios for interviews and "cattle calls." The paycheck stubs I still have indicate that I worked the most in the years 1942-49, ages five to eleven. I drew a fair amount of unemployment during those years (at least $1,100). The whole affair was confusing to a kid who felt he got no reward of any sort for what he did.

Although I did not understand the economics of my role in the family, from the age of five or so my mother taught me how to do my own banking. My experiences in setting up my own accounts and dealing with the very pretty and nice teller at the Bank of America, Miss Tumigas (whom I called Miss Tummygas, to her amusement), were undoubtedly an influence on the fiscal management role I've been comfortable with most of my life.

I remember vividly the calls when I had to be on the set at five in the morning; I would jump up and down on my bed, screaming and crying at my mother until she talked me into cooperating. Then it was off to the smelly and unsavory makeup department at one of the Hollywood studios, usually a screened-off room in a corner of the set or lot where we were shooting that day; some joker would try to make my face look dirtier than it was by slathering greasepaint all over. Then, if it was a period picture, off to wardrobe, where you put on scratchy horsehair clothes from Western Costume, designed by sadists. This was particularly true of Lord Fauntleroy suits, Eton suits with bow ties, and little boy Victorian togs with plusfours and knickers for films such as *Gaslight*, *Meet Me In St. Louis*, and *Centennial Summer*. On this last picture I remember well the difficulty of getting my pants down to go to the bathroom in the twelve-seater outhouse we had on location. Some old man extra then asked me to zip him up! I said no and ran out the door.

Clothes for fantasy or swashbuckling films were fun—to look at. They were also educational, although I'm not sure I ever thought of them that way. Once, when I was five, on a three a.m. call for a picture with Lionel Barrymore and Margaret O'Brien, we were supposed to be Leprechauns. They stuck spirit gum and long pointy ears on us, and we worked with smudge pots and smoke in a mysterious garden scene. The gum and the clothes sent me into a scratching frenzy!

Although I never liked the business much, it wasn't entirely negative. The best times were when the dreaded makeup and wardrobe process was over; when I was a bit older, I sometimes got to sit on the set and play cards, football or hide-and-seek with friends all day because the director and cameramen wouldn't get around to shooting the scene we were scheduled to be in. One time in the week or so I was working in *Another Side of the Forest*, we weren't called to shoot for several days, days of free box lunches and cavorting about Elysian Park. The sets for historical films were always fascinating. We ran around the old fake houses and store fronts, or the castles and the moats, or along the Nile, the Mississippi or the Ganges rivers, giving us a rough idea of what the world looked like even before we were in school. If they called me to work under the hot lights, amid mazes of wires on the ground and the aroma of new construction (indoors or out), where the man would clap two sticks together and yell "action" and "roll 'em," I would usually be finished by no later than four nor earlier than two o'clock. Then I would go home, either with my mother or a sister—in those very young years. My mother would stay on the set with me when she wasn't teaching ballet; when she was teaching, it was either Harriet, Pat or a welfare worker. When I got older, I'd go to my mother's place of business to wait for her, and then my late afternoons were spent roaming the streets, theatres, and magic shops of Hollywood. Most jobs lasted two or three days, but I don't think there was much time between them in the early years before I started school.

My fondest movie memory at about five years old was *Gaslight* at MGM. Aside from the itchy, smelly clothes and, to a kid, the seemingly unnecessary pancake makeup, my few days there have given me lovely memories. We worked both inside and outside on a studio lot. There was a street scene where we boys and girls were playing and Angela Lansbury was always somewhere about. One interior scene turned out to be something extraordinary. I recall clearly talking seriously to Charles Boyer and Ingrid Bergman as we walked one morning from the extras' dressing room toward the cameras. How lucky I was to be acknowledged by these tall and gracious people. They smiled and spoke to me very sincerely and asked me how I liked being there. I felt like a grownup. Then we shot the scene where Gregory (Boyer) became jealous of Joseph Cotton in the Crown Jewel room of the Tower of London. I was only in the crowd of tourists viewing the instruments of torture and the jewels, but those facsimiles and the executioner's block made a lasting impression on me. I believe it began my lifelong interest in English history and literature.

Most of the Hollywood personalities I worked with were nice to the extras, especially to the kids. Some of the child stars were not fun to be with, however. Butch Jenkins was snotty and didn't like me because we both had a crush on Margaret O'Brien. Dean Stockwell borrowed a Yo-Yo from me on the set of *The Boy With the Green Hair* and wouldn't give it back. I wanted to slug him when he told me to buzz off, but I was chicken and my mother wouldn't let me anyway because he was the star and his mother was watching. These things happened when I was eight or nine. In a year or two, I was to encounter Dean again, this time as a rival actor, a competitor for the boy lead in *The Green Years*. I lost, but was hired as an extra for the film. I remember that in a church scene when I was to kneel behind him, the director changed my position because I looked too much like the little thief.

Of the adults, Frank Sinatra was the only really unpleasant person I remember, distant and uppity. I worked with him on one of his first films, a holiday trailer at MGM. Each nation was represented by a kid of a different nationality, and I was Great Britain (who knows why? I'm not even English). We gathered around a Christmas tree to watch as Mr. Sinatra crooned some seasonal ditty. After the shoot, we kids grabbed our autograph books from our mothers and rushed up to get his signature. At first he ignored us and kept talking to the men around him, but finally he said something like "Get these kids away." Then he turned on his heel and walked down the street. My sister, Harriet, has an altogether different perception of him. She recalls him treating all the children to ice cream.

There were those stars who really liked working with kids, or at least made us think they did. One such was Van Johnson, who would scuffle and joke with us between takes. In one scene of *The Bride Goes Wild,* I accidentally shot him in the forehead with a rubber-tipped arrow. He laughed, and we just went right on shooting. I can just see Sinatra doing that!

Red Skelton was also very understanding about the sand I kicked in his face in *Excuse My Dust.* We were shooting a scene on a beach where he was wooing this girl while they lay on the sand, and I was to run by and kick sand into his hamburger. After about three takes, I finally got the sand in the sandwich instead of his face. He never complained.

David Niven was fun, a real prince. I was with him and Jane Wyman for two weeks on *A Kiss in the Dark* when I was twelve. I was in a pack of Boy Scouts he was leading, very ineptly I might add. Niven performed all of his own stunts, like stepping into a snare and being lifted leg first into a tree. We admired the fact that he did the stunts himself. He would talk to us and point out things in the park where we were shooting (I think it was Elysian in L.A.). Both he and Jane Wyman willingly gave us autographs. The director on this film, Delmar Daves, was not aloof like I remember most directors. He gave me his autograph in Old English calligraphy.

At about this time (twelve years old) I remember a pleasant two-day job at Twentieth Century Fox with one other boy in a film starring Hedy Lamarr. We were fishing from the end of a pier and spying while Hedy and her boyfriend smooched in a dinghy. It was a nice way to earn $100 a day, and I remember feeling disappointed because I did not get more jobs like that.

At eleven, I did get one role that promised to work into something a cut above bit player. I landed the part of Squeaky in *Rusty Pays a Debt*, part of a series of films about a German Shepherd and his pals. I felt very satisfied because I was told I was better than any of the other kids who read for the part of Squeaky. I got third billing, after Ted Donaldson and Darryl Hickman. Although I thought I was on my way to being in "THE MOVIES," I didn't feel it was that important at the time. All I remember is going to the lot every day and having fun with the other kids and the pooch, who was easily the grandest dog I had ever seen. Most of the film was shot at Columbia Studios on Gower Street in Hollywood, but there were several exterior shots on one of Columbia's location ranches.

I think I would have done better if someone close to me had shown an interest in what I was doing. I didn't have much trouble memorizing my lines, but I distinctly recall that no one in my family would run lines for me without bitching. But I always managed, and my scenes went well, until I got a double dose of poison ivy and measles!

The poison ivy was acquired during a shot at Columbia Ranch in which Ted Donaldson's character and Squeaky were pulling a drowning man to shore after Rusty had rescued him from his sinking car. I felt awkward doing this to begin with, as we had to drag the man through the brush lining the bank. Since we wore our own clothes in this picture, I knew the itching I felt the next day was something else. Two days after that I came down with measles.

Sadly, I was laid up in bed for the next month, and a stand-in had to be hired for the rest of my scenes. Most of my business and lines had already been filmed, but disappointment and guilt were high. I had blown my chance to be a star. No one, not even my simple but comfortable Aunt Mary (mother's younger sister) who came to visit me one day at our house on North Beachwood, could make me feel like I hadn't let everybody down. I was actually reprimanded by my family for causing the studio to hire another kid to finish my job.

In this scene from Rusty Pays a Debt, *I have a temperature of 103°—the klieg lights were fires from hell!*

By September of 1948, I was back at work playing Andy Clyde's son in a short comedy. My big moment came when I was to pull the trigger on a supposedly empty shotgun pointed at a pillow on the living room couch, blowing a hole in it so that it landed, feathers and all, around Andy's neck. Under the hot lights I was still weak and had trouble holding the shotgun, let alone firing a blank into the prepared pillow. A thin wire guided the pillow over Andy's head. I think it took six takes to get this right; either I ruined the scene by telegraphing my shot (I wasn't supposed to know the gun was loaded), or the prop man working the pillow wasn't able to place it on Andy's head. We got through it, and I probably could have worked in more Andy Clyde shorts (he was also my Cub Scout master in real life), but by this time I was concerned with convincing my parents that I cared more about studying and being at public school than being in films.

I never had a large role again. Whatever enthusiasm I had for working in films completely deserted me. Perhaps this was meant to be. Whatever the reason, I was getting pissed off, having to mess up my normal life as a teenager with this crap that nobody among my family or friends cared about. I hardly ever saw any of my income. My father and mother had separated, and I was living with mom, attending LeConte Jr. High in Hollywood and hating almost every minute of it. When you attend public school and return from a week or so on a picture bearing a pink slip to account for your absence, your peers know and make fun of you for being "in the movies." Certainly they made fun of me, and I got in some good fights over this on the playground.

I kept going as a would-be actor for a few more years. Somehow I got into the Ma and Pa Kettle films, and a host of other little jobs whose main merit was to keep me out of public school for a time. The most memorable one was with Dan Dailey in *The Pride of St. Louis* when I was fourteen or fifteen. The scene I remember was shot in a stadium around L.A. As Dailey was leaving (he played

Dizzy Dean), I rushed up with a bunch of other kids and asked him to sign my baseball. If you look at the closeups of the video, it's easy to see that I was pretty bored with the whole thing.

My last work was in a Charlie Ruggles comedy for live TV, which by 1950 was just beginning to nurture the behemoth of the sitcom. This so-called comedy, sported a group of kids on a porch fighting and pestering the hell out of Charlie. Good show I guess, but it was to be my last, and that's why I remember it; I liked TV, the people and the whole bogus rigamarole, even less than film work. School work and a reasonable future were calling, and I felt there was no future for me in movies. I didn't relate to the work in a significant way, and I really had little talent for acting or even doing walk-ons! I became very vocal about this between the ages of thirteen and sixteen, and finally my parents did not force me to continue.

LeConte graduated me a free teen, and I headed for the desert to live with my father and attend Coachella Valley Union High School.

Chapter 4

MORE MIXED BAG

I have gotten ahead of my story, largely because my memory of the exact time an event occurred is too hazy to claim accuracy. So, let us return to those thrilling days of yesteryear!

It seems as if there were many family gatherings and outings during my early years, for I do retain impressions of sunsets on the hill at North Beachwood, of waves and the seashore, of the smell of pine needles and the squawking of blue jays. Sometimes my father would pile us all into an old Hupmobile and take us for a picnic on the beach or in the mountains. These trips almost always included, my grandparents, an aunt and a cousin or two.

Wherever we went and no matter how alluring the country we passed through, I was always relieved to get home to North Beachwood, my toys, my friends and the world I had created. Somehow my dominant memories of those days spent in Laguna Beach or Lake Arrowhead (a distant relative's cabin) mix the thrill of adventure with sunburn, sand in my toes and clothes, and doing lots of things I really didn't want to do. Everyone was so serious. And I wasn't having as much fun as everyone seemed to think I should. I always felt I should have enjoyed it more for their sake.

I didn't like the beach, running in the sand and getting my fair skin burned, then having to spread cocoa butter on it and getting it mixed with gritty old sand. But it was fun being with Harriet and Pat and sometimes my older cousin, Joyce. I liked the mountains much more than the beach; there were things to do up there, and it was cool and shady among the brooks and pine needles. I couldn't swim then, and that is what one did at the beach. To this day, I don't care to swim in the ocean, although I am a very good swimmer in a lake or pool.

My memory of learning to swim is extremely vivid. It happened at age four or five, and did not involve the beach, Lake Arrowhead or any family member. This is strange, for my father was a very good swimmer. I was given lessons with a bunch of kids from our neighborhood at Bimini pools in L.A., where there were many different sizes of pools. I spent much of my time there jumping into each of them and splashing around, until one day I mistak-

The De Kay family at Christmas. I'm in the center with my Teddy Bear.

enly jumped in the deep end of one and was very frightened when I opened my eyes underwater and saw that I was in over my head amidst the legs of all the other bathers. Automatically, I just began to swim and never have had any trouble again (in fact, much later in my teens I won a swimming award at Black Foxe Military Academy).

The only cousins I had at that time were Jackie and Joyce de Kay, my mother's brother Jack's kids. Joyce was about fifteen, so I didn't see much of her. With Jackie, who was a few years my junior, I had sort of a warring truce relationship. We roughoused and played ball and did gymnastics, but Jackie was so much better at everything physical that we developed a kind of rivalry. He and his parents thought I was weird because I wanted to play games in the house or listen to records. But it was always fun on some level; my parents would take me to Jack's home on Moorpark Drive in Sherman Oaks for a weekend, and often I'd stay overnight. Later, my relationship with Jackie became distant. I never saw him much and still don't to this day.

But my greatest pleasure was being home with my magic tricks or playing with the kids in the neighborhood, or sleeping for part of a warm summer or fall night on our large, round stone front porch at the top of the stairs which led up from the driveway. Many nights I would lie awake on this porch either listening to records on my portable record player ("Don't Fence Me In" by Roy Rogers and the Sons of the Pioneers was a favorite), or travelling on my mattress through the freedom of the air and stars to the Moon. Sometimes I wonder if this actually foreshadowed my later interest in astrology.

I took great delight in learning and practicing simple magic tricks. I would put on shows in the archway between our living and dining rooms where there was a step up that formed a neat little stage in the dining room, and I pretended the living room was filled with an appreciative audience. These acts were much more satisfying than the acting done on movie sets. I would arrange things in the house because I liked the elegance and spaciousness of the place and the smells of the furniture, my father's tobacco, and books. Especially the books, for although I couldn't read yet, I delighted in their odor and feel. I've always been told that I had a large vocabulary as a child, and certain memories cause me to believe that I did; so perhaps I could read a little before kindergarten. I certainly have no memory of not being able to read a little. I may not have known what those books were, but I loved them. There was my father's set of Shakespeare, seventeen small volumes bound in red leather which resided on the tall record (78's) cabinet in the living room; I had to climb on a chair to see or touch one. I rarely did so because I was in awe of their look and feel.

I was in awe of the five-foot shelf of Harvard Classics in the dining room. Later in life I was to know all these books and their authors intimately, but I have never gotten over their majestic presence in my childhood home. Those books had no pictures, so at the time I stuck to my magic manuals, comic books and, not too much later, the Oz books and the Hardy Boys.

There was one little girl named Joyce Lambeau with whom I spent quite a bit of time. One thing about Hollywoodland; it was and still is fixated on sex. So it was definitely not a prudish environment in which to come of age—even if that age was five! This heightened awareness of sexuality was not always healthy, more often than not it led to a premature self-consciousness of the body.

Now my parents were definitely not liberal about natural urges or functions, although my mother had given suck to the daughter of a friend at the same time she nursed me—one kid on each tit! Mrs. Lambeau was liberal, and more than once when I went to their large home up on Belden Drive. She would bathe Joyce and me together. Between these two little girls, I got a very healthy and precocious introduction to female anatomy—without shame!

The little girl my mother nursed was named Paulette Frankl. We became so close the girl wanted to marry me — a bit later, when we were three or five years old. My mind boggles at this memory, but it did happen, as I not only remember the event but I recall that my Uncle Bob took home movies of the entire proceeding. Reportedly, what happened was this: when Mrs. Frankl asked Paulette what she wanted for her fifth birthday, she said that she wanted to marry Bobby (everyone called me this then). So, being rich, her parents obliged—with a reluctant groom who had to be bribed with a new magic trick or comic book. Even then I had experienced enough of my parents' marriage to know I didn't want one. The ceremony was held on a sunny Sunday in the Frankl's large garden somewhere in North Hollywood or Beverly Hills, and for elegance it beat anything I have experienced since. It was something like a Hollywood set, a clean and manicured lawn on the crest of a hill overlooking the home, spacious and flowery, pansies and the smell of springtime. Paulette and her maids of honor (who were all bigger than she) were dressed in white lace and veils and corsages. I was dressed in a navy blue sailor suit, and I remember wearing a captain's hat and feeling very strange. There was a minister. I can still see Paulette throwing her bouquet to a gaggle of tittering little girls.

Another time I was introduced to an adult role inappropriately was when I was dressed in a professor's robe for some function. I felt grand in cap and gown, and knew that someday I would be part of this world which my parents did not understand. To this day I regret not fulfilling this vision of the academic life that began as a childhood game and developed into a lifelong desire.

Something told me I was growing up in a hurry, but nothing told me that it was out of the ordinary. I grew up in a kind of time-warp, with unstable and unsettled results that required a lot of re-navigation. I was pushed into adult activities before I had a chance to experience childhood. I would often play grown-up, pacing the dining room floor like an expectant father, and feeling very adult.

My parents did not offer me great opportunities for self-expression. Once I embarrassed my parents by appearing before a guest with my privates hanging out of my Dr. Denton's. This happened one evening at North Beachwood; my parents wanted to introduce me to a Mr. Biberman (the shocked man's name). I did not know I was exposed, but reacted by tittering when I saw the surprised and silly expression on the man's face. I was promptly hustled off to bed, and I never saw Mr. Biberman again. Perhaps it was because Herbert Biberman became a victim of the Hollywood blacklist scandal, and not that I scandalized our home.

Whenever I behaved well, on a set or anywhere, I was rewarded with enchiladas at the Spanish Kitchen on Melrose or a French dinner at Maison Gaston in faraway downtown L.A. For a really special treat we went to one of Clifton's Cafeterias. I loved Clifton's because I could hide behind the waterfalls or in the chapel. I think I got some of my love of the woods from enjoying many meals in those surroundings.

My lifelong love affair with Mexican food began when I was a toddler. This is perhaps a strange taste for a non-Hispanic child under five, but I have warm and detailed memories of sitting in a high chair at the table in the spacious banquet room of the Spanish Kitchen while the waiter brought in steaming plates of beans, rice and cheese enchiladas. Occasionally, the entire family would eat there, and these are really the only pleasant memories of family mealtime that I have. I have carried those childhood experiences in the Spanish Kitchen into every Mexican restaurant since.

Not all of my earlier experiences were with adults. Some games were played with other kids in the neighborhood, mainly hide-and-seek and, after I started school, kickball. The three children I was with the most in those days were Joyce Lambeau, Brent Wilson, who lived a few doors up the street, and Bruce McPheeters, who lived several blocks away. Joyce had a big yard up on the hill with swings and rings and a jungle gym, and I got to be pretty good on those. Showing off for her did my young ego good. The most fun of all was sliding down the iceplant on her hill and getting my butt stained green. Brent often played with us, but I remember his grandmother, an old harridan named DeShazo, was so overprotective that he rarely got to go out; if I wanted to play with him, I usually had to go to his house. Bruce didn't play with us often either, although his folks were not overprotective; he just lived too far away, near the markets at the bottom of the hill.

Bruce was a sometime friend because his parents thought that my being in movies set me apart from normal kids. His father was a badminton champion, and I remember that's where I wanted to learn to play the game—at his house, where all of the necessary equipment was at our fingertips. But for some reason, we never played on his court which was pink clay, so I learned on the asphalt court at our nextdoor neighbor's up the hill.

Brent was the best male friend I had then. We were born at the same time in the same hospital. His mother, Avis, and mine had met there. So we were both Scorpios, and hence kids who were difficult in many of the same ways. Brent had it rough; most of the time he was in the care of his grandmother whom nobody liked. We shared toys, and when I went to his home we would play detective, put on theatrical puppet shows or sing and dance and play the piano in his living room. We even shared a dog I had found in a shack on the dirt part of North Beachwood Drive. We named her Lady. She was a black and white fifty-seven varieties pooch, part Cocker Spaniel, and when Brent's grandmother decided he shouldn"t have a dog, Lady became my pet and she stayed at our house permanently. Lady became Ladybug, and eventually just Bug. Bug was a special dog, and loving, always with me at home. She seemed to know everything, and wanted to help me to know too. Losing her several years later, when I was eight or nine, taught me a great deal about grief. To this day, I don't know whether Brent stole her, or an irritated dog-sitter (Viva Nelson) dispensed with her. And I have never had another dog—or wanted one.

When these three kids weren't around, I had an imaginary playmate. In some ways, he was a lot more fun. He didn't talk back and he didn't want to do something else when I wanted to do magic or play with my father's tobacco or throw a tennis ball against the wall. His name was Hogie, and he understood me. He was a necessary part of my life until Jr. High School. I knew very well he was imaginary, but I got a lot of comfort out of talking with this other self about my problems. He certainly helped to aleviate the boredom I felt in the company of my family.

He and Bug and Mexican food were definitely my "security blankets," the links between my family's fantasies and the truths of living in the "real" world. There was always discomfort when I had to return home from the real world. My home life was not based on reality.

Of the time I spent with the neighborhood kids on North Beachwood Drive, my fondest memories center around summer and fall nights, especially Halloween. This was a very special holiday in the Hollywood hills, and I will never forget the trays of candied apples that Spring Byington used to put out on her porch for us trick-or-treaters. My mother or sisters took me out trick-or-treating before I was five; what I recall most is being fascinated with all the spooky stuff, and creating a Ghost Room in the round room or wine cellar in the basement of our home. Every year from the time I was four, and maybe even earlier, that room was decorated with black and orange drapes on which cardboard witches rode broomsticks, skeletons clattered, bats swerved, goblins grinned, and spiders and cobwebs dangled (the last two were there naturally). There were also booby traps for anyone foolish enough not to heed the warning on the door, KEEP OUT. Here I would tell fortunes on Halloween night, and all us kids would sit around in the dark daring each other to get up and walk around and, when I was older, to make out.

Although I had many fist fights, mainly with Brent, Bryce Worthington, Bruce, and Michael Allen, we were not a violent bunch. There was a lot of play at being Dillinger, Hopalong Cassidy and Red Ryder, but we knew it was playing based on our weekly viewing of the serial and feature films at Hollywood's Hitching Post Theatre (where we had to check our cap pistols at the box office). Many of these serials were filmed at a cave in the hills near our neighborhood, and we loved to imitate the actors when the cave wasn't being used. The cave had two entrances, one large and one small, and a stream ran through the smaller one. There were several rooms in the cave varying in size, parts of it totally dark, which necessitated our bringing flashlights. Often the rooms were used for scenes but mostly they photographed the entrance. Today, watching those exciting cliffhangers on TV is fun because in most cases I can identify the locale.

There was no conspicuous violence in the families that I grew up with, although everyone suspected the Worthingtons, the Allens and the McKees of dastardly goings-on behind closed doors. In fact, I was so averse to seeing anything actually suffer that when, at the age of five or six, someone stepped on my pet chameleon, Little Joe, I cried. I also bawled when I killed a bird with a slingshot. When I shot a lizard through the head with a BB gun, I terminated my career as a big game hunter.

Christmas was always a big event at North Beachwood marked by extravagant celebration and many guests. According to my parents we were poor, but at the holiday season you'd never have known it. My father, who drank very little and only on Thanksgiving and Christmas, had intermittent bursts of physical gusto inspired by Mr. Schlitz and Mr. Fitz (his names for any brand of beer or bourbon). Under the influence of these friendships, he would drag a big green pine up the front steps into our vaulted living room on Christmas eve. My mother and sisters would hang decorations while I played underneath the lowest branches with the electric train my uncle Bob had given me one year. When finished we would all sit on the couches, and the adults would drink Tom'n Jerries and eat tamale pie. Maybe there would be a fire in the fireplace (after removing Scorchy Burns), and we would toast marshmallows. Adults played Chinese Checkers or listened to the radio, and if we all made it to midnight, each of us would open one gift. When, invariably, we saw that the gift was something we didn't want, we went to bed. I always prayed that Santa Claus would do better and bring me a gift I wanted in the morning. I had faith that he must be out there somewhere, but I wondered why he never seemed to visit our house. Perhaps he was stuck in someone's chimney, I thought. I never heard the patter of hooves on our roof, although I do remember seeing Santa when, at age three, my father had held me on his shoulders at the Hollywood Christmas Parade.

On Christmas morning, everyone reaped a bountiful harvest of useless and, by accident only, useful loot. After the unveiling of presents we got ready to leave our comfortable hearth to make the rounds of family homes. I never cared for this ritual, as it meant tearing myself away from the warmth we had created in our home and dressing up in clothes I didn't like or feel good in. It is amusing that such experiences, so small in the scope of things, make up so much of childhood memories.

First, it was off to Jack and Ruby's in Sherman Oaks; or Bob and June's in Montebello; or Frances and Perry's in Pomona (here, at least, there were cats, and I could pull their tails); or Mary and Larry's on Melrose (I liked this one because it was near the Spanish Kitchen—the restaurant had a special magnetism even though it was closed on Christmas Day). We would stop at each family home, collecting and dispensing more loot each time; and then, the *piece de resistance*: everyone met at the appointed hour at Nana and Dad's three story house on Tremaine Avenue in L.A. Jackie and I usually ended up fighting, and being relegated to the backyard; the adults sipped Manischewitz and exchanged platitudes in the front room while my grandmother and aunts cooked the shit out of a rabbit or a chicken in the kitchen. Rarely did they serve a turkey. My mother would contribute what was left of her tamale pie to the meal. Despite appearances, there was really very little substance to these gatherings, which originated out of a sense of obligation to begin with. At last we would wish everyone a merry Christmas, and gratefully head for home—to begin gathering energy for a repeat performance the following year.

I could hardly wait to get back home to my toys, my dog, and my friends. Sometimes, although not often, Joyce Lambeau and her mother (or Brent, or the people who lived downstairs in the apartment off the basement) would come over on Christmas night. In those cases, the day always ended on a pleasant note. I could go to bed believing that Santa was alive and well, and hoping he would do better by me next year.

Christmas was one example of how my mother used the money I earned, as well as her own and some of my father's, to spoil me. I was given plenty of gifts, so I couldn't complain; but rarely did I get anything I truly wanted. I would typically receive useless toys or ill fitting clothing or something I had absolutely no interest in, such as a calender or toy duck or scratchy shirt. Never a magic trick or a book or stamps for my collection--things I truly wanted. She did it completely innocently. She didn't know what else to do, so her attitudes arose out of panic. And as I've already mentioned, my father offered very little help in the way of parenting.

My mother beat me only once, when I was four or so. It was in the Broadway Department Store on Hollywood Boulevard. She had taken me shopping for a book, as a reward for being a good boy at the studio that day. I couldn't make up my mind which Oz book I wanted, and after exchanging my selection four times, she decided she'd had it with me. She grabbed my pirate cap pistol which was in my belt and began whipping me with the butt. She chased me up and down the stairs and finally caught me by the arm and dragged me out of the store! There was no book that day, and she refused to read to me that night. Undoubtedly I deserved some measure of discipline, but a pistol whipping? I still shudder when I remember seeing the black and blue marks on my body. I remember this vividly, because nothing like it ever happened again—just as when my father took the razor strop to me when I threw the pillow in the butter.

I got back at her, though. She had four or five canary cages hanging in our sunroom at North Beachwood, right off the living room where the piano was. One day I grabbed a perch from a cage, which was lying on a table, and methodically whacked every white piano key so that each was chipped on the front! I got my ass tanned for that one, too, but just an ordinary spanking. What was worse, her true revenge was that I had to begin piano lessons.

Chapter 5

SLOW TO START

This child was prisoner to the womb . . .
—The Winter's Tale

Looking over these pages, I find the detail with which I remember the good or humorous things of childhood fascinating. This is in marked contrast to the more generalized feelings of the dreaded everyday activities.

I do have a distinct and embarrassing memory of trying on a little girl's flowery print dress when I was five and stepping through the French windows from our living room onto the front porch to model it for myself and the folks in the neighborhood. Perhaps it was some kind of reaction to the piano lessons and, besides, I wanted to see what a girl's clothes felt like. But I felt naked in the dress, and quickly took it off, never to go drag again. From then on I became very defensive about wearing only what I felt comfortable in. Still, my mother tended to overdress me when I started kindergarten. In fact, I can distinctly recall my teacher, Miss Howe, reprimanding her for doing this and risking making me sick from overheating.

I loved to put on shows for my family and for the neighborhood, which must have seemed strange. I distinctly recall reading to my parents from the Bible at Easter and Christmas when I was five or six, and staging an accompanying religious service! As age and the piano drove me out of the house, I moved my act outside and into the garage.

I would stand in the middle of our cement driveway and declaim a small piece I had written, loudly (undoubtedly silly and vaguely obscene); or perform a magic act or mimic a radio show I had heard the night before. I wrote a skit with a neighbor boy we called "Asses are Glasses," whose main character was a bootblack named Butshine, and I treated the neighbors to that. Often passersbys would stop, shake their heads, and move on. We kids used that driveway as a stage for everything—roller skating, dancing, fighting, acting, fencing, basketball and archery, and even Easter egg hunts. The twenty-five feet from the front of the driveway to the garage door was a perfect distance for enthusiastic but careless bowmen, and that garage door became full of arrow indentations. We often missed the flimsy straw target, sometimes intentionally.

A tenant in the downstairs apartment, Sy Simons, hung a basketball hoop above the garage door, and many weekends and evenings were spent shooting baskets. Basketball always won out over piano, and Sy was a wonderful coach as well as a father figure. When all this started I was demonstrating signs of a small boy's need to grow, so the folks were probably relieved when the time to start school arrived. Ballplaying in the evening continued for a few years, and something like an unofficial Little League team developed here with the kids in the neighborhood and later with the local Cub Scout troop. Mainly we just goofed around with the ball and the rules of different games. My mother was den mother. Once I slugged her in the chops by "accident" when she tried to stop a fight I was having with another Cub Scout during a basketball game!

I began Cheremoya Avenue Elementary School reluctantly. It was only two miles from the house, and after the first year I rode the public bus with other kids from the neighborhood. I walked the half mile to the bus stop in front of the drugstore at the entrance to Hollywoodland,

and then took the bus the rest of the way to the school on the corner of North Beachwood Drive and Franklin Avenue. We each had books of ride tickets, which typically lasted one month. The bus stopped at a gas station across the street from the school, but for the trip home in the afternoon, it stopped right in front of the school. Here there was a big circular planter we could sit on to wait, in the middle of which was a huge Cheremoya tree.

I disliked the introduction of the strange ways of school and the outside world into the comfortable life and environment to which I had grown accustomed. I was told repeatedly that I had to be on my best behavior because of my sisters' brilliant record at this school. They would be a hard act to follow. All the teachers would expect me to be as good as they were. As it turned out, they didn't even remember my sisters.

My memory of my first day of school is of a bunch of kids lying on the floor in a big room at nap time. My mother was holding me by the hand, trying to keep me from squirming. I wanted to leave; this scene didn't fit my view of the world. For one thing, some boy lost his bowels right in front of me, and I was scared because I had never seen or smelled shit like that before—all lumpy and yellow like it had curry powder in it. You can bet I was homesick!

Anyway, the poor kid's mess was cleaned up, and I stayed. He later became a good friend because he liked magic and performing, and I recall going to his big home near director Cecil B. DeMille's and playing in the big stone garden and puppet theatre.

I liked most of the other kids at the school, and after I got over the initial trauma and made the adjustment to kindergarten, I began to assimilate the experience into what was normal for me. The only time I got dirty looks from the other kids was when I'd come back from working on a picture. Somehow the word got out that Bobby was in movies. You would think, that in a Hollywood elementary school, that would not be unusual, but it seemed to be. Most, but not all, of "Hollywood's children" attended professional or private schools, not public. Also, many of the extras and bit players came from outlying communities.

The other thing that disturbed me was that I did not excel at sports. I was always the last one chosen for kickball. This wasn't because I was bad at the game, but rather because I didn't mix well with the other children. I guess I didn't take the game seriously enough for them; still, all I wanted was to be chosen.

I never went home for lunch; it was too far, and I preffered the company of other kids to the loneliness of eating in an empty house. Either my mother or my sisters packed a lunch for me, usually in a brown bag. Sometimes I had a lunch box with a thermos of milk. The lunches were always good, although sometimes I would share or exchange items with other kids. My favorite lunch was a tuna sandwich, an apple, cookies and moo juice. At recess I would have a lemon with salt, or some Kool-Aid powder, licked with abandon from the palm of my dirty hand. I never bought food at school until junior high, and then not often.

I did not like many of my classes at all until the sixth grade. They seemed pointless. After I learned to read well, I really didn't pay much attention to them. What I enjoyed most was playing with the other kids in the yard at recess, or after school. For at least two years, maybe from six or eight, I was appointed monitor, passing out kickballs and basketballs. I got pretty good on the overhead bars and the rings and at tetherball, but I was very envious of boys and girls who could jump higher for the ball and hit it harder.

What I did outside of school informed my future considerably more than my actual classes. I've already mentioned how much working on movie sets aided my learning about geography, history and period costumes. I also think now that the quality of the schooling and the study habits developed in the studio schools were in some ways superior to public school. Certainly not always; most of the schoolrooms on sets were dismal, temporary spaces created by old green and olive drab partitions and filled with cheap furniture and stage props. They were cold and dank. As a general rule, the teachers or welfare workers were old crones who had seen better days and whose hearts and minds were elsewhere. Most of them were good teachers when they wanted to be, and I do recall lying to them a lot about what I was taking at Cheremoya and Le Conte so I could get the benefit of their knowledge on subjects that I was really interested in, like chemistry and the history of magic! A notable exception to this dismal state of educational facilities at the studios was the Little Red Schoolhouse at MGM, a permanent feature of the studio, where it was pleasant to spend mornings in school.

I must have had many peak learning experiences in grammar school, but I can't seem to recall any, except learning to read and write fluently. The countless hours spent studying penmanship, spelling and grammar dominate my academic memory of the years through fourth grade. My spelling has always been good, but my handwriting is ghastly (so was Shakespeare's, which is my only consolation). My peak learning did not happen at Cheremoya, which was a place mainly for socializing, goofing off and getting away from the movie sets.

Eventually, I took charge of my own learning process. I received plenty of encouragement but very little help from the adults around me. My parents were fully capable of tutoring me with homework and introducing me to the ways of the world. They simply chose not to. My mother helped with homework a little when I was in the fourth, fifth and sixth grades, but not much; my father never showed much interest in my schoolwork at all—except once, when I was in high school.

If I daydreamed in class, it was usually because I didn't relate at all to what the teacher was talking about. I paid closer attention to fantasies in my head about becoming a magician, or, later, a tap dancer. These were much more interesting pursuits than taking ballet lessons at my mother's studio.

By the time I had learned to read well, I had lost interest in most of what I was supposed to learn and set about to absorb all I could about the world of stage magic and prestidigitation (sleight of hand)—and philately (study of postage stamps), which became a passion after my sixth grade introduction to all those beautiful South American and European issues.

Events prior to the fifth grade were pretty routine at Cheremoya, except for my periodic movie absences and preoccupation with magic. Like most boys, I disliked my teachers and could find something monumentally wrong with each of them. Their names still sound to me like a Rogue's Gallery to be dealt with gingerly, if at all; ascending through the grades of initiation: Howe, Craig, Pedersen, Fullerton, Crouch, Craig again, Ashe. Mrs. Ashe was the only positive influence, giving me a lasting interest in South America and history in the sixth grade. The other lasting influence was undoubtedly Miss Howe, in kindergarten and first grade, a stone faced old maid whom I associated with the witches in *Snow White* and *The Wizard of Oz*.

Mrs. Ashe was perhaps the first woman who stood up for me; at least I remember her that way. My sixth grade class had done so well in the first half of the year that she had decided to let the whole lot of us skip the next semester and go right on to junior high. Naturally, she consulted with each set of parents first, and my mother was the only one who didn't want her child to go on with the rest of the class. "He's not emotionally up to the rest of them," she said, and Mrs. Ashe said that even if that were true, it would do me more harm to hold me back while the other kids went on. I had done just as well as they and had merited the promotion.

Being a mama's boy, I accepted my mother's decision. Literally, I had no choice, so I rebelled silently. Later that semester I got back at my mother by allowing some pre-Colombian artifacts she had lent my class to be broken (they were then mended by Mrs Ashe's husband, who worked in a museum). This event may have been the first in a long line of promotions that I was not able to or could not accept.

I did develop a crush on one of my teachers once. After a year in junior high, I convinced my parents to use some of my money to send me to Mar-Ken, a private professional school (most of all, I wanted to get away from the bullies at Le Conte). Mar-Ken was about a block from Cheremoya, and I gladly entered it at about age twelve. At Mar-Ken I felt I could be myself and, most importantly, the other students didn't give me dirty looks for working in the movies. So, hormones relaxed but not yet raging, I fell in love with Miss Boyd, a lithesome and luscious blond of 27 who, for one glorious week, was the substitute for our regular Medusa of an algebra teacher, Miss Voorhees. I yearned for this wonder with all the intense romantic passion of Errol Flynn in the swashbucklers I had spent so much time imitating. I was very embarrassed in her presence because I felt she must know that I wanted nothing more than to nestle close to her voluptuous body. I was even more embarrassed when her boyfriend came to pick her up after school. A prepubescent pecadillo, the pain of which was intensified by the fact that my first crush on a classmate at Cheremoya, Joann Phillips, had been ripped from me when Joanie was promoted to the next grade. I had had crushes before, or at least a little boy's longing to be close to a lovely girl. At four, I had pursued as well as possible one of my mother's pupils, Irene Walpole, who was several years my senior; I recorded songs for Irene and called her on the phone hoping for encouragement. The adults thought it was cute.

Getting along with my parents was not an issue, because we were not close as a family. To give them credit, they did send me to a public school, except for that one semester at Mar-Ken. They believed there were better teachers there and that it would be healthier for me to grow up with "normal" kids my own age. I saw more of my mother than my father. If I wasn't working in a film, most days after school I would take the bus or streetcar down to her dancing school, above the Greyhound station, and hang around Hollywood Boulevard, romp through the Warners or Pantages theatres, or one of the magic shops. There were three of these on or near the boulevard, and what one didn't have, the other did. The owners must have loved me because I spent very little money; I just hung around talking and getting people to demonstrate tricks. The Joke Shop on Cahuenga Boulevard opposite Rainbow Studios, where my mother taught ballet until I was seven or eight, became my favorite haunt. Between six and eight years of age I did buy a number of my favorite tricks: a red bottle that hung in mid-air by a rope, Chinese Wands, the finger guillotine, the linking rings. Of course, I got into practical jokes there too, and many times my father and grandfather fell victim to the joy buzzer and the whoopee cushion! My father did not take this at all well, but Dad (my grandfather) usually laughed with me.

Despite all the extra-curricular activity, I never came home with a bad report card. Neither were they more than "Satisfactory"; after the fifth grade, "outstanding" became a more frequent mark. I never got an "F," even in those early years when magic, chemistry and comedy patter absorbed most of my interest.

The most positive influences in my life during those years were men: Eddie Ocknoff, Sy Simons and my Uncle Bob. The women who stand out as having been significant to my development were my mother, my grandmother, my aunt Frances, Barbara Eshbach, Viva Nelson and Lola Moore. And, although I did not realize it at the time, Paramahansa Yogananda became one of the most influential persons in my life.

We were not a church-going family. In fact, my father was against any kind of organized religion. However, it must have been thought important for me to attend Sunday School. Although I don't recall ever actually attending a service, I have a certificate from the First Presbyterian Church near Gower Street that I received for memorizing Bible passages (although I don't recall ever attending a service). At about eight years old, my mother began taking me to services at the Self-Realization Fellowship on Sunset Boulevard to hear one of the men who has guided my spiritual life in one form or another ever since, Paramahansa Yogananda. The usual ritual was that we would attend the Sunday service at ten a.m., and then have a Sultana Salad in the Temple restaurant afterwards. These were magic times, and every week when Yogananda was giving the sermon, I got to kiss his hand, and he blessed me. These Sunday mornings at the Temple went on until I was eleven and then stopped; Yogananda's influence on my life and interests did not surface again until I reached adulthood, when I turned earnestly to metaphysics and the Science of Religion.

Barbara Eshbach was a piano teacher. I did everything in my power to avoid the woman. This was practically impossible because she was my mother's best friend, and she came to live with us at North Beachwood when I was eight or so. A former Brobdignagian, black haired opera diva, she also taught voice. I remember her towering presence looming over me at our mutilated keyboard and waving a metronome. She mercilessly beat time as I ploughed through Czerny and Thompson exercises. She allowed me to learn the "Habeñera" from Carmen, but that was it as far as real music was concerned. All I did was practice those damned exercises! When I heard a classmate at Cheremoya play "Golden Earrings," Barbara was completely deaf to my entreaties to learn the same thing. From then on we were at war, and I would never again touch a piano. A few years later, Barbara moved out of the house to one she purchased on Cahuenga Terrace, and as I became older she became more of a friend, with whom I learned to play pinochle (better than piano) and discuss Catholicism. Years later, when I was taking philosophy in college, her blind faith in Catholism caused me never to see her again.

Viva Nelson was another one of my mother's friends. For several years, I was madly in love with her daughter, Norma Jean. Norma Jean was studying ballet with my mother, and Viva would bring her to our house on North Beachwood for private lessons, or my mother would drive to their home on Ardmore. My nine-year-old infatuation with this lovely and talented thirteen-year-old never got off the ground; in fact, I was downright embarrassed because she was so much older, a shame that was reinforced by the situation and which took me years to overcome. Viva helped me with schoolwork, especially English grammar. It was while waiting for Norma Jean's lesson to be over one afternoon that I had my first introduction to fortune telling. It may be that this incident planted the seed of my future as an astrologer.

In back of Viva's home there was an old trailer occupied by two women who read fortunes using astrology, cards and palmistry. This was right up my alley. By this time I had already read a small book by Cheiro on palm reading, and *Astrology for Everyone* by Ralph Lyndoe. I had even read fortunes for neighbors on North Beachwood for fifty cents. After the ballet lessons, we often stayed for dinner, and I usually managed to sit next to Norma Jean. After the meal she would wash the dishes and I'd dry them. Then the four of us would go back to visit with the "gypsy" ladies. The evening would begin with Norma Jean playing "Clair d'lune" on the upright piano (which I wouldn't get near). Then palms would be read, after which we talked about astrology. Cards were spread out like a fan on the table and then interpreted. In the process I was taught a great deal about about this rapidly developing passion. My mother did not necessarily approve, but she didn't discourage my boyhood brush with metaphysics; no doubt she assumed it was simply a passing phase. One of my chief interests today is the tarot, and

I'm sure that is rooted in these evenings too; but I have no memory of these women using or introducing me to anything but regular playing cards.

Card playing was a feature in the lives of several women in my younger years, and it is a wonder that I didn't turn out to be an avid gambler. Poker, not fortune telling, was Lola Moore's game. Lola was my movie agent, a full-bodied nurturing lady with huge legs and a heart to match. She was a good friend to me, as well as to my mother for at least sixteen years, and I think most of my work in films was through her. Her home and her card parties were famous in Hollywood, and I always liked to go there; the atmosphere was always warm and the food plentiful and delicious. Her niece, June Hedin, was my first genuine crush, the baby I mentioned in Chapter 3 as having replaced me with Claudette Colbert. Again, she was a bit older, but not out of range. A beautiful Nordic blonde who set my gonads aflame. We did a lot of things together over the years until I was sixteen. Although I considered her my girlfriend, our relationship was always platonic, a fact which I still regret.

My father was a brilliant man, and could have played a much more significant role in my life had he chosen to do so. I was my mother's son in his eyes, and he gave her full responsibility for me. Occasionally he would play catch with me (and cuss me out for not throwing the ball straight at him so he didn't have to move), go to a baseball game, attend a magic show or two (Dante and Blackstone at the Biltmore in L.A., and one I put on myself when eight or nine at Bert Wheeler's magic store and theatre on Hollywood Boulevard). I believe he helped me with my homework—once.

One of my most vivid memories of him is in connection with the beginning of my study of Shakespeare when, at the age of twelve, he took me to the premiere of Olivier's *Hamlet*. I had devoured the play in that red-bound set of his. I loved the story; perhaps this dysfunctional family was not too unlike my own! I even had a grayish cat at this time named Miss Ophelia. My father encouraged me in this interest, but he did not think I understood Shakespeare at all. Just the same, he took me to the film at least twice; I just wish he had discussed it with me. Nevertheless, he was an honest, moral and respectable man, and I am proud to be his son.

Eddie Ocknoff lived in the apartment downstairs when I was five or so. He was a musician, and I remember his kindness to me and the fact that he brought me souvenirs from his tour of duty during the war years in Egypt: a Gurka knife and a copper serving tray. I learned later that he had snatched the tray from the butt of a waitress in a Cairo dive. He often told interesting stories like that. To this day, I wonder if they were tall tales or not. I believe my mother enlisted him to give me piano lessons; the project was mercifully terminated when Eddie moved out to get married after his service in the army.

He had met Trudy in the service, and although they moved across town, I still saw them once in a while. When I was ten or eleven Eddie wrote the score for a musical revue my mother staged at the Wilshire Ebell Theatre in Los Angeles, titled *Christmas in June*. Trudy and my mother became good friends, and it is because of Trudy that I got to know the teachings of Yogananda. She and Eddie had introduced my mother to the church, to the point where the three of them studied Kriya Yoga under Yogananda. In fact, Yogananda asked my mother to become a devotee and disciple at the Mt. Washington retreat, but she used me as an excuse not to do so.

Anyway, my last memory of Eddie was at about seventeen when he came to see me after I had started college. I can still see him looking out the restaurant window at a svelte bundle of young female pulchritude and saying something like, "Ya know, kid, if she doesn't watch it, some day some old fart like me is gonna jump all over her."

Shortly after Eddie moved out of our downstairs apartment, Sy and Betty Simons moved in. I remember a lot of things about both of them, but in particular it was Sy who took charge of my afternoons at home when school was out, the years from seven to ten. He taught me to play basketball and even installed a hoop and backboard above our garage as I have mentioned. We built model planes together, and he furthered my interest in stamp collecting. He and Betty had a player piano, which fascinated me, but by then pianos, by their very presence, scared me, so I let him play it after I learned to load the rolls. This relationship continued until Sy bought a home elsewhere.

After the Simonses moved out, my mother rented the apartment to a voice pupil of Barbara Eshbach's, a Frances Farwell. This woman was tall, in her late twenties, had a great voice, and at age twelve I immediately fell in love with her. She humored me and always sang when I asked her, especially "La Vie en Rose," a la Edith Piaf.

I don't think my Uncle Bob was ever at North Beachwood except for Christmas, when it was time for his family to come to our house, and one night when he reluctantly came over to tutor me in algebra. My earliest memory of him is when he taught me to box in my grandparents' garage at their house on Tremaine Avenue. It was a disaster, but at least I tried. Bob was pretty kind about my ineptitude, but I don't think he ever understood it completely because he was a natural athlete. He and his wife June lived in the lower apartment of that triplex on Tremaine when I was six, but soon bought a large home in Montebello. He did teach me a bit about boxing, but being small and afraid of getting hit to the point of being a scaredy cat, I related much more to other things like his cameras, June's steel guitar, and just playing around with him. Later, I worked at least one summer, when I was fifteen or sixteen, in his machine shop on La Brea, keeping the metal filings swept up and learning to run a lathe.

The big thing was his yacht, docked at a pier near Redondo Beach. Bob was the entrepreneur of the De Kay family, having built De Kay Machine Products from scratch with government contracts and inventions like a toy steam engine, a kind of jiffy-stitcher, and a rivet gun. For at least six years, occasional weekends were spent on his yacht, until I was thirteen or fifteen. Most of my time on board was while the boat was docked at the pier. But once, much against the wishes of my mother, Bob took me out beyond the harbor to the ocean in one of the ship's dinghies. This must have been before I was six, because my memory is that I didn't know how to swim yet and I still had a fear of water. I had a life jacket on but it was a wild ride which Bob made wilder in his wish to upset his sister. I remember the exhilaration of cutting through those choppy waters while my uncle steered the boat into the breakers, laughing all the while because he could see I was enjoying it so much—even though I was quite scared.

One summer we took the yacht to Fourth of July Cove at Catalina. I was fifteen and so was my girlfriend, June, who was along because her aunt and ward Lola Moore had been invited to come with us as she was still my motion picture agent. I had survived my parents' and North Beachwood Drive's lessons of sexual miseducation, and the desire to sleep with June was excruciating! I had the urge but I was so inexperienced I had never even heard the expression, 'to screw.' When I learned it, I was somewhat embarrassed, because I was sure June knew it; she attended the much more sophisticated Hollywood Professional School. Today I believe she had similar urges toward me. But nothing, and I mean nothing, happened. After initial hostilities at being thrown together in intimate situations, we had a few close encounters and vague displays of affection. I didn't even have the courage to take things in hand and masturbate, although I had learned this delicate art at age eleven. Instead, I spent the afternoons rowing around in a dinghy and getting sunburned, swimming with my uncle or swabbing the decks. I think June and I may have gone ashore and hiked around once, but I never saw her much after that trip. It took me awhile to connect her presence with the lump in my trousers; I actually thought that this tumescence meant I was sick! I didn't even have sense enough to ask Bob about what I felt.

Soon after that, Bob's son Robbie became old enough to take all of his dad's time, so I didn't see much of my uncle anymore. I missed having this active and admirable man's man to look up to; and even though Robbie and I got along well, Bob's family and mine gradually grew apart. Also, my interests were now in things like chess and girls, not in boxing, machine shops, or boats.

When, in the after school hours or on weekends, the neighborhood kids and I weren't watching a serial at the old Hitching Post Theatre on Hollywood Boulevard or playing basketball on my driveway, we were playing a form of baseball or softball in the street, or Monopoly under the flowering pomegranate in our patio. We did just about every sport you'd expect kids in a temperate climate to do, including roller skating and riding a bike. I became a good skater, although I never did master going backwards, much as I never learned to crawl as a baby. But I took to bicycle riding quite readily; I rode all over the Hollywood hills, around Tremaine Avenue in L.A., and in La Quinta. My father was dead set against my having a bike, because I had totalled a neighbor kid's bike careening down the curves of Mulholland Drive. The kid had not told me there were defective brakes on the thing!

This was the one activity in which I welcomed my mother's participation. Often on weekends, when I was nine or so, we would drive out to North Hollywood and rent bikes. There were lots of bike paths there, and we would ride around for several hours. I think she felt as if she had to do things with me that my father would not do. We went to a lot of movies in the years before I reached my teens, and he never went with us.

The most bizarre and unusual influence my mother had on me during these years was through her ballet teaching. Much to her credit, she never tried to teach it to me or put me in a class with her girl pupils. I studied drama, tap, and music with other teachers who were not in the same school. But she did promote social relationships with her girls. I even accompanied them to movie sets like *Hans Christian Andersen* or to out of town engagements like Signal Hill or the Scheherezade Pageant of the Riverside County Date Festival, which my mother staged for several years. There was ample opportunity for hanky-panky when the mothers weren't looking; but, much to my regret and chagrin, I have to be honest and say that there was hardly any. I was too naive, even when some of the girls encouraged my attentions. One little girl slapped me when we were at the top of the Ferris wheel on the midway in Indio; I damn near fell out! After that I was always the perfect little prude of a gentleman — a real fool amidst a sea of young feminine pulchritude. Let me tell you, there were some luscious, firm and sexy little girl bodies in the group. I was tortured by them almost daily until my mother quit teaching full-time when I was fifteen or so.

My early experience with adult women was friendly and caring. In contrast, my sexual experience with young women was skewed; but it was non-existent. Although I dated a few women in later years, it was usually a disaster. It took me many years to connect the urge that had resulted in the masturbatory rites of the tower (see chapter 6) with the urge that drove me to want to merge with these lasses. I trace much of my lack of success with women to these unconscious, frustrating years; I wanted them to care for me, but I never learned to give them what they wanted or needed. Perhaps this was due to the lack of male guidance, emotionally and physically.

My mother was a caring person, but she didn't know how to show it. She would cling to people and do things for them until she either made enemies of them or drove them away. My grandmother is an example: on one Sunday drive, when out of my mother's hearing, she said to me, "Robert, can't you ask your mother not to call me on the phone so much?"

The most common event my mother shared with her mother for many years was attending blind auctions. What they got was mostly junk, and on most of their trips I was carted along with the boxes and furniture. They did strike it rich on one occasion when I was age seventeen. They bought a big steamer trunk for $2. Under the dirty laundry, which filled most of it, were several valuable rings and a striking post-impressionist watercolor. What was significant for me was that my grandmother gave that painting to me. I still have it, and today it is worth $1200. Such moments of kindness and graciousness serve to tag our memories and shape our attitudes.

Gertrude Staton de Kay (Nana) was always kind to me. An enigma, she was about as close to an artist as her family got. Her painting was a mystery to me, and I don't remember ever being curious about what she did as she sat all day at the easel in her sunroom smoking Camels and drinking cream and sugar with a little coffee in it. She was a good still life and landscape artist; sometimes she painted her scenes on China and dishware. Two of her paintings hang in my living room today. As far as I know I'm the only grandchild of whom she painted a portrait. She was never very affectionate with me or with anyone else, but I respected her because she did not try to make anybody be someone they weren't. I think she respected my sensitivity and intelligence; she had the good sense to give me that watercolor, knowing no one else in her family would appreciate a work of art. Nana succumbed to cancer at age 74.

In some ways my Aunt Frances appreciated me as a child more than my parents. She was childless herself, and so took a sincere interest in her big sister's kid. She related to me as a male child, doing things and taking me places in ways my mother would not.

I did not see her very much until the late '40s, but when I did it was always memorable. By that time she and her second husband, Perry Hack, had moved from Claremont to the desert near Palm Springs. They also bought a small horse ranch near Idylwild and named it Pine Meadows. I spent many weekends there learning to ride, herd cattle and hike. These were precious days spent away from the cerebral and restrictive ways of the city down below: the movies, school and general familial confusion. I was more of a city person even then, but I could not wait the two weeks or so to get up there to the soughing of the winds and the smell of freedom in the pine trees. I became fairly adequate at horseback riding so that it became my job to run off the neighbors' cows when they strayed onto Pine Meadows.

When Aunt Fran saw my skill, she gave me a horse. She and Perry had acquired a beautiful bay gelding named Flax and, probably after much deliberation and squabbling with my parents, decided to make me the owner and to house the animal at the Hollywoodland stables! I was thrilled, and now I rode every day after school when I was not at the mountain ranch or the desert. I still marvel at how much my aunt must have wanted to do this, for it could not have been easy transporting the horse from Pine Meadows, a drive of well over 150 miles. She accomplished this herself by pulling a horse trailer over mountain roads to the Jack Rabbit Trail leading from the desert to the formidable Hollywood Freeway! Years later, I mentioned this and other memories to her while dining at the Iron Gate Restaurant in Palm Desert. She responded by giving me the deed to a lot she owned in New Brunswick (a wooded and green piece of delta land Perry had won years before in a poker game). Aunt Fran had many faults, but lack of generosity was not one of them. So Pine Meadows and our homes at the desert in La Quinta were my salvation between the ages of nine and fourteen.

World War II was over, and my parents decided to take a vacation from each other. I am still unclear why my father went to the desert to join Fran and Perry. There was an economic factor. He was out of a job, and Indio, California seemed like a good place to build an insurance business again, but this did not adequately explain the separation. It was, perhaps, more an excuse to separate amicalbly. In any event, this left me at North Beachwood with my mother and a gaggle of assorted roomers, including the Simonses downstairs. My sisters had both married and had homes of their own, Pat in Berkeley and Harriet in Silver Lake.

Chapter 6

PRE-ADOLESCENT FOLLIES

*'Tis not good that children should
know any wickedness . . .*
　　　　　—The Merry Wives of Windsor

Adolescence snuck upon me pat, like the catastrophe in an old comedy....

After the usual childhood diseases of chickenpox, mumps, measles and whooping cough, I emerged a fairly healthy, spoiled and too-smart-for-his-own-good specimen of young manhood. The doctors at school never found anything wrong with me, although other more competent practitioners usually did. (This syndrome was to follow me my entire life). The former would invent diseases just to scare me and fill me with shame.

I remember vividly when I was twelve one medico in Le Conte looked at my pubic region and commented, "Stop playing with yourself and that ring around your penis will go away." Well, now, this was entirely wrong; something there at the base of my penis itched like fury, but it wasn't from jacking off. I hadn't the courage to do that. Something there got scratched a lot all right, but it wasn't for pleasure. I told this genius that but he was dead set on making me feel guilty.

When I came to masturbation it was in a most dramatic, flamboyant and traumatic way. In the interests of being truthful, let me say that at the age of eight or nine, I was totally unaware of my sexual nature, which is not too surprising because sex was such a taboo subject in our house that I never even thought of myself as having any sex organs! I did not associate the fumbling of an old man in an outhouse who asked me to zip him up on the lot of *Centennial Summer* with anything except something I would not do. I did not have the foggiest idea where babies came from, nor did I care; and I certainly didn't know that thing between my legs was for anything other than peeing.

At the entrance to Hollywoodland, flanking North Beachwood Drive, there stood two gigantic stone towers, one on either side of the street—pointed, black phallic and Freudian sentinels which announced to the approaching motorist the underlying psycho-structure of the neighborhood he or she was about to enter. Standing as if they had grown out of the very earth and sidewalk, these imposing erections had appeared in response to the community's need for an air raid warning system during the war years. One entered them through a wooden door inside an alcove off the sidewalk, and then ascended to the turret via a steel ladder attached to the stone wall. Three-fourths of the way up and off to the right or left there was a small room hewn in the rock which one could step off the ladder into; its original purpose was probably to house sirens or some kind of warning device. Opposite this room was a window where, in later years, I would spend many blissful afternoons after school feeling very adult, talking dirty with other kids and smoking cu-bebs (which my grandmother gave me) and cigarettes (when we could pilfer them). For some strange reason, it was only possible to enter one of these towers; the one in front of the tailor's shop and Beachwood Drug had been sealed off.

On its way up the street from Cheremoya Avenue School, the bus stopped to disgorge its passengers a few yards from the open tower, before turning around to head back toward Franklin. How many kids used that place for some nefarious purpose is not known, but I am sure my little circle of half-pint perverts were not the only ones. We were mostly boys, but there were one or two girls who were in training for rebellion against society. To my knowledge and their credit, Joyce Lambeau and the other girls I associated with never went up there. Actually, nothing ever went on in that small room anyway, except boasting, smoking and dirty talk. The older, sophisticated kids in the neighborhood had no interest in being there; we were their social, intellectual and emotional inferiors.

Inferior we may have been, but when it came to subterfuge and doing things on the sly, we had few equals. We raided our homes for items with which to furnish the stone room. A small table, chairs, ashtrays, a telegraph set, candles and cameras for photographing our exploits for posterity, made their appearance there. I am amazed now that we got them up that ladder. I think I spent more time up there than I did at home. Once or twice, to find out what it was like, I did go at night; it was really spooky in that old tower!

After we got settled in, one little kid decided to impress us all by proving that he could masturbate, a word which was unknown to me. What was the mysterious secret he was about to reveal? A demonstration was scheduled for the stone room on an afternoon after school. He bragged about his manual prowess, and did everything but send out printed invitations to what was sure to be a first in recorded history. Even his sister pimped for an audience. Finally the big day came, but he didn't. It was pathetic; here was this nine year old trying desperately to yank his prick off (at least it looked that way to us). Most of us had little idea of what this kid was doing that would prove him more grown-up than we were. We just stood there in that dank, stone room watching this clumsy ritual in awe—awe that he would be so stupid as to manhandle himself in that painful fashion. He asked for a handkerchief to catch the liquid in, perhaps to save it for posterity. Was he going to bleed? He called what he was expecting jizz, but it never showed up. Even if he had been biologically up to this task, doing it in public would have constipated the performance. His gyrations got so furious that we started to laugh; one by one we jumped on to the ladder and descended to the street, leaving our brave, throbbing companion high and dry.

The poor kid never lived down his humiliation. He was not very popular to begin with, but now he had little chance of raising his standing. To give him some credit, I had several fist fights with him which he usually won, although I can remember a couple of occasions when I did best him with my wits when my fists proved inadequate. We were about the same age and once, when we were eleven and I was learning fencing, I parried and thrusted him from my house to the Hollywoodland market a half mile down the street.

There was lots of sexual play in my life about this time, both with girls in my neighborhood and my mother's pupils. One night when I was nine I caused my mother and Viva Nelson much grief when I brought them one of my father's condoms. I had snitched it from a drawer in his room. They got very serious so I knew it had something to do with sex. It may have been evidence to my mother of my father playing around, but I feel rather it had to do with her anger at his fear of having another child.

My curiosity continued but never got very far. I played house and doctor with two older girls and had a crush on at least one neighborhood girl with whom I came close to heavy petting.

Ruthie and I lay on a bed one night at North Beachwood and kissed a long time; as I recall, Joyce Lambeau and Ruthie's brother were on the other twin bed doing the same. We had a contest to see who could go the longest, and who could French kiss the best. Ruthie was a bit older than I and may have been sexually aroused, but I don't remember feeling anything except the pleasure of being in a girl's arms and doing something our parents wouldn't like. Perhaps if we had French kissed a litttle longer, I might have risen quickly to manhood, in the beautifully moonlit bedroom off our patio, which at that time was my sister's.

I am mortified that the reality of sex was almost nonexistent to me until I experienced my first wet dream at the age of twelve. Sex was, I believe, covered obliquely in a biology class at Le Conte, but I must have been memorizing comedy patter or something because I have no memory of this other than some slides of male and female bodies.

The wet dream occurred one afternoon after returning to North Beachwood from a trip to the desert. I was very tired, and went to my room and lay down on the bed. I dozed pleasantly for a spell, and then was awakened by this warm, pulsating goo in my crotch which seemed to be coming from an exploding penis! I screamed and ran to the bathroom unzipping, and then tried to eject the entire mess into the toilet, penis and all. Instead I had to wipe it off with a washrag and stuff it back in my jeans. I went back and lay down, sure that I was dying. I observed my state of feeling and health down there for many days, hoping that I would live and too ashamed to mention this horrifying incident to my mother. At least until I figured out that I wasn't dying.

She did explain it to me, and I vowed I would never have another wet dream because it was too messy. So much for resolutions.

Sex was an important part of my life at this time, only I didn't know it. I was in Mar-Ken professional school, and one captivating girl kept asking me if I had a "dic." God save me, I thought she meant dictionary! Her name was Jaqueline, and, at fourteen, she was the quintessential dumb blonde. In matters of girls and sex, I was her male counterpart!

Fortunately, the mixed messages of these years eventually unscrambled, but only after years of analysis and therapy.

Chapter 7

A TALE OF TWO CITIES

Fair is foul, and foul is fair . . .
—Macbeth

Uncle Perry and Aunt Fran had found La Quinta, California one night in the spring of 1947 while looking for Palm Springs. They rented an old ranch in a grove of Tamarisk trees, and it became their weekend home for the next year or two. They liked living in this hamlet so much that they moved into it permanently. Perry suggested to my father that he join them, as it should be easier for him to find work selling insurance in Palm Springs or Indio. My father moved into the old Administration Building which they had also rented, right next door to the old Post Office in La Quinta, one quarter mile from the ranch. Why he moved in there I can only guess; he liked to be independent, and may have felt that he was already imposing on the Hacks' hospitality and should not move into their home. The ranch house had plenty of room. He lived in several places during the next two years. I got to know them all, as I visited him every two weeks with my mother. The 250 mile round trip must not have been easy on her.

I was eleven, attending Le Conte Jr. High School and working in pictures from time to time. My mother was teaching ballet, and starting a children's talent directory with my agent, Lola Moore. My father established Boles & Scott in Indio, which became one of the most successful mortgage, loan and insurance brokerages in the Coachella Valley. Later it became Pearson, Scott & Company.

I was ten when my father left the house on North Beachwood. It wasn't so bad; I thought I'd see him every two weeks and, more importantly, I liked the desert where I could ride bikes and horses and hike. Also, I got to move into his old bedroom at North Beachwood, although by habit I still slept occasionally in my mother's bedroom or my sisters' old room. I had plenty of space now, and I took to growing plants hydroponically in my sisters' room where I had set up a chemistry lab. I also created a photography darkroom in the spacious linen closet between my mother's room and the bathroom.

At the Hacks' suggestion, my mother invested some of my money and her own in a lot in Pomona. This was the first in a string of real estate deals that was to influence my life considerably. It was also one of the first demonstrations of my mother's real estate acumen. Looking back now, except for the fact that my parents were separated, we weren't doing too badly in the post-war years. Visits back and forth from La Quinta to Hollywood continued all through junior high.

When my father formed Boles & Scott in 1949, my mother must have figured it was time he stopped moving around in rented rooms. She made another investment, this time in La Quinta; she put $800 of her earnings and mine down on an old Spanish-style stucco house on Avenida Navarro. It was a most livable, cool little one-story house that had been built in the '30s, with five date trees in the front yard, and three bedrooms—one for each of us! How great it would have been if we'd been able to live there permanently and leave Hollywood. However, it was to be my father's home and, while the purchase of it went some way to heal the rift between my parents, that was fine by me as long as I could visit every two weeks.

I had a lot of fun in that house, right up through the

first semester of high school. As I had my own room right from the start, it really felt like a space that existed just for me. Many were the crystal sets I built there—I strung antennae all over the yard. For some reason, having to do with the atmosphere in the desert and the surrounding mountains, reception on these sets was better than on the regular radio. I had a microscope and a chemistry lab in there too, and books—the Hardy Boys, Zane Grey, Earle Stanley Gardner. When we'd visit, I'd read at night or play cards with my father. In the summer after all were asleep, I'd climb out my bedroom window and walk in the moonlight. Sometimes I'd go swimming at the Desert Club about four blocks from our house—usually past midnight when it still was near one hundred degrees in the still and starry desert night. My mother joined me for a walk once. Sometimes I would pretend I was hunting coyotes in the scrub and tumbleweed off the rutted dirt roads, especially when we stayed at the ranch with Perry and Fran.

The only thing I didn't like about these bi-weekly jaunts to the desert was the chores. My father would save them especially for me, particularly sweeping the porch and vacuuming the house. Sweeping at the desert is a Herculean task, at least for a kid with less than perfect coordination, and it was impossible to keep that porch free of sand. Then there was mowing the lawns; the front yard wasn't so bad except around the date trees. But the back lawn became a battleground and a challenge—a battleground on which I fought all the gnats and mosquitoes in La Quinta, and a challenge to my muscles due to the huge, thick green area around the septic tank. This skirmish I went through every two weeks, and if for some reason I didn't get to the desert for three weeks, this war was sheer hell. I learned to cuss eloquently, especially with no one there to hear me except the scorpions, date beetles, sidewinders, and cockroaches!

Sometimes I'd go over to the corral at Fran's ranch and take one of her horses for a canter in the wash, or sit on a bale of hay and talk to the horses. The mare, Lady, was grand, and I rode her a lot, all over the desert but usually not far from home. She was even gentler than Flax, the gelding Fran had given me and boarded at the Hollywoodland stables. In the log fence corral we had built at the back of the ranch house, Fran and Perry kept three and sometimes four horses: Lady, a feisty stallion named Bones, their foal Starlight, and, at first, Flax. Bones was nothing but trouble, and once gave my Uncle Jack a harrowing ride all the way to Palm Springs because he allowed no one but Perry to control him. But Starlight was a lovely animal, and one of the real estate developers Fran worked with named a street in the new development of Bermuda Dunes in her honor, Starlight Lane.

My grandparents usually accompanied my mother and me when we visited my father. Nana must have painted pictures there, for she did several landscapes of ocotillo and sand dunes and the lavender Santa Rosa mountains. My Dad (grandfather) was a diamond in the rough anyway, and the desert seemed to accentuate all his quirks and unique, exasperating energies. He was

The ranch at La Quinta.

always working outside clearing land, painting, sawing wood, or building something. I have memories of him sweating away in 122 degree heat, naked in the sun and enjoying every blistering moment. The two of them loved the place. I loved and respected both of them, which I'm sure influenced my feelings about the desert in general. However, our enthusiasms for the desert had very different roots. Theirs was physical, while mine was young, imaginative and emotional.

The whole family seemed to like the desert for one reason or another, so a real estate deal was made. By 1950, Perry and Fran had bought Pine Meadows Ranch in the San Jacinto Mountains above the desert. In La Quinta, they had built a small house next to ours on Avenida Navarro, and decided to spend summers at Pine Meadows and winters at the desert. My parents and grandparents then bought the old ranch in La Quinta. I'm not sure what the economics of this transaction were and just how much of my money went into it. Suffice it to say that it was a very wise move.

In June of 1950, the owner of the ranch, T.O. Brooks, who was also the postmaster in La Quinta, was willing to sell the entire parcel of 20.9 acres for something like $6,000. The water pump, which supplied the houses and the land from an underground lake, and electrical equipment, were purchased for an additional $10, as they had been on the property since 1915.

This suited me just fine. I was attending Le Conte Jr. High in Hollywood and hating every uncomfortable moment of it. I was constantly harassed by bullies, partly because of being in the movies. I did not enjoy any of my classes, with the exception of Print Shop and Metal Shop. I could not wait to leave town every two weeks for the quiet and reasonableness of the desert or Pine Meadows, where I could feel free to be myself. No movies, no bullies. Plenty of fresh air, bikes, books I liked, BB guns and horses. My father had several intellectual-type friends, and I could discuss chemistry or magic with them, and even learn about the stars with a big telescope that belonged to one—which on clear and crisp desert nights was a magic in itself.

I have no recollection of graduating from Le Conte, which seems strange, as I had spent two and a half years trying to make sense out of the experience of junior high. Even the semester I had been at Mar-Ken Professional School had not helped; I felt like a social and emotional misfit when I had to go back to Le Conte. I had little problem at either school academically—except boredom. The desert, just in time, opened doors for me; the problem was that it was a sometime thing because my mother did not move us there.

I convinced my mother to let me go live with my father when I escaped from Le Conte at age fourteen. By this time, I was not working much in movies, and North Beachwood had lost its charms. So I moved to the house on Avenida Navarro, and if my dad (I called him that now) did not exactly welcome me with open arms, that was overwhelmed by my joy at being free, away from my mother and her friends, and especially the damned film business. I would attend high school in this environment, not at Hollywood High to which most of my classmates were sentenced.

My father's basic contributions to my life at Avenida Navarro consisted of a broom, a vacuum, a lawn mower, and dinners of dehydrated and charred ground round with boiled carrots soaked in butter—and an occasional game of Casino. Later, when I was in high school, he did introduce me to three books which shaped my thinking about the world: *The Theory of the Leisure Class*, by Thorsten Veblen; *Our Plundered Planet*, by Osborne; and *Apes, Men and Morons*, by Ernest Hooten. There was also some talk of Joseph Wood Krutch and Wilhelm Van Loon. In return, he discovered Orwell's *1984* and Arthur C. Clarke's non-fiction when I became interested in them. The sad thing is that he never discussed this wealth of knowledge with me.

Chapter 8

THE BIG SLEEP:
HIGH SCHOOL YEARS

My salad days,
When I was green in judgment.
—Anthony and Cleopatra

Coachella Valley Union High School was located about ten miles from the Navarro house and, at least at first, I was glad to be going there. It was an attractive school whose totem was an Arab (to go with the sand, palms and dates of the area). Its ancient bus picked me and three or four other kids up every morning near the Post Office in La Quinta. For me this was a new way of getting to school, since I had always taken public transportation or walked to Cheremoya or Le Conte. I was enrolled in the usual high school fare: English, algebra, physical education, Spanish, typing and the only course I did well in, driver education. In fact, as a project I plotted the first set of stop signs in La Quinta, and most of them still stand. I wanted to take French, but my father convinced me that Spanish would be the more useful language. The school had its share of bullies, but I managed to attract only one or two in my half year there—including a sadistic gym coach who took great pleasure in seeing me nearly kill myself daily on the football field where he held class. He chewed tobacco and carried our gym equipment around in an old laundry bag. He impressed his pupils because he was something of a rebellious slob compared to the uptight rigidity of other teachers, but when he made me try to run the high hurdles with an injured foot it was no joke. No matter how hard I pleaded with him, I awakened no compassion; it finally took a note from my doctor stating that I had run a palm frond through my bare foot while stringing an antenna in my back yard, and the wound had become infected, festered and required surgery. By that time, he had almost succeeded in emasculating me and several other boys on those damned high hurdles.

The other bully was a kid named Roman (must've been a barbarian from the hills). He latched on to the fact that I had big ears and, to him, as it had been to some rather unhappy delinquents at Le Conte who had tried to cut off my ears with scissors, he took this as an excuse to call me names, hit me, swipe my lunch, and otherwise humiliate me and degrade himself. Actually, the ears had nothing to do with it except to give him ideas for verbal insults, which usually consisted of some slur on my movie work. In his eyes (and certainly in my own at the time) this socially unacceptable work rendered me inferior, and as such I had little right to existence—especially within his jurisdiction. However, I must have discouraged him when I failed to get too excited over his attempts to scare me. To bolster his ego, he tried extortion once—but that didn't work either.

Now this asshole lived just outside La Quinta on a large ranch, and so rode the same schoolbus I did—a balm to my soul which made me very anxious about leaving home every morning. I dreaded the moment the bus would stop in front of his house. But two things made these rides tolerable—they postponed the agony of the schoolday, and the presence of a busmate, Sally Kuykendall. I took great pleasure in observing her every move on the bus. However, when Mr. Schnabel, our driver (also the typing teacher), finally coaxed the old clunker of a bus onto the campus, my libido turned quickly to Joy Olson. Sally never noticed my fickle ways.

Joy was a joy to look at as well as being intelligent. When she was around, I was alternately jealous and aroused. She had all the brains in English and algebra, and sitting behind her blonde locks in these classes did nothing for my self-confidence. I also envied what I knew of her personal life; she was the daughter of Olson of Olson & Johnson, an ice skating comedy team. She lived in the relative opulence of a large house on a knoll by the highway through Indian Wells, a house I coveted with all my heart (and would to this day, were not that area a virtual nightmare of traffic and development).

Between my father's total indifference to my dislike of this school, his home cooking, the sadistic gym coach, the low caliber of instruction in every class, and my desire to return to the city where there was always something to do, I knew I had to leave the desert if I wanted to grow emotionally and intellectually, and to acquire the experience needed for a career as a man of the world. Also, I had a hunch that attending CVUHS was not ideal preparation for college.

Nevertheless, I had some wonderful days at the desert. I loved the climate and quiet. The mountains and plains were soothing and beautiful. Throughout my life, I have periodically returned to the desert. During this period, I had become close friends with two boys who lived in La Quinta—Merrill Chapman and Jerry Rambo. I wanted desperately to make living there and going to school work; I loved the Navarro house and the ranch and the horses, and was learning a good deal about how to grow into a man from Uncle Perry and Les Shockley—a cowboy friend of the family from Hemet. In fact, I was so sure it would work that I cajoled my mother into letting me cash in a savings bond to buy an Arab class ring! But on top of all the negatives pointed to previously, the shit really hit the fan when I brought home my first "D" on a report card—in typing. To my expert typist father, this was a disgrace.

So, when the semester was over I moved again—back to L.A. with my mother, to live with my grandparents and attend Los Angeles High. I had just turned fourteen.

My mother had, during my absence of six months or so, co-founded a casting directory for young screen actors called *Junior Artist*, with Lola Moore and Cosmo Morgan—a broadcaster, impresario and former magician who gave me a lot of his old illusions. Today I am amazed at how much can transpire during a short absence. One wonders what dreams and ambitions lie hidden in those we are closest to. Mother was living with her parents at their triplex on Tremaine Ave. in L.A., and it was to this menagerie that I returned. Los Angeles High School was four blocks away, so I could walk, sparing my mother the need to buy me a car. A "cozy" family situation was created: Aunt Mary and her kid Lonnie had the top apartment; Nana and Dad the middle; and my mother and I the bottom apartment.

The house on Tremaine was old, but it was comfortable and in a lovely, peaceful neighborhood. I loved the cool, grassy back yard where, after school, I threw knives, swung on the clothesline, learned to fence and played catch with friends from school or the neighborhood. These afternoons passed too quickly. All too soon, the sun would wane, leaving me to the ghastly ordeal of dinner and my grandmother's cooking. These meals, served in a dirty white kitchen booth, were so nondescript as to defy both taste and memory. About the only thing I remember is that my grandmother would get her baked goods from the Helms man who stopped by daily. But she never served us the fresh breads, always last week's. My grandfather got so upset at one meal he threw an old doughnut at her.

Next door to us lived a family named Crawford. The father, Bob, was very athletic and used to include me in the fencing lessons he would give his boys. He probably would not have done so had he known I had the hots for his wife, a lithesome creature of twenty-five or so. On several occasions she would take me to join him at a fencing class in Hollywood. Each time I would lust after her mightily and silently in the car on the way home, especially after a heavy workout with the foils. However, I was the only one who got foiled; nothing ever happened.

They trusted me to sort of babysit their sons: Bobby, 8 and Johnny, 4. These kids were interested in many of the things I was. I remember fencing a lot with them (because of their father's coaching, Bobby was somewhat better than I). After school, I often wrestled a bit with them and taught them to play football. This was not always fun, as they both had bladder trouble. Several times I had to make excuses to not play with them. I have never heard about Bobby since, but Johnny went on to act with Chuck Conners on TV in "The Rifleman." I would like to think that in some small way I influenced the talent and attitude that helped him get there.

Across the street lived a Jewish family which celebrated Hannukah, not Christmas. They were friendly, but the adults hardly ever spoke to the Gentiles who lived next door or across the street. However, they didn't prohibit their kids from mixing in, and we often played together.

Up the street lived Jill Oppenheim, better known by her later married name of St. John. I, of course, rapidly developed a crush on her. It came to naught, although I did date one of her close friends. When Jill became one of my mother's pupils, we insulted each other and fought like cat and dog, much like brother and sister.

The ethnic diversity of our neighborhood was reflected in the student body of L.A. High. I remember thinking that the Jews and the Asians were brighter than most of us Gentiles. That may have been due to the fact, which I observed first hand in the homes of my friends, that these families put greater emphasis and value on education than did Gentile families in general. I had, for example, a chemistry tutor named Irv Drasnin in whose orthodox Jewish home I spent many hours; and my best friend for three years was Myron Shan. I was very jealous of the brilliant Chinese boy in my geometry class, and of the glib Hungarian who, besides speaking his native tongue and English, studied three years of Spanish with me.

I walked the three or four blocks to school every day, the most pleasant minutes of the school day. Although I spent three-and-one-half years doing this and attending what was then the second highest ranked (academically) high school in Southern California, I cannot say that this was a memorable time in my life. Eventful, perhaps, but not memorable.

All during junior high, one of my preoccupations had been the study of chemistry. This had begun in a fascination with chemical magic. As years went by, the fascination evolved into a serious pursuit; I had managed to get my hands on several chemistry sets and a microscope. Even on North Beachwood and in the desert, I built fairly large laboratories, and spent much time poring over books on elementary experiments, test tubes, retorts and alcohol lamps. By L.A. High time, I no longer had such a setup, but I did use the school lab occasionally. I decided to become a chemical engineer. Earnest study toward that end began.

So my major field of study was to be in the sciences, which seems to me now a strange choice for a boy who later became a librarian and consulting astrologer! At any rate, I remember that, although I had to take many courses I did not care about, I enrolled in all the chemistry, physics and biology courses the school had to offer, at least until I discovered that I had no real aptitude for any of them. Physics and algebra were absolute disasters during my entire tenure at L.A. High; for some reason known only to right brain theorists, I did passably well in chemistry, biology, and geometry. But English, music appreciation, and play production were the subjects I excelled in. Due to my success, I dismissed them as unworthy of serious study, and certainly as a part of my future.

The reality of actually being a chemical engineer was obviously not for me. I vividly recall the teacher saturating our classroom with chlorine gas one morning. I thought at the time he was fairly stupid to build a paper tube supported by beakers and flasks to conduct the gas he generated out the window. I sat in amazed silence and waited for the entire Rube Goldberg setup to collapse, which it did, loudly. The classroom cleared fast, the students coughing and spluttering. I thought, "Here is a man giving me B's, and he can't even demonstrate a simple experiment." That day figured importantly in my decision to abandon the sciences. Perhaps when I lost respect for this teacher I had admired, my enthusiasm was lost, too.

I had a few good friends at L.A. High. One was a Jewish boy named Dick Warnick, who looked and acted a bit like Danny Kaye, an actor I wished to emulate. Dick had tremendous talent on the piano, which I both admired and envied; I wondered why any guy would want to spend time with one of those cursed things, but I was envious of the popularity he enjoyed because of his talent. Ironically, his father told Dick he should be like me, who was studying fencing and acting in movies! Dick and I enjoyed each other's company. We played chess and studied together, although I seem to recall we had few classes together. Our friendship had a public outlet too. Since I could tap dance and do comedy routines and he played the piano (boogie, pop and semi-classical), we were pretty much in charge of class talent shows. I remember one talent show I directed and emceed during our senior year. I wowed 'em with comedy patter and a stumbling rendition of "Tico Tico," and Dick splendidly played pieces by Cole Porter and Gershwin. This time was a highpoint in our friendship, but sadly not in the annals of showbiz. Still I'd like to think these events had some class; for like most people, when I look back over the waters and hurdles of life, I hope to have had some kind of impact.

The end of our friendship began when, after three years, Dick got his folks' permission to go down to the desert with me for one long weekend. He and my father did not get along and, truth to tell, I saw a side of Dick I had not seen before. Even at sixteen he was picky; he rewashed all his eating utensils (maybe this was because he was kosher, although as a kid I never thought to ask). In addition, everything was always in the wrong place for him. I agreed with his judgments about my father, but his fussiness was a little too much for me. He was, afterall, a Virgo. In most things we had fun though, and we laughed uproariously about my getting him into the "gentiles only" Shadow Mountain Club; I told him he could just walk right in, and he did. To my father's credit, he was fully prepared to withdraw our membership had they given Dick any trouble (he was not anti-Semitic and had not been aware of this prejudiced restriction in the club's policy when he joined).

As with most high school friendships, ours ended at graduation when Dick went on to USC and I to UCR. We had been able to be creative outside of classes, and in a big way I think this made the otherwise insipid and even painful experience of high school a bit richer for each of us. Without Dick and my other friends, Fred and Myron, the positive aspect of the high school experience would have been greatly diminished. Friendships are often what hold us together during times of growth and change.

My friendship with Fred Sansone managed to outlast graduation for a few years, but then that ended too. Fred and I had some high school classes together, but mostly we just goofed around.

One summer we decided to go to Mammoth Lakes near Bishop, Calif. After much protest from my parents, we took Fred's panel truck and his younger brother, Spike, and headed for the Sierras. We were to be gone two weeks. When we arrived at Horseshoe Lake after a drive of some two hundred miles, there were no campsites available. So we just waited until nightfall and parked the truck where it shouldn't have been, in a stand of pines near the lake. It was on a small incline, so the sleeping arrangements that night were none too comfortable. The truck pointed downward toward the lake, and I slept half the night with my head hanging down between the seats; at midnight, two of us changed positions, and I then had my head pointing up the hill. It is a wonder no one came to chase us out of that restricted area, or that the truck didn't roll right into the lake.

When morning finally came, we decided not to rough it and walked down the road to White's Lodge for breakfast. Over ham and eggs we concluded that since we were here, we had to rough it the rest of the time; otherwise we'd have to face our parents and their lack of faith in our ability to make it on our own. That afternoon we spent fishing off the rocks and trying not to fall into the lake. On returning to the truck that evening, we found that our original campsite had not been disturbed; so Spike and I fixed up a fire and an outdoors sleeping place while Fred caught dinner and skinned it—a procedure I gladly left to his experience of camping with his father. I can truthfully say that neither before or since have I had trout that tasted as fresh, crisp and delectable, nature's gift to the palate and stomach of a young man on an adventure. The only culinary experience that has come close to the rapture I knew then occurred years later in Newfoundland: freshly caught cod, prepared at the table!

The next morning we decided to move on to another lake. We drove up the mountain and parked by a stream, which I promptly fell into while trying to take some photos from a precarious position on a narrow log "bridge." We dubbed this enchanting spot "Camp Mountain Dew," and other campers gathered 'round our fire at night, too; we stayed at Camp Mountain Dew for a week, fishing, cavorting around naked and singing, hiking and, I vaguely recall, tempting fate and park rangers. At this point, we had achieved some kind of teenage apotheosis with all this fun, and decided to go back to civilization. We had proved that we could survive without our parents as long as we had enough of their money. We drove back to Los Angeles happy and rested and feeling independent, only a wee bit guilty about not having stayed the allotted two weeks. My mother and relatives at Tremaine were sure I had had some dreadful experience because I came back sooner than expected or wanted. Fred and Spike got warmer receptions. Whenever we saw each other the rest of that summer, we always laughed and talked about our week of living dangerously.

Several years after graduation I saw Fred again on one of my trips to L.A. from Riverside. We had lunch at the Carnation Restaurant on Wilshire Boulevard. He was majoring in engineering, and Spike had also gone on to college. Since I was an English major by this time, we hadn't much to talk about but our indelible and inescapable memories of Camp Mountain Dew.

Considering the intelligence of the friends I had, I should have gotten better grades in high school. But their IQ's didn't rub off the way I would have liked. We usually did some kind of studying together and, most of all, I did so with Myron Shan. Myron, the "brain," never got less than an "A"; he lived nearby, so he'd come over to study whenever I asked him. More often, I'd ask him over to play chess or do something not related to studying. We used to go to the library in downtown L.A. and to the L.A. Philharmonic. I could at least talk to Myron. He and Len Slevin were my confidants and buddies at lunchtime; we had reserved seats on the window ledge in L.A. High's back quad, between the buildings and the ROTC unit.

Throughout my high school years, I remained determined to study the sciences. I didn't really abandon that goal until college. As a result, much of my high school academic life became uncomfortable drudgery. However, I did have some positive experiences that influenced the decision when it came time to choose majors in college. One was an English teacher named Mr. Ruby, whose first name I never knew. He taught eleventh grade, and introduced me to such books as *A Lantern in Her Hand* by Bess Streeter Aldrich, and *Arrowsmith* by Sinclair Lewis. I felt these books contained something I had to understand. It was in this class that I got my first taste of creative writing, which must have worked on me subconsciously, for I was too obsessed with chemistry and physics to consciously pursue it in other than a somewhat dilatory manner. I remember that Mr. Ruby tried to encourage me, but I didn't seriously listen. Later I learned that he had taught Ray Bradbury when he was at L.A. High, and Bradbury was one of my idols when I was learning to write in college.

The other big influence in English was in twelfth grade world literature class. I don't remember the teacher's name, only her stone face. Let us say that I was not her favorite pupil, despite what Mr. Ruby might have said about me in the teachers' lounge. She took every little mistake I made as an opportunity to ridicule my budding literary interests and ability. She mocked me when, in a class play, I gave Moliere's Sgnarelle a Jewish accent! Not nice—at least I was trying. Eventually, she decided to help me, despite her obvious distaste for my erratic behavior. She guided me through Euripides' *Alcestis*, and gave me personal attention for which I'll always be grateful. She also supported my position when I questioned the wisdom of leaving the Porter's speech out of *Macbeth* in our high school text. When I brought in the results of some genealogical research I had done regarding troubadors and Medieval romances, she lost no time in showing it to the class and telling the English Dept. about it—proving once and for all that when I excelled, she could be very supportive. But I was just too wordy, and she criticized my writing unmercifully.

One girl named Georgia Rhodee, whom I was, of course, madly in love with, sat right in front of me in that class, and it is possible that her presence rattled my pubescent equilibrium enough to substantially affect my book reports; in any case, dear Georgia almost always got better grades than I did on these papers. To give the teacher her due, she took great pains to explain to me exactly what I had done wrong, and she was always correct. I owe a great deal to her for this. I never did get next to Georgia, thus endangering the myth of my quest for a woman.

The other teacher who had a positive influence was John Essick. Mr. Essick taught physics, was something of a genius in his field, and was a grade A jerk with a cynical view of humanity that would have put Diogenes to shame. Every day before class he would put some aphorism on the board. Of them all I will never forget "Mud Thrown is Ground Lost"—which should be the motto of all political campaigners today. I thought it incredibly funny and, although I didn't consciously understand its deeper meaning, it was shortly after this appeared that I stopped calling him names behind his hunched back. I tried to understand physics on a more than rudimentary level, but it was hopeless; I never got more than a B out of this man, most often a "C." I'm sure he thought I was stupid, because he knew how hard I worked—my homework and lab experiments were done meticulously. Somehow, I usually came up with the wrong answer. It may have been that neither chemistry or physics was answering my basic question of "why." Why is the universe the way it is? Why do people behave the way they do? I think Mr. Essick knew that the study of physics was not fulfilling for me on some level, and that I was getting very little for the time and effort I put into his class, and so he did not encourage me. By the time I had struggled through Physics II, the die was cast, and we mutually agreed that I should look elsewhere for academic satisfaction.

As you can guess, physical education was not my strong point, either. I had locked horns with it all through Le Conte and CVUHS. At L.A. High it was no different, perhaps even worse at times. Except for the gym teacher. Homer Graves was no sadist like the martinets I had suffered at the other schools. He had some brains and compassion, and it was mercifully obvious to him that I could not perform on the track or the football field in the manner that either of us should like. He knew I was sincere and tried, but he also knew that for some reason I could not do well. So for most of my physical education periods he put me to work in the office, or doing something to help out the class like monitoring, refereeing or scorekeeping. Then one day in my third year he told me he needed someone to hand out equipment and supervise the locker room, someone with "an impeccable record." I flipped when he said he meant me, and from then on I spent physical education periods herding a bunch of guys, handing out baskets of gym clothes, basketballs, etc., and running errands on campus. Not a bad way to get out of breaking your ass trying to run high hurdles!

The other teacher in the Physical Education Department, Mr. Chasson, didn't care for me at all, and I sure as hell didn't like him, although he did hone my swimming skills. He took great delight in taunting me during gymnastics—when the rope climb, the sidehorse and the parallel bars proved too much for me. However, in the pool I got back at him; I had had lots of experience over the years, plus training at Black Foxe Military School one summer. So I could swim, and that pissed him off, as well as the fact that Graves had put me in charge of the towels. He would give me difficult laps, and put me in a bad position when we played water polo. These I could handle; but, I had not learned to high dive yet, and he was quick to latch on to that. However, I must say that I did win through intimidation—by him. I won in that I learned to dive fairly well—after the fear of going off a twenty-five foot board left me. I never did learn to do a backward dive, though, for maybe the same reason I never could skate backwards. He picked up on that fact, and damn near caused permanent damage when he made me go off the low board backwards. I refused to even try the high board, although I had mastered it frontwise. He never forgave me for challenging his authority. I believe he was disciplined for almost causing a poor boy who had a deep fear of water to drown. I will never forget Chasson forcing this student to crawl, shaking, out to the end of a diving board.

My favorite class was music appreciation with a woman named Nightingale. I don't believe she sang, or had been a nurse in a previous life, but she cared about her students and nurtured each according to his or her needs. She introduced me to a book I still read from time to time, Aaron Copland's *What To Listen for in Music.* She got us all free passes to the Los Angeles Philharmonic, and usually Myron or Len and I would take the bus downtown to these concerts. My family gave me condescending looks when I began buying classical records of symphonies and bringing them home to play on my Aunt Mary's console phonograph. Mary was the only one in the house who listened to music, even though it was mostly Lawrence Welk, Spike Jones and Ken Griffin. This could be because she had had Mrs. Nightingale years before and through her ministering had acquired a love for music. When it came time for me to do a unit paper for this class, Mary very kindly let me see her old paper, and use many of the pictures of instruments and composers she had saved.

Now there was in this class one young lady of exceptional beauty who, with exquisite finesse, orchestrated all my gonadic fantasies and set them to music that would make Ravel's "Bolero" seem like a fox trot. Trouble was, I was totally unconscious of the fact that this was the state of affairs. She wasn't unconscious of her feelings, and this made me hugely uncomfortable in her presence. It was hard, because she sat right in front of me. Her father was, I believe, an orchestra leader, and we talked a little about him and what a musician did. I was too embarrassed to do more, because, by this time in my story, you, dear reader, know perfectly well what I wanted to do. I went through the entire year not knowing how she felt, until the last day when she signed my yearbook with affirming and inviting terms of endearment!

I had lots of fantasies about women in those days, but I never did anything about them. If I had, things might have been a lot better, including my present absence of a romantic relationship. But that's another story...

By this time, I had maneuvered my way through one

year each of chemistry and physics. I was beginning to get the message that the sciences were not for me. I didn't know what was, but I really liked my English classes, and I was spending more and more time reading and looking up things at the Memorial Library across from the school on Olympic Blvd. I started reading most of the titles for which I had read the "Classic Comic" years earlier, especially the adventurous and swashbuckling ones. I devoured Dumas, not only the *Three Musketeers* series but everything he had written. I wanted to be a Musketeer, but instead settled for giving written and oral book reports in English class. Sabatini, Hugo, Eugene Sue, London, Doyle, Shakespeare—these authors and their magic became the focus of my attention, and I was quite content to put my homework in the sciences on the back burner. To hell with chemistry, here was matter more attractive! Spending afternoons after school, until time to go home for dinner in the Tudor-like atmosphere of that little library became fairly regular, when I wasn't at an archery range, taking fencing, or wasting time at home playing with my cousin Lonnie or the Crawford kids.

When I had exhausted Dumas, reading everything including encyclopedia articles, Shakespeare took over via the duelling scene in *Hamlet*. Such preoccupation was necessary to stave off the boredom of living with my family. It was lovely just to be at the library in the midst of that room full of books, and eventually I began taking the bus downtown on Saturdays to the big main library on Hope and Olive. Here I got my first exposure to real research and using a card catalog, but I thought most of the librarians were weird creatures—albeit kind and helpful ones. Also, I did not like having to find books using all those numbers on the spine; after awhile, I knew the areas of the library that interested me well enough to abandon their use.

All this led to a marginally healthy obsession with genealogy and the fine facility for this at that downtown library. In rummaging through old papers, I came upon a manuscript written by one Charles Augustus de Kay about the origin of my mother's family in medieval Picardy, bringing this history down through the French and Indian Wars. I had finally found a De Kay I could relate to! And the colorful medieval and adventurous setting of this story was right up my romantic and fantasy strewn alley! At the library, I discovered that Charles de Kay was a well known and respected literary light of his day—a graduate of Yale, author of several books aside from the manuscript, master of six languages, Consul General to Berlin, and founder of the Author's Club in New York. Right away, I knew I could identify with this great-great-great cousin, and to other long-dead European de Kays who had been writers, artists, and architects, as well as a few politicians and financiers. Elated, I began to spend most of my time with these people and their times; I learned a great deal of history, and if it did not readily fit into my study of literature, I somehow forced it to do so—with the noteworthy result that I was not always wrong! It was at this time that I began to understand how to conduct more in-depth research in a library, and most of my free time was spent in the Genealogy Division of the main L.A. library.

The family was somewhat underwhelmed when I announced that I had completed my revision of Charles' manuscript, given it a title, and added footnotes, pictures and clarification from historical sources. Everyone wanted a copy. At least they were paying attention to me—despite the fact that very few of them ever read the book. Uncle Bob offered to pay for the typing of the copies, a deal which he tried to get out of when I called him with the bill. I got much better reception from the New York De Kays, who had corresponded with me during the entire two years of my young life that I had spent on this project. Years later when I became a librarian, the book, *The Kays of Picardy* , was added to the Charles de Kay collection at the Denver Public Library.

During this period the family at Tremaine took two

summer trips that were to have a significant impact on my future. The first was with my mother and grandmother to visit my sister Pat and her family in Berkeley. It was fun, but that's not why the trip so influenced me. On the way up from L.A., we stayed for several nights at a rustic camp of cabins somewhere between Monterey and Berkeley, descriptively named "Piddling Springs."

I had seen my first Shakespeare on film at the age of eleven, but here at fifteen the magic time of the theatre really began—in the sweet night air and majestic pines of this resort. I cannot remember the name, or why it was there, but nearby there was a small outdoor amphitheatre. I cajoled my mother into leaving my grandmother in the cabin one evening and taking me to a performance at this wondrous place. I remember that we saw a most exciting production of *Romeo and Juliet* with a lovely Juliet and an apothecary shop that moved. During the intermission, there among the crickets and the nightsounds, I had my first lengthy conversation with playgoers. One couple listened to my every word for the entire intermission and for quite a while after the show. They then told my mother, who had been talking to her neighbor about travelling or something, that they had never heard anyone my age who knew so much about Shakespeare. This may or may not have been true; the moment plays before my mind now as if it happened yesterday! The result of this was that she was persuaded to bring me back the following evening to see *Twelfth Night*. I think the music, fun, and language of this play, and the performance of a very young Ed Winter as Feste, convinced me, on an unconscious level, that I no longer wanted to study the sciences. My questions about the universe and the life of man were to be found in works of art like these plays and the exchange of ideas with other people! I have since seen a great deal of theatre of all sorts, and even been a vice-president in a Shakesperean Festival, but nothing stands out like those two evenings at "Piddling Springs."

The summer of my sixteenth year also stands out in my memory for very different reasons. The family at Tremaine decided to take a trip by car to see some property they owned in Montana. It was a time when I really got to know my grandfather, who climbed over the hills and meadows of this limestone and once copper rich land near Anaconda and Butte as if to the manner born. He was evidently remembering the days when he hauled limestone out of this quarry for the Anaconda Copper Mining Co. I remember him crawling in and out of mining shafts with me and my grandmother's nephew, Louis Staton. Ed de Kay was then seventy something, and was to live at least ten more years. It is true that the property is beautiful, and he and I even located an underground spring that runs through it that no one else had been able to find. I still own eight acres there.

The place and people that I can never forget from this trip have nothing to do with beauty or Lost Creek, and they gave me a deep feeling for the plight of the blue-collar worker. This was when we visted some of my grandmother's relatives in what I can only call the "Living Hell" compound of the ACM Co. These poor people were, for the most part, dead to life, zombies, truly victims who gave frightening meaning to Tennesee Ernie's song "Sixteen Tons." Not only did they owe their souls to the company, but there was an evil and threatening sense that no matter what they did they would never get out. Their bleakness and misfortune dramatically drove home to me how lucky I was to understand and enjoy things like Shakespeare under the stars—stars which they could never see because of the all-pervading and oppressive nature of the mines, in which the men toiled and the women struggled to overcome. I was never so glad to get out of a place in my young life. This is one of the grimmest lessons I have ever learned, and it could not have been learned out of a schoolbook.

When we "resumed speed" and returned to L.A., I was getting ready to graduate. In L.A., weekends were taken up with either study or genealogical research, or mowing the huge and incorrigible front and back lawns. So my time at La Quinta every other weekend was a kind of reprieve or retreat. Instead of study and research, I biked and rode horses, played cards (Casino, Gin and Canasta), and swam. At night, I read science fiction and mystery stories and, in a burst of companionship and literacy, my grandfather read and discussed Clarke's *Childhood's End* with me. This was quite unusual for him, for as much as I admired his ability to work efficiently around Tremaine and the ranch and appreciated his wry sense of humor, his usual behavior with me was to ignore anything artistic. Also, from his viewpoint, having fun was something one rarely allowed oneself, and only if time for it was planned and structured, never spontaneously. This was especially true when he was home at Tremaine.

So I can't say I was sorry to be leaving, although overall, the experience of L.A. High and living in such an ethnically diverse neighborhood had developed an understanding of my fellow man—if not intellectual and emotional prowess. There were things I'd miss, but surviving with the family was decidedly not one of them. Most of my college bound classmates were going to UCLA, but I had decided, with my father's help, on the new campus of Letters and Science at UC Riverside.

It was with a mixture of excitement and apprehension that I looked forward to living on my own in a dormitory. So it was with a kind of relief that I received my mother's announcement that she was going to buy a house in Riverside. I could live with her while going to college. Everyone told her that she should not do this, for my sake; and I only feebly protested because to my seventeen-year-old vision, comfort looked a lot more conducive to studying in college than adventure. She vindicated her mothering by pointing out that UCR would have no dorms; all students would have to live off campus. Living with her might be pleasant, but even then I felt something would be missing.

The graduation ceremony was made memorable by my father. As we graduates filed off the stage he stood up in the audience and yelled at me, "Good for you, Buck." I was reminded at that moment how fortunate I was to have given up any notions of living at the desert while going to high school.

Chapter 9

AWAKENINGS: THE COLLEGE YEARS

There was a small party at Tremaine the night of my high school graduation. Of my family, only the inhabitants of the Tremaine house were present. My Aunt Mary's stiff return of my victory hug served to throw cold water on my new freedom. In fact, from what I could discern, no one seemed sufficiently happy for me. I began to wonder if this shindig was not an unspoken ritual celebrating my imminent departure!

At any rate, shortly after graduation I left for Riverside. Disregarding my protests and the advice of her friends, my mother rented a small house on Central Avenue near Riverside City College for the two of us to share. Months before, when I had settled on going to UCR, my parents had decided to purchase one of the new tract homes Riverside was developing in Phoenix Plaza near Arlington Street. The rented house on Central was a place to live while this was being built.

The prospect of living with my mother was distressing. No self-respecting American male of seventeen should tolerate such a thing. But from my point of view at the time, it was an arrangement of convenience. Once I accepted the idea, it didn't seem so bad; physical comfort is always seductive. This delusive attitude did nothing to further my self-esteem or my emotional growth. However, in spite of my embarassment, my mother going off to college with me did have some redeeming purpose. The house was centrally located, and again I could walk to the campus. My mother being there also served to bring my parents closer together again.

UCR had accepted me on the condition that I attend Riverside City College first for one semester to make up a one-unit shortage from L.A. High, which my high school counselor had overlooked—an annoyance, but one from which I truly benefitted because I experienced an academic awakening there. I truly enjoyed RCC, and I received "A's" in almost everything—except acting and education, in which I earned the obligatory "C". But the miracle of that first semester was my very real academic breakthrough in astronomy and anthropology with Dr. Elmer Peck encouraging and cheering me on.

I loved these courses and, as a result, I began to approach studying differently. The subject matter came alive under the enthusiastic direction of Dr. Peck. Field trips added a lot, especially in astronomy; I recall viewing constellations under optimum conditions at Barton Flats. My high school friend, Fred Sansone, came down from L.A. for the trip. Dr. Peck treated me as an equal, and I believe it was this attitude of recognition and acceptance that ignited a deep desire in me to learn.

Dr. Peck, as well as everyone else, called me "Dr. Scott." Our discussions on moon motion and parallax reached epic proportions. For the first time in my life, I raised the grade curve of the entire class—in both anthropology and astronomy! Our textbook was Alter & Clemenshaw's *Pictorial Astronomy*: I treated it as if it were the Bible. When the course was over, Dr. Peck wanted me to go on to advanced studies in astronomy when I got to UCR. I did not do so because the math—trig, calculus and more algebra—scared me off.

Anthropology was even more of a joy. In addition to

the text, *Cultural Anthropology* by Goldschmidt, I devoured Ruth Benedict, Clyde Kluckhohn, Margaret Mead and A.L. Kroeber. When I read some of Kluckhohn's *Mirror for Man* to my father, whom I cornered on one of his weekend trips to the Riverside house, he thought it was too hard for me. Dr. Peck did not, and many were the sessions when he taught me reverence and respect for science—even though I had given up on chemistry and physics. I did continue the study of anthropology at UCR, and several times Elmer Peck would drop by my house for dinner and to discuss my progress.

I almost stayed at RCC because of Dr. Peck. Through him I had at last discovered a love for the pursuit of knowledge. However, the lure of a new campus and a four-year college eventually won out. I enrolled at UCR in February of 1954. This was the newest college in the University of California system, built on the grounds of their Citrus Experiment Station in Riverside. It was a spacious, open campus with lots of green lawn, red brick buildings and the smell of new beginnings.

Although it is axiomatic that a person's college years are a high point in his life, it has always been apparent to me, from the day of orientation, that mine were to be a special journey of unfolding, and truly becoming aware that I was a valuable and creative human being.

While I thought little about myself and the world around me in high school, when I got to the university I was shocked into awareness. The feeling was so different from high school; here people were alive, and anxious to discover the truth of their existence. This was completely alien to the mental and emotional desert I had experienced during my years at La Quinta and Tremaine. At both RCC and UCR I felt like a viable person and so became such. I was Bob Scott, not a rusticating and vegetating automaton. I felt expansive. In high school I had been content just to find a spot in the corner of a world where everybody else went about the business of living; I felt lucky if they didn't invade my space and let me live in my hum-drum way! College changed all that. To my amazement, here was a world of sentient beings whom I could relate to, who saw me as an equal, who brought me out of the corner into the light of realization that it was all right to want to create a life outside of the narrow, stifling parameters established by my family and the attitudes I had adopted.

At any rate, something quite wonderful happened inside me on that sparkling spring day when I entered the Physical Education building with the other new students to hear Provost Gordon Watkins. All the new sights and sounds of the campus, the swimming pool outside the gym and, most of all, the delicious feeling of merging with people my own age doing what they needed and wanted to do, made me extremely eager to have Dr. Watkins tell me what going to UCR was all about. This was the first thing that my father had ever pushed for that I felt was right for me; he had talked me out of going to UCLA or USC.

I sat down in the large gym and listened to this interesting little son of a Welsh coal miner tell us how we were going to work our butts off; that if we had any delusions about a four-year loaf made with Pop's dough we might as well go home to Mama. I, of course, had no such delusions; I was there to work, by God! Little did I know...

Visions of Dr. Peck ran through my mind, although Watkins gradually convinced me, and everyone else, that we did not yet have a mind. Elmer Peck's influence on me was very evident; he had awakened my hunger for knowledge with personal attention and appreciation of my need to learn. For a brief time, Peck and Watkins were at war in my psyche, but I soon saw that they were the same persona.

My first two years at UCR are best characterized as absolutely joyous. I discovered the capacity and range of my mind, even though my grades were rarely higher than "B." Being on that campus was like acquiring a whole new life.

During the summer of 1954, I moved into the Clifford

Street house which had been completed by the somewhat dilatory builders. At last I had a new room of my own; my mother had her bedroom and my father his, although he was only there every other weekend. The time in between, he lived at the Navarro Street house in La Quinta. There was a fourth bedroom which was reserved for my grandparents, and which was later rented to Ted Leicht, one of my classmates.

With the campus five miles away, I now needed access to a car. We had only one—an opalescent green DeSoto, which my Dad used at the desert. Another vehicle was purchased—a white '52 DeSoto, which I liked because it was a two-door and the nearest to a new car we'd ever had. However, my mother was to have chief use of it, to drive to Los Angeles every other week for her work publishing the *Junior Artist* casting directory, and on occasional weekends to the desert. I could have it every other week, and when I did not have it, I rode to and from school with Ruby Humphrey, a neighbor who worked in the cafeteria at UCR. With careful scheduling, a car was available to me most of the time.

When I had the car, I spent most of my time on campus. I loved being there, even when I wasn't in class or using the library. To me it meant freedom. I ate, studied, and even slept there. By my sophomore year, several other guys in my class and I had appropriated a classroom in the humanities building. The room was used for classes about once or twice a week, and it had a large locker in it where we stored books and other paraphernalia. Here, for almost four years, I would study between classes and often late into the morning, before going to sleep on a table in one of the seminar rooms or on the couch in the women's restroom. Many of us did this at various times, and we almost never had an "incident." Once, a campus cop rousted me at three in the morning; he had seen the light on and came up to investigate, pistol drawn. He recognized me at once, as I had troubled Captain Shroeder numerous times with improper parking on campus—usually in a reserved slot or in a hidden spot in back of the library. Another time, a cleaning lady surprised me early in the morning reading poetry on the couch in the women's restroom, but there were no complaints, and everyone around campus knew and accepted that some of the students did this. The comfortable little room at the new Clifford Street house provided an anchor when I needed to go home.

The customary silliness of freshman initiation was pretty low-level at UCR in those days, with the exception of having to wear the stupid blue and gold beanie every day of one's first year. This concession to mass idiocy was most notable in our huge Humanities lectures which required the attendance of all 147 students! Everybody just seemed to go along with such things.

The outstanding feature of this student body was a serious approach to education. Instead of stressing sports, UCR put emphasis on intellectual accomplishments through organizations like the "Order of the Great Stone Face" (I never joined, as I thought it was just as silly as its name). Also, the student body voted down fraternities and sororities. There was no housing on or near campus until UC acquired the old March Field housing project, named Canyon Crest, in 1955 or 1956. This section of tree-lined streets dotted with one story ticky-tacky bungalow type houses was about a half mile from the campus—which came to be known as "the Harvard of the West."

I liked all my classes, even physical education, but it was humanities that changed my world. The attitude and study skills that I had learned at RCC were intensely applied to this course. To begin with, I loved its structure: Tuesday and Thursday lectures, and an hour-long seminar on Monday, Wednesday, and Friday. This was a new way of learning to me, structured and yet allowing freedom to study and learn related knowledge within the parameters of that structure. All my classes at UCR were structured for a maximum learning experience, especially the small, intimate seminars, so much so that I really had quite an adjustment facing me when I later went to graduate school at the University of Oregon.

This re-birth, for such is how I see it, was like being thrust suddenly into a foreign culture, an unrecognizable planet.

I did not have to work to put myself through school. College was not the expensive business it is today, and, while we didn't have much money, I don't believe my attendance was a hardship on my family. Tuition was $70 a semester, and my father usually paid that. If my parents had asked me to, I would have worked during the summers. I tried to twice anyway, once as a janitor at a coffeehouse in downtown Riverside—it lasted a week! The other, after my marriage, was as a library clerk in the Humanities Division. This job I held onto for almost a year and a half! I didn't earn much, but it was enough to keep us stocked up on beer and textbooks. Perhaps I should have done more, but it relieves guilt now to know that I had already, through my film work, contributed to the family coffers.

Summer vacations were usually spent in La Quinta and, when it got too hot there, in Riverside or at my grandparents home in L.A. There wasn't enough money for much else. But it was fine with me. I studied a lot and took correspondence courses—one memorable one in Shakespeare from UC Berkeley the summer after my freshman year. Then, there was the ranch in La Quinta to take care of, as well as the Navarro house. Most people got away from the heat during the summer, but we went to the desert. It seems funny now to think that I spent a good portion of those four college summers mowing the lawns at both houses, swimming, tending horses, playing cards and reading—often aloud, to friends, parents and other desert creatures.

On the whole, it was a pleasant and productive time—except when I had to do things like paint the rear house at the ranch, or help with one of my family's renovation projects. I was always more than happy to get back to the university and civilization.

The courses that fascinated me most through my sophomore year were humanities, biology and, marginally, Spanish. Within these disciplines I increasingly became focused on how language and literature, history, anthropology, and philosophy shaped our world. Study of these subjects occupied most of my waking hours, while nights were occupied by nasty dreams of those two damnable requirements which had to be satisfied before one's junior year—American history and civics, and physical education. I loathed civics with all my heart, especially the way it was taught—and I had to take the state exam twice that year before passing. Writers of American history were so dull and supercilious compared to ancients like Herodotus and Thucydides. Of course, the Greek historian, Bury, and Caldwell's *Ancient World*, were also tough going, but poetry and literature added glory to that history.

My two years in physical education were a comedy of errors that sometimes bordered on tragedy. This requirement could be satisfied by taking an elected activity each semester, thereby earning a half unit—should one survive; the remaining half unit was bestowed on us by an unmentionable and horrifying course in mental masturbation called "Sports Appreciation." The only thing I will say about this menu of weekly lectures by semi-literates is that it was based on a mammoth textbook which we all had to read, covering such socially significant activities as Lacrosse, ping pong, the size of a regulation tennis court and Olympic swimming pool, rugby, croquet and, I kid you not, tiddly winks. At the end of each year we were presented with a two-hour written exam on this reading and lecture series. At the end of two years, we who had survived burned these textbooks en masse.

My physical education electives were really not too bad—it was just my performance in them. Golf, swimming, archery (taught by a Brunhilda named Schlundt) and social dancing (the written test would have stopped Arthur Murray). In golf, I became the first student to place a left hook through the windshield of the campus police car, further endearing me to Captain Schroeder. In swimming and archery I did fairly well, as I had years of experience in both. In social dancing I purposely was klutzy and discourteous because by then I resented the time taken away from my studies by these grossly cretinous requirements. I squeaked by with a "C," after completing a two-hour written and 'experiential' final. In my senior year, a year and a half later, for some reason which I will never understand, I elected to take weightlifting. The class met at 8:00 a.m., and I had just gotten married! It became my first and only "F," as I attended two classes all semester.

It soon became apparent that my best subjects were philosophy, history and English. Since UCR did not offer a major in anthropology, I elected to major in English, minor in philosophy and history, and squeeze in as many upper division courses in anthropology as I could. The teacher and founder of the Anthropology Department was Dr. John Goins, a brilliant and gifted man in his 30's who was the sole instructor in this field. He was an avid researcher and had spent some time in a village in Bolivia named Huyculi, studying the Quechuan peoples. We had some discussions about my interests in archaeology and cultural anthropology prior to my becoming an upper division student, at which time I enrolled in several of his classes.

Two of my fondest memories of him surround the philosophy, manufacture and drinking of beer.

Near the end of my sophomore year, he and Homer Aschmann, head of the Geography Department, invited two students, Greg Figgins and myself, to accompany them to a dig at the Indian caves in the hills above Newberry, California. Also with us were Dr. Goins' young son, Tim, and a newspaperman from the Riverside Enterprise named Patterson. It was thought that some momentous discovery was about to be made! We did get a write-up in the local paper. This was an honor of sorts, but it was rough work. The only things I discovered were not to wear tight jeans on a dig, and the joy of being tired after a day of sifting sand and digging inside a three-foot high cave. Eight-year-old Tim, who was small enough to get into one of the cave openings inaccessible to us, made the big discovery of the day : a sinew-wrapped sheep pellet, which Tim's father figured to be some kind of fertility amulet used by the former cave dwellers. We then stumbled down off the mountain into Victorville, our dust-filled academic noses headed for the nearest bar. I was not much of a beer drinker then; I just didn't like the stuff, and initially refused Dr. Goins' offer. He said that I had earned it and insisted. Being thirsty and euphoric as well as bone weary, I accepted that frosty golden glass with the white crown. I have never tasted anything like it since.

One of his most fascinating lectures occurred on a warm spring afternoon in 1957 in a course called "Peoples of the Andes." It covered the brewing of chicha, a native fermented liquor, and the ceremony and mystique surrounding the drinking of it. Dr. Goins described the process in detail, complete with diagrams on the blackboard (which was green, like my face after hearing how this brew was made). The women of a village would sit around chewing a sacred bean, then spit the resulting wad into a communal pot. When it was full, the pot was set aside to ferment for perhaps several days. The liquor was then boiled and strained through several stages until the liquid came clear. The first pourings were used for everyday drinking, while the last clear pouring was reserved for ceremonies only. When one drank this, the first portion was always poured onto the ground as a propitiatory gift to the Earth Goddess. After this lecture, I took my beer drinking seriously.

When Dr. Goins died of illness several years later, I made a trip back to the campus to pay my respects. The university established a library named after him, and, at a later date, I donated my collection of pre-Colombian pottery and jewelry to be displayed in his memory.

I made several friends on the faculty as well, and I believe it's accurate to say that most of my instructors liked me better as a friend than as a student. These friendships were the guides and touchstones of my college years.

The best remembered and perhaps most intellectually influential of those after John Goins was and is the philosopher Philip Wheelwright, a glorious and brilliant man who picked up where Dr. Elmer Peck left off in his concern for my intellectual growth. He was head of the Philosophy Department, and I took many courses from him after I made that subject my minor; but I was first introduced to his indirect and incisive way of teaching in humanities lectures. Most of the faculty gave lectures from time to time in this course, and some were more memorable (and tolerable) than others. Philip's lectures were among the best, and of the same quality as those lectures he delivered at Oxford and Cambridge as a guest scholar.

The closest thing UCR had to a student union in those early days was the basement of the physical education building, which housed a bookstore, a coffee shop, and an area for study called "The Catacombs." It was cool, and coffee, which I had learned to consume by the potfull, was five cents a cup, including refills! I may have learned more here during informal discussions with instructors and professors than in any classroom. In about two years, the 'combs were closed, and an old barn on campus was converted to be the agora of students and faculty.

Dr. Wheelwright did not come there very much, perhaps because of his age and status as one of the top four philosophers in the nation. Wherever they took place, our talks were always lengthy, especially the ones on Socrates and Plato, Heraclitus, the poetics of Aristotle, and T. S. Eliot's "Wasteland" and "Little Gidding." Once, he spent an hour on the etymology and onomatopoetics of the word "shit." Through his wonderful teaching by indirection, I began to understand the profound vastness and scope of human knowledge.

Sessions at his beautiful home overlooking one of Riverside's parks were coveted, and our class had several; we were, however, dismayed when he informed us that he listened to Wagner while correcting our papers! "A's" were difficult to come by, but they were a high reward from this demanding and caring man. In my junior year, when I began to shake from an invisible condition no doctor could diagnose, it was Philip who came to my house to convince my mother to take me to his chiropractor. But the treatments were to no avail in dealing with the tremor. Philip was sure then that I was a victim of "original sin," and to this day I am not sure that he wasn't right. Also, he was one of the few people to support me in my decision to marry in my senior year. "Bob," he said, "it is a grand thing!"

In those first two years of college I needed the support of intelligent people who cared, and I got just that from outstanding educators in all the fields I studied. In humanities, Al Lewis was an exceptionally communicative guide and friend during humanities seminars and in those informal discussions in the Catacombs and the "Barn." In English, Mortimer Proctor was that special little pixie of a man who eagerly opened doors that shed light on language and literature. Like every other man in her class, I fell in love with Betty Gray Edwards, who made Spanish begin to come alive for the first time. John Vasek and Irwin Newell created an interest in biology which I had not thought possible in high school; even dissecting a rat did not completely turn me off, although the sciences, save astronomy and anthropology, still gave me no answers to life's dilemmas.

In my sophomore year, I began to take some upper division courses in my major and minor because I had covered the introductory work at RCC. Dr. Milton Miller of the English Department became a good friend and mentor, as did Dr. William "Bloody Bill" Arrowsmith with whom I studied Ancient Greek and Roman history. Between "Bloody Bill" and Dr. Wheelwright, I gained a reasonably thorough knowledge of the ancient world and its philosophies. Milton gave me a basic grounding and love for Renaissance and Restoration literature, although he had a very conservative idea of what constituted an "A" in any of his courses! In my senior year, he accepted me as editor for the new literary magazine, *Mosaic*, which we founded. He remains a friend to this day.

Although I loved the Clifford Street house, by the end of my sophomore year I was beginning to feel stifled. I had a very good friend and study partner named Charles Preble, a philosophy major studying under Dr. Wheelwright, who was willing to share a house with me at Canyon Crest housing near the campus. We got one other student to go in with us, Ed Dalton, a brilliant physics major. Housing in the Crest was pleasant, and ours was a duplex, the other side occupied by two women we never saw. Scott, Preble and Dalton, Inc., became famous for its parties, late hours, and the many women who passed through.

Let me add that most of these women were not coming to see me. I led a monastic life, and was not even studying for the ministry, like the Anglican, Charlie Preble.

Being on my own agreed with me, although I still took my laundry home to Clifford Street every few weeks. I began to get A's and B's consistently, and to have a real feel for English literature, philosophy and the Greek language. Spanish was still my required language, but I had begun Greek because of my interest in Greek philosophy and culture. Dr. Arrowsmith taught classical languages, but according to Charlie, who had been injured in his Greek class, "Bloody Bill" had a habit of firing chalk at anyone who made a mistake at the blackboard. So I felt relieved when the school brought in Dovering Evans, a Welshman from Oxford or some other prestigious English school, to teach Beginning Greek. He, at least, did not throw chalk, but I got an elbow in the ribs many times because of misplaced iota subscripts!

I considered myself socially inept, so I turned to studying late into the morning every day, including Sundays. Eventually, I turned day into night. This went on for two years. I would go to bed when classes ended at four or 6:00 p.m., and sleep until midnight. Then I would get up, eat breakfast and go to work. It was quiet, and it seems in the early hours one is somehow more alert—especially when one is the only one up in the house, sometimes on the block. During breaks, at three or four in the morning, I would run around the still streets or fence and talk with some other night studier (never anyone from my house). My radio was permanently set on KNX for "Music 'Til Dawn." I'd work until seven when I'd leave the house for the Barn and more coffee before classes began. This was a great routine. After a few weeks of this procedure I felt no strain or tiredness, and I never took drugs (except No-Doz, coffee and cigarettes!) to stay awake. So all was agreeable at the duplex on Avocado St., and Mr. Preble could have his numerous girlfriends over any time as long as they didn't make too much noise. He had set up an altar in his bedroom, so I figured they were usually praying for one thing or another.

Ed Dalton could not take our humanistic household for more than one semester. When he departed, we took in Lester Prestwood, an English major who proved to be compatible and shared my hours. I had the larger bedroom since I had moved in first; Charlie had the smaller bedroom, by choice, and Les had the living room. Les was a sound sleeper; I remember a party we once had in the living room with people drinking, playing chess and talking all around his bed, and he slept right through it!

One night a few weeks after he moved in, Les and Preble were in the living room waiting for me when I returned from the library. They had a reasonable request: that I abandon the large bedroom for the smaller one, so that they could room together and leave the living room free. At least they asked me before moving my stuff out. I said I didn't want to do this, as I had become accustomed to the room. I pontificated, yelled and argued that I needed the space. Preble smoked his pipe and tried to look disinterested, while Prestwood slouched deeply in his armchair and chain smoked. Preble was afraid Les and I would fight it out physically, so he removed my fencing foils from the room. But my histrionics had some effect on Les and, when I observed that he could move in with me without disrupting anyone, he lit another cigarette and relaxed. Since we were both in English, that made it harder for him to disagree.

I could see I was winning, but when I rose from the typewriter case I was sitting on, I grabbed the back of a chair with my right hand and immediately noticed that my arm would not stay still. I thought I was shaking with anger, and perhaps in a way I was. It quieted down very quickly, and I didn't think of this incident again until several days later. Les accepted my offer and moved into my room. Charlie was, I'm sure, secretly pleased that he didn't have to switch bedrooms, and for the rest of the year we got along very well.

When I mentioned this incident at Clifford Street to my mother, she was sure the shaking arm was a sign that I should move back home. Of course I told her no way! My uncle, Jim Scott, who was living there at the time, was sure I was quite ill and seemed pleased that at last he had discovered my Achilles' Heel. My father did not have to deal with this as he was in the desert, desperately managing his own affairs in getting Pearson, Scott & Co. started. As for me, I felt fine, so I ignored what they said and went about my business for the time being.

Back at the Crest, the second semester of my junior year settled down into the usual collegiate morass of wine, women and song. Or so it was for my two carefree roommates; for me it was mostly study. Charlie helped me with Greek once in a while, and Les, since we had some of the same classes, read English with me occasionally. When he got the lead in UCR's production of *Playboy of the Western World*, I worked with him on the lines and the director's blocking. This was an appropriate role for him: he ran through women faster than Charlie. Whenever there was trouble in his relationships, the women turned to me for consolation! I didn't know what to do with them, but I sure wish I had. It was a perfect set up, and some of the women were quite wonderful. But I didn't do anything, although I'm sure now some of them would not have minded if I had: they belonged to Charlie and Les. Or so I thought!

I slept for two days after finals that year and entered the ranks of "A" students in English and philosophy at UCR. Les warned me that I'd get bed sores when the third day started, so I reluctantly got up. Beer and pizza flowed freely for a week, and I renewed my friendship with Captain Schroeder.

Our housing situation on Clifford Street finally came to an end. Campus Housing wouldn't renew our lease for another year. And in addition to this, I said something to Ann (one of Charlie's women) about Preble that pissed him off. He retaliated collegiately one day by putting an old toilet seat in my bed. He got very cool with both Les and me after that, and I believe Les just moved back home. I no longer felt comfortable living with Charlie, so I was glad he moved to another house. Perhaps the most positive return on my tenure with Preble was meeting Mary, who would later become my first girlfriend in the realm of the physical. I returned to Clifford Street for the summer, living with Uncle Jim and my mother and spending part of the vacation in La Quinta with my father. At any rate, by the beginning of 1958, my senior year, I was back at a new house in the Crest with a new set of roommates. It was right across from the old one on Avocado Street, which was still being fumigated.

How I got into the new house, which had the exact layout of the old one, I never knew. Bob Walker was a long time pre-ministerial student friend of both Charlie and myself. I had met him at CVUHS years before, as his home was also in the desert. He became my roommate, along with Joe Winkler, a classics major whose libido knew no limits. In the course of the year, he had to be bailed out of the Tijuana jail at least twice. We had an unlikely household, and some of the things that went on there would make the Victorian author of *A Secret Life* blush. (At this time, this book and *Catcher in the Rye* were both strong influences on me.)

In the old house people got some studying done. In fact I'd say that that was the dominant mode of behavior there except for the intermittent screwing around. In this house, screwing around became dominant, and studying intermittent. I had a bedroom all to myself, so I continued my midnight routine of studying 'til dawn. This got ludicrous after awhile, because Winkler and his pals were usually carousing 'til dawn in the rest of the house. I don't know what Walker did, but I suspect he prayed a lot. I began spending more time in my carrel at the library, and at Clifford Street. In this atmosphere began the most important year of my young life.

If I didn't come through with many A's in my junior year, I can say that I never got lower than a B, and I almost made the Dean's List. More importantly, I met two people who would change my life forever: Eldon Smith and Mary, my future wife, a dark haired poetess of extraordinary talent. Eldon was a brilliant history major and a fine drinking buddy.

Near the end of that year, Eldon and I set a new standard for studying, drinking, chessplaying and ludicrous behavior which tarnished the reputation of the Humanities Department for years to come. I didn't join Winkler's escapades because to me they were frighteningly real, like spending time as a guest of the Mexican government. Also, I hated his attitude toward the many women who bestowed favors on him; he was physical with them and even slapped them around. Eldon, on the other hand, idolized this guy.

I happened to be present on the one occasion I know of when a woman gave Joe Winkler what he deserved. It took place after a party at our house in the Crest. Joe had spilled beer all over my records and thrown up (spaghetti) in the bathroom and in my bed, where he had taken one of his women before I got home. By the time I did get home, he had left with her, and others had tried to clean up after him, especially Bob Walker, my other roommate. At the urging of everyone except Bob, I got as drunk as I've ever been, challenging every man there to a fencing match on the lawn amongst the coupled bodies. Finally I decided to walk it off and stumbled toward my girlfriend, Mary's, Crest house. How I got there was a miraculous testament to human stamina, for I was beyond falling-down drunk; I can still remember dragging my sweaty carcass over her lawn and up the front stairs. I aimed for a pin-point of light on her porch and bawled out her name. She lugged me inside, but there was no way little Mary could have gotten me onto a bed. Thankfully, her roommates were out. I sat there on the floor, painfully incoherent as I tried to tell her about the mess back home. She offered a few commiserative words before I passed out, breathing tears, frustration and nausea. The next day Winkler moved out of my house.

It turned out that Winkler had been abandoned later that night in an orange grove where he had driven the woman in order to screw her. He had passed out, and she threw him out of the car and drove off with his clothes. When he came to, he had to walk home in the raw. I was home when she returned his clothes several days later, and we had a good laugh.

With Joe gone, Bob Walker was my surviving roommate. He and I got along well, except during the tombstone incident. Oh, I remember it well. . .

One night in October just before Halloween of my senior year, Eldon, Mary and I were at my place drinking and playing chess. Mary was preparing food in the kitchen, while the men drank from quart beer bottles and struggled with a Ruy Lopez or Nimzo Indian Defense. Walker was at the library, and all was warm and serene. Then I made the mistake of capturing Eldon's queen. He exploded as if a bomb went off under his chair, much like his hero Napoleon was said to have done in similar situations; chess pieces and board flew all over the room. He grabbed his bottle of beer, shook it, and squirted me full in the face. I retaliated in kind, and before Mary could stop us, the chessboard, walls, table and curtains were soaked and dripping. In exasperation, perhaps, she grabbed her own bottle and proceeded to shower us. When the three of us collapsed in a heap, tired and laughing, there was not a drop to drink.

An officious neighbor reported the ruckus to the campus police and, even though I offered Schroeder a beer when they arrived, he said he was going to keep the house under surveillance for a month. Well, we decided to give him something to look at, at least on Halloween. The next afternoon we picked up an old tombstone from the Riverside cemetery and set it up on the lawn in front of the house. However, its presence went unappreciated by the patrolling cops, and we were not even asked to remove it. The joke had failed, but before we had a chance to take the thing back to the graveyard, Walker dragged it into the house and set it up in the living room as an altar! This did not seem fitting behavior for one studying to be a minister, and I told Bob so. He was chagrined, and Mary and I ended up taking it back to the cemetery. It is possible that this incident had some effect on Bob, for he didn't become a minister. Although neither of us had anticipated the direction of our lives, he, like myself, later became a librarian. When we met again years later I found he had married a woman with many children, and had one of his own.

There were many such incidents during this year. I was playing harder and studying more effectively. English, philosophy and history became my joys, except when I was carousing with Eldon or courting Mary. Eventually she and I moved into the university Canyon Crest apartments and lived there for two years before tying the knot at the County Courthouse.

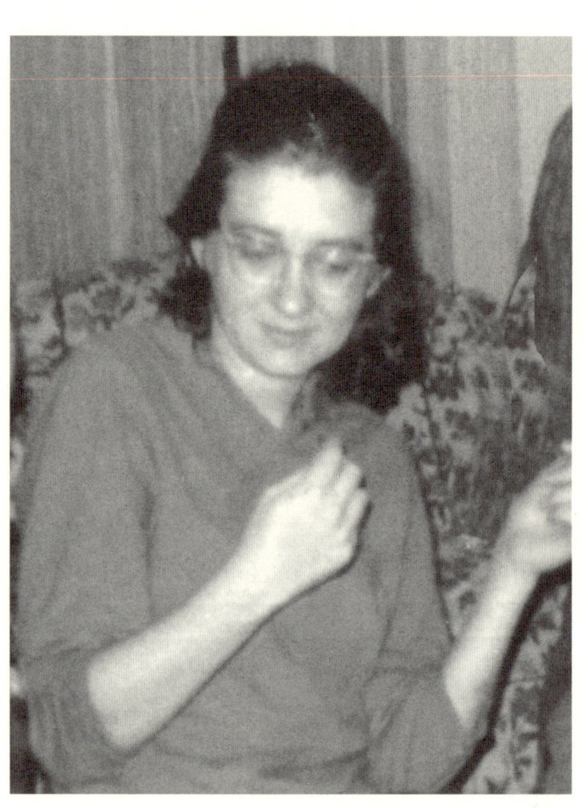

Chapter 10

THE MARRIAGE CONTRACT, OR, WHAT'S WRONG WITH THIS PICTURE?

> *Look down, you gods,*
> *And on this couple drop a blessed crown!*
> —The Tempest

Mary and I married on a hot September afternoon in1958, after driving around Riverside all morning getting up the courage. It was a sweaty and lifeless ceremony, witnessed by the judge's secretary. Mary was seventeen and I was twenty-two. A late bloomer, I really had had little intimate experience with women before Mary; in fact, she was the first woman I ever slept with. She was also an English major and didn't seem to mind my lack of confidence or maturity.

Now our meeting came about this way.

During 1955 and part of '56 I had known her as the girlfriend of one of Charlie Preble's friends, Jim. We did not pay much attention to each other, except during some of those interminable bull study sessions in the Barn where we were the only English majors at the table. She seemed to enjoy my gift of gab, and by the time Jim left UCR to go into Officer's Candidate School in Texas that summer, she and I had become good friends. Jim, who had also become a friend, asked Eldon Smith to take care of her for him. I was not the only unrealistic romantic in our group.

Mary and I became emotionally intimate long before Jim left. She revealed to me that her father had raped her during the Christmas holidays when she was seventeen. I'm sure it was the trauma of this experience that destroyed much of her self-esteem. (How much my own self-esteem was compromised by marrying her became clear only later.) Although Jim knew about what happened with Mary's father, it may have been my comforting and simple acceptance of her as a virtuous woman that won her away from him. Yet, although we shared a relatively healthy marriage in our eight years together, there always remained a haunting sense of emotional maladjustment, shame and guilt. I sometimes wonder what would have become of us if we had dealt more directly and thoroughly with Mary's incest.

Another event that contributed to our shame occurred while living in an apartment on 9th Street. We tried to finagle the continuance of Mary's scholarship money by not telling the orphanage that she had married. We did not succeed, and as I recall we did not intend to actully defraud them, although we were briefly tempted.

We moved out of that apartment after our first year of marriage and back into University housing near the campus. This seemed to change our luck and attitudes toward life, something that needs a lot of work in an Aries-Scorpio union. Fire and water tend to boil.

Although it was small and ticky-tacky, Mary and I made our square box of a house quite liveable—certainly for student housing! Everybody we knew loved it and had a great time there. There was never any shortage of beer or music. Even the UCR Poetry Group, which Mary and I started with Professor William Elton, occasionally met there. I turned the small bedroom into a study and a lifelong habit was born. It was there that sheafs of paper seemed to roll out of my hand and typewriter, including my senior thesis on Dylan Thomas. I also corrected papers in the dim light of that room the year I was a teaching assistant in English. Mary had decorated the living room with enough chairs and day-beds that we could accommodate groups of students and teachers, and I learned to cook for them (mostly spaghetti) in the small and often catastrophic kitchen.

One Saturday afternoon when Mary and I were showering together, a Jehovah's Witness came to the front screen door. From the shower I could tell who it was and, since I had no love for these creatures, I went to the door naked with Mary following. The guy retreated hastily, leaving a "Watchtower" and one of their versions of the Bible on the stoop, babbling something about Paradise lost. The campus gestapo were not thrilled with us either, especially the night we soaped each other and bathed in the sprinkler on the front lawn.

But probably the most magnetic attraction in our home for those who did like us was a little grey and white pussycat named Montaigne. Everyone loved him, and he was friendly. He was given to us as a kitten, and I named him after the great French thinker I most admired at the time because he kept making essays at the doors and windows. Montagnus Pussus Cattus. He slept in an old fencing mask which hung in our closet, and he followed us everywhere. Because she could not bear a child, Mary treated Monty like a son. He ate when we did, read when we did (I think he got through the Comprehensive Reading List for the honors program in English before we did), slept when we did. We were blessed with his presence for only a few years, and it was a major tragedy when he died from poisoning in 1960.

We usually left the house and spent Christmas and New Years with Mary's folks in Pasadena and Altadena. I have said that Mary came from an orphanage, but it was actually a girls' home in Covina where she had been placed because her parents could not afford to keep her at the time.

When we married, I got to know her parents, Iris and

Paul. Iris lived with her parents, Frank and Grace McLean, in an old hillside house in Altadena. Many were the nights that she, Mary and I sat up until nearly dawn discussing such subjects as Schopenhauer and Poe, consuming onions and wine! Grace was a fine painter after the styles of Titian and Michaelangelo, and she had carved the altar at the First Episcopal Church of Pasadena. It is a pity that she and my grandmother De Kay never met, for Grace's sophistication about art, her gentleness, common sense, and love for her husband, Frank, would have been very nurturing to Nana in her last years. Their home was eccentric to say the least, with the vacuum in the grandfather clock, the walls covered with Grace's paintings, and a buzzing wasp hive lovingly hung in the bedroom. But it was warm and comfortable with the grace of human companionship and conversation, and I met many incisive minds and hearts there—where in earlier days Upton Sinclair had been a regular guest.

Her father, Paul, did not live with them, but down the hill in Pasadena with his mother. I was prepared to hate him, but, although I never truly forgave him for what he had done to Mary, he was not an unlikeable man. Strangely, I was very pleased to find out later from a letter he wrote to Mary that he didn't resent me either, but actually liked and respected me! Paul was also very intelligent and had passed on these genes to his daughter. He had read to her extensively when she was a young girl, an enduring act of parenting, however deficient he may have been in other areas.

He was, among other idiosyncrasies, fiscally irresponsible. He was a knight of the road and had lived as a genuine hobo; I recall having driven him several times to hobo jungles along railroad lines where he would wave goodbye to me and Mary and hop a freight. But for all this he was reliable at times, and not a moocher.

Throughout the six years of our marriage, Paul came to see us only a few times, although I'm sure he always knew where we were. He showed up at the Crest house after Mary and I had been married for almost a year, and after that only once in Oregon where he impressed all our friends with his ragtime piano playing and encyclopedic conversation. The man was a brilliant raconteur whether sober or after several quarts of Gallo wine, but a six-pack of beer would turn him into an uncoordinated fool. He could have dropped in on us anytime, for he had the capability of getting anywhere he wanted within the continent in a matter of days or weeks. He never asked to stay in our home.

The one time Paul did borrow money from me, he paid it back within two months out of wages earned picking cherries in Washington state. We only heard from him once after our first year of marriage, but I have never forgotten his attributes nor what was hidden behind his thick eyeglasses: a blackguard and a reprobate.

While Paul was not the father-in-law of choice, I genuinely liked Iris.

Shortly after Mary and I were settled in our Canyon Crest home, several events occurred which changed my relationship with the De Kay family.

My mother had thrown a number of temper tantrums about the marriage, and had even spied on us in her efforts to sabotage our relationship. I remember waking at three o'clock one morning to see her staring in at us through a bedroom window!

Another disturbing event occurred in 1959. My cousin, Joyce, and her husband, John Osborne, had just bought a new house in the San Fernando Valley. They gave a housewarming party one Saturday and invited the whole family. Since Mary had not yet met any of my relatives aside from my parents, I thought this might be fun and enlightening for all concerned. Enlightening it was, fun it was not.

It was the usual middle-class family rumble. Since I was anti-Catholic and not very religious at the time and Mary was an Anglican, we could hardly contain our laughter when we were told that they had had a priest sprinkle holy water throughout the house!

Mary and I felt ignored at best; few talked to us. We were sitting alone on a sofa in the den when I heard my mother's voice behind us. She was sitting with my Uncle Bob in the living room which was separated from the den by a windowed partition. What we heard through the shutters made us both sick; my mother was sure "that girl" was not good enough for her son, and would Bob make a pass at Mary to prove that to Robert? I was shocked into silence; here were two of the people I loved and respected most actually planning a vicious, fraudulent and criminal act against me and my wife! Mary started to sob quietly, and left for the bathroom. I heard Bob agree to this subterfuge. I went to the kitchen for another drink.

During the rest of the day and into the evening, Mary and I stayed very close together, and at one point I even put on a public display of our affection by passionately embracing and kissing her before everybody. Hours had passed, and I thought that perhaps Mom and Uncle Bob had reconsidered their little scheme. Bob had done nothing, and Mary was beginning to relax. Then, as we were leaving, Bob put his arm around her waist in a very non-avuncular fashion and held her wrist behind her back; he did this plainly so I could see him squeezing her arm as I was walking behind them. While he tried to charm her he also undressed her with his eyes. I lit into him verbally as I was no longer the little kid he had been so good to years ago. I tried to get physical with him, but male relatives pulled me off.

My father drove the car on the way back to Riverside, and Mary sobbed with her head on my lap in the back seat. In the front, my mother was silent—as well she should have been, to have initiated such a juvenile and hurtful act. I was livid, and could speak only to comfort my wife. My parents dropped Mary and me off at our home in Canyon Crest, and then went to their home on Clifford Street.

The next day was Sunday, and when I drove over to Clifford St., Mary would not go with me. When confronted with the fact that we had overheard the plotting session, my mother had the posturing naivete to ask that I call my Uncle Bob and apologize for attacking him! I refused, but a few weeks later gave in and called to apologize for cussing him out and hitting him. He wouldn't talk to me, and I never saw him again. He died a few years later, so I will never know the truth of his motivation. I only know what I heard and saw. It has not been easy to forgive him, until recently. And I can never forget the pain he caused.

This event was perhaps one of the threats that eventually undermined our marriage. Mary had been devastated by her father, and now by her mother-in-law. I was confused and ready to strike out at anyone. Our marriage probably didn't end at this time because our relationship was still in a discovery stage. I don't believe we were yet in love. We needed to grow into that. The thought of separating did not become an issue because of a shared intuition of a life unfolding together. And, of course, we had to stay together because of Montaigne!

Then again, it is not improbable that Mary stayed with me out of sympathy. The shaking condition had worsened, to the point that, by the middle of my senior year of college, I could barely hold a pen to write. Marriage was a refuge and a comfort which enabled me to finish college. Without Mary, I doubt even now that I would have made it through UCR, let alone graduate school.

I experienced intermittent episodes of shaking which occurred regularly for at least three years. These were a source of major frustration and psychic pain. It wasn't my entire body that shook, only my right arm and hand, and there were times (when I was not called upon to write), when there appeared to be nothing wrong. I hadn't a clue as to what was happening. Neither did Mary, my parents, nor the doctors at the university. California Physicians' Service sent me to nerve specialists, muscle specialists, osteopaths, chiropractors, psychologists, psycho-analysts, naturopaths, and witch doctors (one even prescribed snake root).

By the spring of 1958, my arm was shaking so badly that I could hardly write or type. Both arm and hand had a life of their own. My thesis got behind because I had to type all my papers, and I certainly was not fast at that and sometimes even had trouble hitting the correct key. When I was desperate, Mary, who was a proficient typist, would type my papers. One professor, Dr. Goins, let me tape record the three-hour final in Peoples of the Andes, and so I passed that course but took incompletes in most others. By June of 1958 I was resigned to staying on at UCR another year; I worked extra hard to complete my thesis, and continued in the honors program in English. I made it all meaningful and purposeful by marrying Mary. I even got a job that summer in the Humanities Division as library clerk, because I knew books and I could file. All of my objectives worked out in the coming year except the honors program—the academic senate felt that, although I may have had the grades, the strain and demands of the program would be too much for me. In retrospect, I am grateful that they made this decision; but at the time it sure hurt, especially as my wife was one of the best students in the school, on the Dean's List, and in the honors program. Also, to augment our income during my extra senior year, she worked part time in the university's mimeograph department.

No one in my family save my mother, father and Uncle Jim would concede that I wasn't just malingering—trying to get out of growing up, and avoiding success and responsibility for myself and Mary by failing to graduate. They felt that because I had remained inappropriately dependent so long as a child, I was now too psychologically and emotionally immature to cope with life as an adult (everyone said this except, of course, my mother). While this was true to a great extent, I felt it had nothing whatsoever to do with the origin of my shaking; but medical science had no other explanation. As I naturally assumed the doctors knew more about my condition than I did, I had to buy into this convoluted and viscious program of denying the obvious physical nature of my condition.

Mary went along with this idea too. However, I'm sure she felt, even as I did from time to time, that something must be organically wrong. She witnessed my daily struggles to write and sometimes even to dress in the morning. Once, when I couldn't get a tie pin into my tie without sticking myself, she broke down and cried—a moment of empathy and love which I shall never forget.

I was now twenty-two, in need of glasses for the first time in my life, and overdue in graduating from college. My marriage to a brilliant girl with similar tastes and interests and as intellectually oriented, unstable and unconventional as I, was comfortable, even if neither one of us was blessed with maturity and wisdom. Our home in Canyon Crest was, for students, quite liveable. Our many friends, students and professors treated our union as a comforting and stable affirmation of the goodness of lfe. We both had jobs and, in addition, I became an assistant teacher for "Bonehead" English that year. And, of course, we had Montaigne.

Except for the shaking, our year progressed routinely for young marrieds in a small but growing western American university of the 1950's. Mary and I got along well, never fought, even when one of us got drunk (which was not often, but when we did it, was spectacularly sloppy). We never got abusive, and when hangovers came we nursed each other through them. Studying together was always productive, although we had few of the same classes, as she was a year behind me. Between us, we had quite an extensive collection of books, about one thousand, and it certainly looked like we were headed toward a comfortable if slightly unconventional married life.

Toward the end of the academic year in 1958, when I

knew I was finally to graduate, I applied to graduate schools. I received a few acceptances and one offer of a teaching assistantship at the University of Wyoming. As Wyoming might have been too much of a culture shock for us, we eventually decided on the University of Oregon at Eugene. We wouldn't be going for at least a year, because we both wanted Mary to complete her junior year at UCR, and I had to finish my thesis; I had my job in the Humanities Division, and she would continue part-time in the mimeo department.

My first priority that year was my senior thesis, which developed out of my interest in poetry. It occupied most of my time, as I had become fascinated by my subject for many reasons, including a personal resemblance to Dylan Thomas. In fact, it was this that first intrigued me when it was pointed out by fellow English major, Ken Harris. At the time, I had never even heard of the poet, as UCR's bias on twentieth century American and European poetry was strictly orthodox: Yeats, Eliot, Joyce, Pound and perhaps Frost or Archibald MacLeish. Thomas was considered a very minor poet, to be read but not necessarily admired or studied. (Years later, my looking like him was noted again by the bartender of the White Horse Tavern in New York when he mistook me for Dylan!

I found the poetry exciting. It hit a responsive set of emotions in my psyche even at its most laconic and obscure. Over the protests of most of the English faculty, but not my thesis advisor, Dr. Thomas Edwards, I got my topic approved by the department. Even Mary did not share my enthusiam for Thomas, although she was tolerant. To make a long story short, I prevailed, and "The People of Dylan Thomas" succeeded in changing a number of attitudes toward a great imagination who was to eventually be recognized as one of the most influential poets and wordsmiths of the twentieth century. Since I also dealt with Thomas' characters in *Under Milk Wood*, the drama department was inspired to stage a reading of the play for voices; although I read for the role of Captain Cat, I was not cast, but I did get to review the production for the school paper. I am proud to have supported Thomas when it was certainly not fashionable in academic circles to do so.

I also came out in support of the poet, Langston Hughes. As drama critic for the UCR *Highlander* and member of the controversial UCR Forum, which brought guest speakers of all sorts to the campus, I was given the assignment of reviewing his appearance and poetry reading. The evening, in Humanities 1000, was surprisingly well attended by white and uptight Riverside residents as well as most of the student body. My review was published in the local paper; it was favorable, analytical, and was full of praise for not only Hughes but black artists in general (Riverside was just getting used to calling Negroes "blacks" instead of "coloreds"). The next evening I got a phone call from a Mr. Valentine, the head of the local John Birch Society, demanding that I retract my support of that "nigger Commie." I was not home when the call came, and I did not return it. There were several more such threatening calls, and the university went under fire for having such subversive and un-American relationships in such a liberal format.

There were side benefits of our policy on the Forum. One semester we invited a naturalist to speak on nudism. He in turn invited Mary and me and another couple, named Bob and Peggy, to spend a Sunday at their camp in the San Bernardino mountains. Couples only. Great. The first thing Bob and I did was worry about getting an erection, a fear which vanished as soon as we got there and were forced to disrobe.

After chucking our clothes in the car, about which Mary was surprisingly prudish, we presented ourselves to the main office where a sun-kissed miss of most firm and alluring loveliness directed us to the secretary inside. The young woman's miraculous tits pointed to a desk over which was slumped the most wizened female body I had ever seen, one of her voluminous breasts dangled dangerously into the type-cavity of an ancient Underwood. Outside, nude men and women played volleyball, creating a kaleidoscopic panorama of breasts, pudendas, balls, and penises flapping furiously in the breeze.

Bewildered because we did not feel excited by any of these displays, we were ushered to wet seats around the swimming pool. The air was redolent with chlorine and the aroma of one hundred or more bare bodies. Relaxing somewhat after being served strawberries on toothpicks by buxom blondes, the four of us dived into the crowded pool. In honor of the occasion, we decided to try screwing under water. Let me tell you now it cannot be done, at least not without extreme acrobatic contortions which we could not perform. Nor were the men able in other ways. Dejected, we got out of the pool. In the course of the afternoon we talked comfortably with many of the people, and our apprehension about being *au naturel* was forgotten. However, this was not forgotten by the helicopters which kept buzzing the place, probably with binoculars feverishly focused.

All in all, it was a free and easy day; we did not accept their invitation to stay for dinner that night. The chlorine had made me lose my appetite anyway. We did go back up on the 4th of July, when the planes and helicopters were really out in force. Later that year, the four of us even tried our own little nudist experiment at Lake Hemet, but it was a limp and disappointing time, as were the sessions of strip poker we organized.

While the Forum fulfilled many of our intellectual, creative, and social curiosities, our intellectual appetites were unbounded. Mary and I took many seminars—small classes which were unusual for undergraduates but possible at UCR because of the small student body and the excellence of the teachers. The most memorable were on Dante (for which we learned a little Italian). The classes on Faulkner and Hemingway were absorbing, taught twice a week by Drs. Gino Rizzo and Milton Miller. I also had a private tutorial with Dr. Herbert Lindenberger on

Modern Poetry. We founded the UCR Poetry Group with Dr. W. R. Elton, who was professor of Shakespeare Studies. Dr. Miller and I were co-founders of the campus literary magazine, *Mosaic*, which I also edited. I got my first taste of library work as liaison clerk for the Humanities Division; and, as I have mentioned, was a teaching assistant in the English Department that year.

Since that year was full and profitable, perhaps it is good that I did take an extra year to graduate. When I did graduate on June 11, 1959, I did not attend the ceremony. I chose to celebrate by getting bombed with my buddies! Congratulatory notes came from Mary's folks, but among my family the accomplishment went unacknowledged. My parents were not speaking to me at this point; in fact, my father would not set foot in our house. The event was noted in the Indio paper because I was George Scott's son and had once attended CVUHS (my father was now vice-president of Pearson, Scott & Co.). I was proud of my intellectual accomplishments and of my marriage to a brilliant and beautiful woman.

The initial plan after my graduation was for Mary to enroll at the Univerisity of Oregon for her senior year while I started work toward a Ph.D. But she insisted that her chief desire now was to make a home for us, and leave the schooling behind. I was dismayed by this decision, as I have rarely in my years met anyone as gifted. I believe her desire was to create something more stable and "normal" than a scholar's or artist's life.

During this period of settling into marriage and trying to figure out our future, I was drafted. College deferments were not an automatic escape from military service in those days; it took a lot of manipulation to get out of serving. I was married and a full-time student, but it was my extensive list of doctors and deliberately faking the intelligence test that kept me out. Classified 4-F by January of 1959, I breathed again, and Mary and I moved back to Canyon Crest into one side of a duplex. Here, serious academics and a bit of growing up commenced.

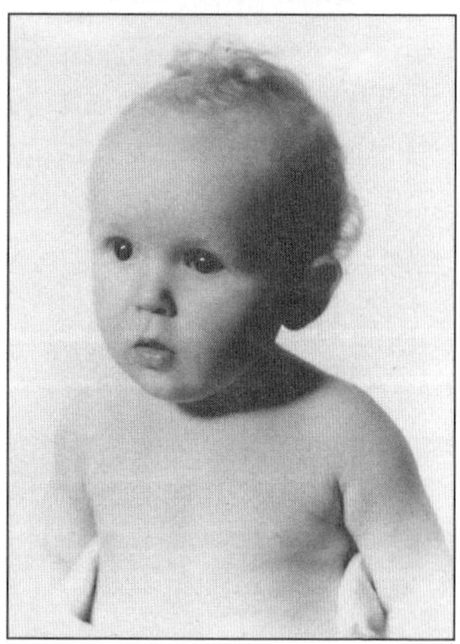

The North Beachwood house where I grew up, myself a bit bewildered at this new world, and mother several years before my birth.

My parents just after their wedding, my sisters Pat and Harriet around the time of my birth, and with my parents in front of the North Beachwood house.

From top left: With my dogs, Cindy and Bug, with my mother, my horse Flax, and with Flame, the movie dog from Rusty Pays a Debt.

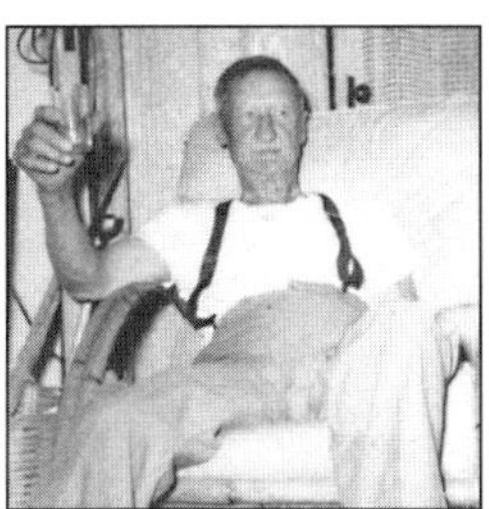

Learning to ride a bike with my father, my grandfather toasting the camera, my first girlfriend June Hedin on Uncle Bob's boat, and Uncle Bob in his rowboat.

From the top: Me with my mother-in-law Iris, my wife Mary, and our cat Monty, my sister Harriet with her husband and child, our cat Geoffrey among his reading material, and my hangout in San Francisco, Papa's Pizza.

Also, I wanted to take some time during this last year of college to get well before the rigors of grad school, and to see more doctors. (At the time I was called for the draft, the sergeant had exclaimed, on viewing my record, "Jesus! This guy's got more doctors than most people have teeth.") We liked our home; everybody at UCR liked us and I guess we were more or less useful and comfortable to have around. We had the poetry group, and social and discussion functions—like the Canterbury Club—to attend at Watkins House on campus. I only wanted to finish my incompletes and my thesis that final year; and I wanted to work with my doctors, mostly psychologists and psychiatrists, to try to get myself to the point where I'd be able to once again perform simple manual tasks without shaking.

The year was a full one: clerking between the Humanities Division and the library; monitoring and teaching English grammar for students who didn't even have a clue how to spell; being drama critic for the school newspaper, the Highlander; and being founding editor, ad salesman and proofreader for the school's literary magazine, *Mosaic* (which Mary and I named and christened and which is, at this writing, still in existence).

The more Mary achieved excellence in her classes, the less she seemed to like academics. She spent more and more time writing poems. I was very proud when she won the school's first "Creative Writing Award" for poetry, and I published the poem in *Mosaic*. Some of her work was also published in the local paper, but other than that, she didn't want accolades. She got on my case once for sending a bunch of her poems to *Ladies' Home Journal*. The reason I did so was because she wouldn't send them herself, and I felt she should share her talent with the public! They weren't accepted. I learned from her then that not everyone has the same attitude I do about their own work!

By spring of 1960, we were ready to leave Riverside, so Mary and I and Montaigne headed north to Oregon in a green four-door Packard. I did all of the driving (the one time Mary had tried to learn she almost put us in Riverside's Lake Matthews!). Our household goods and books were put into storage, to be shipped later. Our union had lasted through two years, and the future promised more of the same.

Chapter 11

THE BEAT GOES ON ... AND OFF

Expectation fainted
Longing for what it had not!
—Antony and Cleopatra

The trip north was Montaigne's excuse to howl from the prison of his carrier. He quieted down only when we got to our first stop in Altadena to visit Mary's folks. After that, it was a real effort just to keep the car on the road because of his lung power! When we stopped to see my sister, Pat, and her family in Berkeley, I was definitely in favor of having him tranquilized by a vet before going on to Eugene.

We experienced a monumental rainstorm going over Grant's Pass, Oregon, and Monty hid his head in Mary's arms all the way to our unknown destination. I remember driving into a rain-soaked Eugene, panicked because I didn't know where in hell we were going to stay that night, let alone live for the next year or so. We stopped at a real estate office run by a man with the ominous and suspect name of Titus. I thought the gods were beginning to smile on us when he told us a rental which accepted pets had just become vacant; beggars can't be choosers, so we took it, sight unseen. It was not classy, but it was a port in the storm, literally. This leaky, musty one bedroom, one story apartment was one of eight units in what affectionately came to be called "Grass Widow Court." It stood on a corner, surrounded by a vacant lot.

What we had in our car was going to have to do until we found something else, for neither of us could imagine putting our stored goods into this dump. We would have to sleep on the couch as there was no bed; and the puke green carpet in the bedroom was full of live water stains.

We made the place fairly liveable and stayed there a good part of that summer. Mary and I looked for jobs, and I was determined to go without therapy because we couldn't afford it. Also, I was beginning to believe that I didn't need it anymore, a belief that is often the last refuge of those who really need massive doses. Montaigne embarked on a life of sleeping and playing inside; for no matter what he did, he could not hurt this choice property! Nothing can ever erase the memory of subsisting on Kraft dinners and green beer; but this gut-wrenching, cheap diet did help us keep the wolf from the door.

I remember very clearly that about the second week, when we were actively searching for jobs, Mary begged me to ask my parents for money. I told her no, that I was sure we'd both find jobs for the summer and that I was going to apply for a student loan for the school year. For me it was a matter of pride because they had said we'd never make it anyway. She finally agreed, and we both cried and blubbered and then made mad love before falling asleep on our Salvation Army bed.

The next day I got a position as a library assistant in the Science Division of the University Library. Shortly after that, Mary became a cataloger/secretary at the Eugene Public Library. We began to feel that our lives were justified. We even skipped the green beer and Kraft for we'd recently discovered a pub that was to become our home away from home for the months to come. In addition, Monty got fed real cat food, not table scraps. We loosened up, became friends with most of our nocturnal neighbors—even with Titus, a prototype of the avaricious, cheap and grasping landlord.

When the long summer of 1960 ended, we had enough money to move closer to the university. We had dicovered a local coffee house on Ferry Street, two blocks from campus. A friendship was formed with the owners, a couple named Adelman. In return for running the coffeehouse downstairs whenever they needed or wanted to leave, they offered to let us live upstairs in this two story house where each room tilted a different direction. We accepted, and the rest of the summer was delightful: lots of friends, outings in the mountains, in the Willamette and Columbia Rivers, and, at night, conversations, chess and poetry over cappucino or espresso. Monty was ecstatic, because now he had a place to run and other cats to play with, and, as in Riverside, he was very popular with the clientele to whom we served coffee and cakes. It is quite likely that many of them came back just to pet him, and see him careen through the front door smashing the Adelman's pottery.

Our next door neighbors were Gordon and Lydia Strother, and we took to each other right away so much so that when Mary and I moved to a small apartment on Alder Street by the Millrace, we returned at least one night a week to visit and get scared big time by their horrible Siamese attack cat—a feline very opposite in disposition to Monty. We were now in the habit of chauffeuring Monty to the neighborhood he so adored every morning on the way to work. Driving to the tree lined street in front of the old coffeehouse, I would roll down the window and let him jump out. He had a mob of pals to run with, and we knew he would be alright for the day. When we came back at five o'clock, he was always at the appointed spot or would come running when I whistled, would jump in the car window and curl up on the shelf in back. This went on daily for several months, well into 1961. Then one day he did not come when I whistled. Mary fell into hysterics, and I was so upset that I went back every few hours that night to call him. After about a month of stopping for him morning and night we became resigned to losing our pussycat. Still, every time we came to visit the Strothers we scoured the neighborhood.

Gordon was an instructor in the English Department, and so he and I often discussed Shakespeare, Pound and T.S. Eliot way into the night. One evening about six months after Monty had disappeared, Mary and I left their house after a session on *Pericles* and Eliot's "Marina." When we reached our car at the curb, there was Monty curled up on the rear shelf just as if he'd never been gone! After that apparent miracle, we tried to keep him home, but his incessant meowing to be brought to the old neighborhood dissuaded us from common sense. He couldn't run too freely at home because our place, although it fronted on Alder Creek, was very close to the freeway. Two months later he disappeared again, and this time he did not return. A friend told us they had seen him dead in an alley, perhaps poisoned. We were sure he'd made it to cat heaven, or wherever skeptics like Montaigne go.

Mary was inconsolable. We agreed that the only remedy was to get another cat right away. So Mary spread the word among her friends at the public library, and I did the same at the university. A few weeks later, someone at the library said they had a kitten for us, but they wanted us to come and get it. The owners of its mother lived way out on Spencer's Butte amidst dirt roads, hills and forests. Mary prodded me into going on a gloomy Saturday afternoon which turned to rain. My car eventually got trapped in mud several feet deep. Needless to say, I got covered with filth, and we did not pick up the pussycat. Besides which, the owners of the cat, who were straight out of *Tobacco Road*, were not exactly hospitable, and they had no phone so we were unable to call a tow truck. With no assistance I had to dig the car out, swearing that I would not have that cat now for anything! Somehow we got back to Eugene.

Since Mary got off work an hour later than me, I used to drive downtown and park at the library and amuse myself until she finished for the day. One afternoon as I was getting in the car after shopping, I almost sat on a large caterpillar which was lying on the seat! On closer inspection I saw it was a brown furry kitten. It had been given to us by the library employee who had asked us to go after it; she felt so badly about the mess we had gotten into that she had brought the kitten to work with her and placed it in my car. I didn't know whether to be happy or mad; after what I'd experienced, I felt this animal might be a jinx.

I picked him up gently and told him how close he'd come to being a squashed pussycat. I put him on the back seat with my parcels, and when Mary came out we drove home discussing what to name him. Since Monty had prospered well with a literary name, we settled on Geoffrey for this one's principal moniker. Geoffrey occurred to me because of a poem written in the seventeenth century by one Christopher Smart while he was doing time in a London jail and had no one to play with except "his cat, Geoffrey." Now, as T.S. Eliot says, a cat must have three different names. Monty had, it is to be hoped, achieved some sort of apotheosis as a result of being Montaigne, Montagnus Pussus Cattus, and Monty. And so, Geoffrey, too, acquired several names: Snatch, J. Pussey, and Jeff. "Snatch" admittedly came later, after we had experienced his behavior at the dinner table; it is also a crude and corrupted vulgate for pussy, which I often felt he was.

As Geoffrey grew, so did our marriage. At one memorable point, Mary even snuggled close and told me in glowing words that she loved me now more than before. Jeff lived on our living room windowsill and took great delight in hissing at our landlord as he made his rounds. Mary and I had friends visit us from California, notably Bill Evans and his current girlfriend; my childhood friend, Richard Ball; and Paul, her father. My parents visited once, to bring me a long-overdue graduation gift (a watch).

I was doing well at work, although I must admit that it was not easy for me to learn the routines of a library assistant. I was a natural at the service desk and in helping patrons, but it was with the manual tasks such as tying bunches of periodicals for the bindery, typing and writing that I had observable trouble. I'd get them done, but always with much ado. Fortunately, everyone in the division was very understanding, especially my bosses, Al Roecker and Ed Thatcher; and my secretary Judy, whose sometimes pissed off and vituperative ministrations somehow soothed and made me more sure of myself as the days went by. I was, after a few months, beginning to feel quite comfortable with the job. Graduate students and professors valued my knowledge in serving them, and I got to meet and talk with such writers as James Michener. By the time Mary's father came to see us, I was proud to show him around where his son-in-law worked. He made a big impression on my co-workers with his knowledge, and I didn't tell them I had just picked him up at the city jail where he had spent the night as a vagrant! In fact, for several nights he entertained all of us with his lively talk and jazz piano playing at The Cellar. In one drunken contest with Pedro, their resident pianist, he was so victorious that the entire bar applauded him!

After six months the assistant librarian at the University of Oregon, Perry Morrison, told me, "Bob, we like your work very much, but we need someone up there who can write." Painful as it was, I understood. At least I had helped to support my family for my first months of grad school. Mary didn't complain as I made the rounds of Eugene looking for suitable employment in hours I stole away from my studies.

We had met a comfortable, intelligent and lovable older lady named Vernette Kilger in one of the used bookstores around the campus. She was a friend of Al Roecker, who felt bad about the necessity of firing me, and she gave me a part-time job at her bookstore. After a week or two of unemployment and with increasing pressures at school, that was all I wanted. I was in therapy with a psychologist downtown, a Dr. Brooksby, and, in addition,

I had committed to a program of copying and translating the Spanish I was reading for the master's degree in another attempt to overcome the writing difficulty.

I really enjoyed working at Prouty's Old Book Store, although making out sales receipts still gave me problems. Mary enjoyed the camaraderie too, and many evenings were passed at the round table in back discussing books with friends. During this time, she and Vernette became close.

Early that summer Bill came with his girl, and the four of us spent several nights camping at Heceta Beach. I almost lost our car in the ocean, as I'd parked it below the tide line. Bill and I also went looking for additional work and ended up picking strawberries to earn enough to say we did. Mary and I were happy, and both earning our comfort and independence. We had many friends, and reveled in the balmy summer evenings by the Eugene millrace, although I did some pretty stupid things when Bill or Ron Enns came by—like stealing bicycles and riding all over town. Later that year I took an additional job parking cars at a lot in downtown Eugene.

I completed my first semester of graduate school with distinction. I was considered an original thinker in Shakespeare studies, and for a time even did bibliographic research in Beowulf studies for a professor of Anglo-Saxon which was later published. My scholarship was sound even if I did get called on the carpet once by a professor for unknowingly echoing someone else's thoughts as my own. The head of the English Department, Kester Svendsen, had promised me a teaching assistantship for the following fall.

Prouty's and Vernette were very compatible for me, even when I had to clean up after her dachshund, Fritz, who always shat in the stacks just in time for a customer to step in it. I loved to go there after classes and shelve books and cozily talk with customers, students and teachers.

With the work I was doing on my psyche and motor

skills, guided by Dr. Brooksby, the future looked as if it would come in with a bang and not a whimper.

Toward the end of the summer of 1961, Mary breezed into the store one afternoon to say that she wanted to go live in San Francisco. I had just been told by Dr. Svendsen that he could not put me on as a TA that fall, but would earmark a post for me the next year. I was feeling despondent, and Mary's news was like an ice cube in my crotch. Because I hadn't been appointed to a TA didn't mean I didn't want to stay and finish the M.A. and then a Ph.D.! But she felt that, as long as I had to wait for the appointment, we might as well spend the year in San Francisco. I was both appalled and attracted by the idea. It galled me that she would have so little faith in me now as to want me to interrupt my graduate work; on the other hand, I was weary, and tempted by the notion of a break— if it wouldn't damage my academic career. I consulted Dr. Svendsen about this and he said that we could comfortably take a leave of absence and that he would notify me of my TA appointment the following summer.

So we packed everything except our books into the car, including Geoffrey, and headed for the Bay area. Our library was put in storage. Our first stop was with sister

Marital happiness? Here, Mary is either kissing or biting my arm.

Pat and her artist husband, Horst Herman Gottschalk, in Berkeley. I drove so long my eyes were bloodshot from the strain; mercifully, Geoffrey had much less energy for howling than Monty, and we all arrived in decent shape. After resting a day or two, we started looking for a place in the City, which even then was no easy task for an unemployed couple with a full grown cat. We finally found an apartment in a two-story house on Beulah Street just outside the Haight-Ashbury district. It seemed an ideal location, a block from the #7 Haight busline and just across Stanyan Street from Kezar Stadium and Golden Gate Park. The landlords were a Filipino couple named Pinero, and they became good friends. We were to live there for over a year and a half, something of a record for us. Perhaps the time seemed longer to me because a plateau in our relationship had been reached. It was the fall of 1961.

Those first months until early 1962 were a nightmare for both of us. My strongest memories are of employment agencies, walking the streets of San Francisco and Golden Gate Park, and of writing. I do not mean creative writing, although I did turn out some short stories at that time; again, it was writing in an attempt to improve the motor functions involved in putting pen to paper. When I needed a break, I would scour Golden Gate Park in search of peace and relief—planting myself on a rock by the lake. I would plunk down in De la Vega Dell and eat a lunch of cheese and tomatoes (poor man's pizza), often writing pages of verse (certainly not poetry) on a pad balanced on my knee. Most afternoons I would take the bus downtown, leaving the old green Packard parked in front of the house, and plod down Market Street and many others looking for employment, following up ads diligently clipped or phoned that morning. Invariably, they came to naught. I would then end up at the public library (where I also had applied), in a restaurant or, God help us all, the Howard Street unemployment office. It was a wacky and miserable time of sore feet and soul, during which I was convinced that I was going to get well by subjecting myself to physical hardship, by taking a menial job well below my intellectual capacities. Even one of those was not forthcoming. I had determined not to continue any kind of therapy until we could again afford it.

Except for depression over my physical condition, Mary seemed happy; I had taken her where she wanted to be. Since at the moment she was more employable than I, we took some of our dwindling resources and sent her to IBM keypunch school. She had gotten a job at Bancroft-Whitney, a law book publishing firm, and I think they were going to pay part of her tuition. For many reasons, her employment there was not healthy for our marriage, but I did not realize this until later when she started spending a lot of time in bars and bringing strange characters of both sexes home.

I settled into a routine of writing, walking the park, seeking employment, partying and getting drunk at night. After a time, I saw my therapist, Dr. John Card (who had been recommended by Dr. Brooksby in Eugene) once a week, for that was all we could afford (and that barely). Writing stories in the mornings came with difficulty because creativity does not flourish when one is distraught over failure to find work, and even less so when one is faced with the probability of repeating the performance in the afternoon. However, it is true that the movements of writing were becoming easier and less crabbed—though it was often impossible to decipher what I had written. I truly enjoyed Geoffrey during these mornings alone after Mary had gone to work, when he would lie on my table or open book (sometimes swiping his paw at my pen), or just sit on the couch staring at me. At noon I would take the bus downtown to start my rounds of likely looking ad-leads and the employment agencies.

At first, I shunned the private feed agencies, but in desperation I finally filled out their forms (every one in the city, I'm sure). At twilight, I would take the bus back home and, after a long walk in the park, meet Mary at the front steps of our two-story house. We would go up and change clothes, feed Geoffrey, and descend again to Papa Pizza's Pizza Parlour on the corner or to one of the many coffeehouses in the neighborhood for pitchers of beer, poetry and oblivion.

One Friday morning after several months of this, and of selling encyclopedias not-too-successfully, the phone rang just as I was writing the last paragraph of a short story. It was one of those high-priced employment agencies on Market Street. They had a job for me if I wanted it.

Within the hour I arrived at Sullivan Co. on South Van Ness. The boss, Joe Spanier, was looking for a reliable man to work the retail floor, selling awnings, camping equipment and miscellaneous items of hardware and findings. I would be one of a staff of about eight serving the public downstairs; the upstairs was used for canvas cutting, storage, and the cleaning of rental camping equipment. It was different work from what I had been used to, he said, but he was very impressed by my attitude, manner, and the fact that I was willing to do this kind of clerking and labor. I didn't tell him that I was expecting a teaching assistantship in Oregon the following fall. In fact I didn't tell anyone I had been to college until I was ready to quit a year and a half later.

My salary would be around $75 a week, starting Monday. I took the job, went home and actually enjoyed getting pleasantly plastered for the first time since we left Oregon.

The work was *very* different, but I liked the place and the people. I didn't even find the rough-diamond clientele and the retail sales techniques of reaching them unlikeable or incompatible. I learned camping equipment thoroughly, canvas products, how to measure for awnings and truck top covers, and uncommon items of hardware. I learned to work with the public, fellow employees, even the boss.

My year and a half at "Sully's Junk Shop" has nothing but good, warm memories of productivity, friendship and relating to all types of people. Except Nerina. A woman (and I use the term loosely) who unknowingly gave me my most enduring lesson in tolerance and self-esteem.

Joe Spanier hired Nerina to work on the floor with me about six weeks after he hired me. He knew she would be good at stock work, inventory, etc., but I truly believe he had no idea of how catastrophic she would be with customers or in working with the rest of the staff. As with everyone else in the store, she elicited both my pity and dislike and, at rare times, my grudging respect and even appreciation. She did, after all, help me in writing out sales slips and didn't try to claim the sale and its gigantic one-half of one percent commission for herself. But in all other respects, this mousy, dark haired, squat clump of Italian garlic irritated me in the extreme; twice I came close to quitting because of her. But Joe, who valued both of us for entirely separate reasons, talked me out of it each time. The second time, Joe promoted me to government procurement, a desk job which effectively got me off the floor and away from serious temptation to homicide. Once, when I came back to the store for a brief period after library school and had charge of the sales floor, I pointedly kept a camping hatchet in easy reach on my desk. Just for her. She must have gotten the message to stay clear of me, for she was fired shortly after that for taking an unauthorized vacation.

I worked there for one and a half years; it would have been shorter had Mary not urged me to stay. Despite the boozing, the juvenile behavior and just plain gleeful antics, which have a habit of taking over when young people live in San Francisco, these were productive times.

In my time off, I did a lot of creative writing and came up with a book of short stories called *Barstool Sagas*. A number of our crew of would-be poets and lechers formed a club we called "The Dirty Old Men." We met every Tuesday night at a local pub, the "Park Vista," where free food was served; we produced a round-robin novel a la *Naked*

Came the Stranger called *Everyman Unbound.* Also to improve my writing, I did a tongue-in-cheek diary of the time called "Journal of a Dirty Old Man."

Mary and I took full part in the cultural life of the city, attending plays, concerts and even an opera or two. The time was full of adventures, not all of which I'm proud of; practically every weekend was spent at our campsite on Mt. Tamalpais in nearby Marin County. Most nights centered around drinking, discussions on various topics, writing together or listening to "Nightsounds" on KPFA stretched out on sleeping bags I had borrowed from work, or dancing around a wine bottle. The most depressing thing that happened during this time was the death of our friend, Eldon Smith, from a brain tumor. He still lived in Fontana, and we were consoled a bit by knowing that El had been happily married for some months. But it was still a shock to have this peace-loving and gentle companion of our college days die at age 26.

While seeing Dr. Card, I became more competent at my job, the shaking and the writing improved—so much so that I began to be able to carry glasses of champagne without spilling them, and to control a pen steadily and legibly. I clearly remember the morning I had a breakthrough on this: I leaped out of bed, went to the bureau in our living room and wrote out two pages of what was surely nonsense—but with perfect ease and readability. Even typing became easier, if not faster.

The day finally came when working at Sullivan Co. could no longer fill my need to be creative and useful. One night as I was dusting off camping equipment just before locking up the store I decided I'd had it, no matter what my wife said. She, after all, had a creative job of sorts, and together we made enough money to have really enjoyed the best that great old San Francisco had to offer.

Kester Svendsen at UO had withdrawn his offer of a teaching assistantship for 1962-63—another reason I stayed at Sully's as long as I did. He wrote me a letter in which he said that he did not feel I could stand the strain of handling classes and grading papers. If there was anything I could have done, that was it; I fell victim to the man's fears. He was not willing to take a chance and make good on his promise now that I was safely eight hundred miles away. I felt this was a major betrayal, and I vowed to prove him wrong—in true Scorpio fashion. By the time I left Sully's I had become quite good at government procurement and had written a specification book for the company. After all, they had shown faith in me and my abilities, where Kester had not.

So that night as I looked out the store window at Van Ness Avenue, my mind searched for something I could do. I recalled Dr. Miller's voice at UCR one fall afternoon in front of the Barn: "Bob, I think you'd make an excellent librarian." Of course, at the time he'd said that I wasn't listening because I had my mind made up to be a teacher. Now I heard it loud and clear, and the idea appealed to me immensely, especially if I could prove to myself that Kester's estimation of my abilities had no merit.

Mary agreed, and I began applying to library schools; I was accepted by three: Berkeley, the University of Denver, and the University of Illinois. Bloomington sounded bleak from the description given by our friends, Bob and Peggy, who had done graduate work at the University of Illinois at Urbana; Berkeley required two foreign languages for admission, and would not accept Greek. So I selected Denver, and we both agreed we'd love to live there for at least a year. It was not cheap, but my folks promised to help us. I also got a loan from DU as I had from UO. Every bit anyone gave us was eventually paid back.

Of course this transition from salesman to library student could not occur without a setback. One day during my last month at the Junk Shop, when everything had been arranged for library school and my train trip to Denver, the cash drawer hit me in the balls and I nearly went through the glass window from the pain. I had had cystitis earlier that year and recovered, so this was a horrible shock. I was also scheduled to go down to Riverside that week to see my parents before I left, but while there my testicles got so big I couldn't sit down. I was flat on my back most of my time there, and in a urologist's office in Riverside. I had epididymytis—a swelling of the glands behind the testes in which the balls get bigger than a grapefruit.

My mother was in Hollywood at the time, so my dad got to witness my distress. He felt so sorry for me that he promised to pay all my bills, something which fortunately I never took seriously. How I made it back to San Francisco on a plane for an operation and to pick up train tickets to Denver I'll never know.

Mary and I had moved out of the house on Beulah Street into a friend's place in preparation for our departure to a new life. This was also the apartment of a man named John whom I later discovered Mary was fooling around with. But he would soon be out of our lives. We needed a place to stay while I recovered from the cystoscopy and operation at San Francisco Presbyterian, until I felt able to take the train to Denver. That I was being a damn fool about my relationship with Mary never occurred to me. All I cared about was recovering, getting to library school and hence on with the life that Mary and I had planned.

When it rains, it pours.

How did I know she was cheating on me? For openers, my gut told me. I confronted her in our kitchen one night. She, of course, denied it. But when she was gone late at night I knew where she was; the light on in John's place, which was just around the corner, was enough testimony. They also acted a bit more intimately than friends when the three of us were together, which was quite often as John shared many of my intellectual interests as well.

On a hair-raising overnight hike on Mt. Tamalpais I discovered he had brought a gun. He brandished it when we were harassed by a gang of black teenagers on the mountain. I don't know what the .45 was for, but he kept it under his sleeping bag. All I know is that I felt threatened by the gun's presence. Despite these incidents and because of our circumstances, I felt that this infidelity was a phase of Mary's that would pass when we created a more nurturing life in Denver. I decided to leave without her and Geoffrey, and she would join me in a few weeks—when the novelty of sleeping with John wore off.

Another friend of ours, Norman Sams, also known as Smily, who was in love with Geoffrey (there was some magic between this man and the cat), rode the train with me and then left Denver for his home in Colorado Springs. Once again, all our goods and books were stored, and my first stop was at a hotel in downtown Denver. The first thing I did was to phone my dad in California and ask for money; everything Mary and I had saved for the move and library school had gone for my operation and hospital stay.

I was still passing razor blades and red urine, so Norm stuck around for a few days until we were sure I was all right. When he left, I began the search for an apartment for Mary and myself after checking in at DU. There I met the man who was to be my advisor for the next year, Stuart Baillie. I was not impressed then, but this little Scot proved to be one of my staunchest supporters. I went back downtown on the bus, grateful to have been warmly received by him and the school.

Eventually, I found a place on Washington Street three blocks from a bustop and the public library. Not elegant, but it would do, at least until I got things started. Lying on my bed which overlooked the street, I was witness to some of the criminal activity that concerned Denver at that time. Lovely. My diet consisted mainly of yogurt and 6.0 Coors beer. The 6.0 beer was a gas, especially since I was not used to the altitude of Denver. I think Mary wrote fairly frequently during my two weeks in this temporary watering hole. At least I'd like to believe that she did; my chief thought was to do what needed to be done and get on with our lives.

I registered at DU and got a part-time job as a page in the Social Science Division of the Denver Public Library. Not much, but it was to see me through the first weeks of library school, although it didn't last for the entire year as I had hoped it would. The work involved shelving books in the department and retrieving patron requests from the basement stacks. There were many miles of stacks under DPL, and the young teenage pages who worked there full-time wore roller skates to move among them rapidly. I walked, because, although I was a fair skater, I had to go between floors; once, when I was searching a shelf, a page plowed right into me and yelled, "Out o'the way, old man." I was 26!

I found another apartment on Logan St. which would be much better suited for the two of us. Again, it was only three blocks from a bus stop, so I was glad I had sold my car while in San Francisco. Also, I didn't look forward to driving on Denver's icy streets during the winter. This one bedroom apartment had wood floors throughout, was unfurnished except for appliances, and would take pets; it was a large building, with about thirty units. When Mary and Geoffrey arrived on a train, we bought enough Salvation Army furniture to fill it up, and sent for our books.

I really liked my work in the library and I got to help patrons once in a while when there were no more books to shelve. Mary had the qualifications now to land a job as keypunch operator at Noble Mercantile, a packing house which supplied meat to places like Rocky-Bilt Hamburgers near the DU campus. We were happy, although I almost got mugged one night walking home from work right outside our apartment.

I looked forward to the day school would start. Mary got a job and seemed to like what she was doing, although I think the work was not as challenging as her job at Bancroft-Whitney. Geoffrey was very glad to have a permanent cat box again, throw rugs he could skate on, and a place to sleep—he spent most of his time hanging out of a cinder block in our home-made bookshelf.

The day came to have my picture taken for a student body card. As I waited in line my back locked up and for a minute I couldn't move at all. I was stunned, as nothing like this had ever happened to me before. Too much squatting while shelving books, I suppose. I finally shuffled to the front of the line and was processed, but that night I could not stand up to walk to work. As I sat painfully on the living room floor, Mary bitched at me for malingering; she was sure I unconsciously did this to myself to get out of working! At that point I couldn't have cared less what she thought, so I gingerly got up and went to bed. Geoffrey followed, and sat next to me as I lay there; at least he had sympathy for my plight. Unconscious or not, it hurt like hell.

In a few days, all was well again and I started classes at DU. After one week, I left the job at DPL because of the work load at DU; I had been at DPL a month, and they told me I could come back anytime. Several months later, I did go back to DPL to do my fieldwork there in the Language & Literature Department, and after graduation they offered me a position at $5,800 a year which I turned down.

Mary was very supportive of me while I was going through the bibliographic battle of library education. Occasionally she would even type a paper for me. She didn't seem discontented until mid-year when she started going to bars again and staying out late after work each day. I had hoped that John was out of her system by this time, but I discovered he wasn't when I saw her mailing letters to him every few days. I must admit that we didn't see each other much, except on weekends when we would go on hikes in the Rockies or just relax around the house reading or talking. I know I was guilty of spending too much time in the library studying and with my classmates, ignoring her, but that is certainly not a unique dilemma in an academic environment.

The shaking condition had gotten better in some ways, due in large part to the relaxed and understanding attitude of my teachers. They let me take my time, even on exams, and my handwriting was becoming almost normal. However, one afternoon when I was through with cataloging lab for the day and standing in a drugstore looking at postcards, I noticed for the first time that the shaking in my right arm was no longer isolated, but that the tremor was also affecting my chest. Nothing was hindering my progress in school or in accomplishing any physical task and, since the episode was over in a few seconds, I ignored it and went about my life as usual.

This library education and training was exactly right for me; I did well in it even by my own standards, and I met the best male friend I have ever had to this day, Charles W. Amick. In many ways we are polar opposites, but in the important ones that make a friendship work we are very similar. In library school, we were nearly inseparable when it came to studying, as our approaches to the subject were almost identical. At one point, we even talked each other out of quitting and going back to selling cars and awnings. We both have had significant library careers, he in Yonkers and I in Fresno. Most wonderfully, our friendship has survived more than thirty years, and from time to time I have the pleasure of getting together with this multi-faceted man and his second wife, Marilyn.

All library students are required to pass a qualifying exam in their third quarter. I passed this, writing in the little blue book with ease. Thanks to my own diligence and the study habits developed with Charlie, I had no trouble with the subject matter. However, at the beginning of my last quarter, Dr. Baillie called me to his sanctum sanctorum and informed me that some of the faculty were of the opinion that I should not be graduated because I would not be able to stand the pressures of the profession. My heart sank. Then, smiling, he said that he could not support their opinion, because of my above average performance and his personal knowledge of my capabilities. I was going to have to enter the world of bookmen and professional librarianship after all. I have rarely felt such relief, and I take this opportunity to celebrate my gratitude to the "pre-shrunk" little Scotsman.

Mary was not at my graduation that June of 1964, and that clearly told me that something was wrong. Certainly she could have gotten off work if she had wanted to. I had not attended my graduation ceremony at UCR, so this meant a lot to me; I was acutely aware that no one was there to congratulate me as I stood on the stage in Master of Arts robes.

Within two days, John arrived from his teaching job that had ended in South Dakota. I pretended to be glad to see him. When he told me he was in love with my wife and she with him and that he was going to take her from me, I registered mock shock by threatening him with the knife we were using to cut bread. Then I ran out the door of our apartment, and cried all the way down Logan Street to Cherry Creek and back; on returning, he was gone. I learned later that he and Mary spent that night in a motel.

The next day Mary came home only long enough to pack a few things, pausing to say she would come and get her clothes the next day and that I could have our entire library, which now numbered over two thousand volumes; she patted Geoffrey and left, not even saying goodbye as I sat there crying. When she closed the door, I sat there a few minutes, then picked up myself and the cat, who seemed to say, "Well, let's get on with it..."

Chapter 12

WATCHING OUT FOR NO. 1

Before I know myself, seek not to know me.
—Venus and Adonis

I did get on with it, by applying furiously for any kind of professional library job I could. The next seven years were to be among the most creative in my life, and as I look back on them at the time of this writing, they were certainly among the happiest and most productive.

In July of 1964, I spent a week in the mountains at Estes Park with my friend, Anthony Good and his family. Stuart Baillie and I had disagreed mightily over the school's decision to cut Tony after the qualifying exams because he had epilepsy, but Baillie was head of the school and also my advisor, so I kept my mouth shut and watched my friend Tony forced into becoming a bookstore clerk.

The mountain air, the chipmunks and the glorious conversation revived me. Tony's four brothers were Phi Beta Kappas, as was his father who was also a Rhodes scholar. His mother was a warm and easy-going person who thought I was just grand because I was so kind to and appreciative of Tony. However, the presence of so much intelligence somewhat overawed me. It became apparent to me that Tony, having epilepsy and thus somewhat slower than his brothers, had suffered much intimidation within the family because of their academic prowess. Yet, he was just as smart, if not smarter, and certainly more reasonable than at least two of them. We all got along wonderfully, and I shall never forget his father's remark when he heard on the radio that Lyndon Johnson had passed the civil rights act. "Well, we're in for a rough ride," he said. We were all Democrats, but that didn't prevent us from being realists. Certain factions in the country would react to this signing in verbal, if not violent, ways.

After a week of hiking, tossing horseshoes, sleeping out in the clean air and being revitalized by the morning chant of the monks in the nearby monastery, I knew I had to go back to my apartment where my landlady was caring for Geoffrey. I had sent out several resumes and been interviewed by a few libraries during recruitment week, and an answer by mail was due. So I reluctantly took the bus back to Denver, abandoning the hiking challenge of Long's Peak.

Sure enough, an offer was waiting for me in the form of a telegram. Geoffrey was glad to see me too, probably because his box needed changing. The offer was from the Ingham County Library System in Mason, Michigan. I would head their reference and book selection departments and coordinate these functions in nine branch libraries throughout the county. My beginning salary would be $5,700.00 a year; by the time I left, it had climbed to $7,100.00. Denver Public Library had offered $5,800.00, but I jumped at Michigan because it offered new challenges and an envionment and culture I had little experience with. It proved, in every way, to be the right job for the right person at the right time.

However, moving to Lansing proved to be something of a nightmare. I put all my books in storage and gave away furniture. The train trip across country was arduous, but Geoffrey, resplendant in a carrying cage, did his best to raise the dead in Dearborn Station. Carrying him, my portable typewriter and a suitcase, we made it into a compartment on a train bound for Chicago. The porter was very kind and even cut up newspapers for Geoffrey's toilet (easier than having to clean up later). When I got the metropolitan opera star out of his cage and settled in the compartment, he sat and stared fixedly at the scenery. He spent the entire trip craning his head to see the passing landscape behind and what was to come ahead. I even went to the dining car to eat and left him alone.

The trip to Chicago was uneventful, except that I left a well-seasoned briar pipe which I had trained since my first year at UCR in the ashtray of the compartment. By the time I remembered this, we were in downtown Chicago.

This night was to be spent at Mary's aunt's apartment as she had graciously consented to put me up. Aunt Mary Grace was, I think, something akin to a librarian herself, and she certainly had no ill feelings toward me because her niece had run off with another man! In fact, we even discussed invoking the Mann Act against John, and laughed. It was a lovely afternoon and evening waiting for my train connection to East Lansing the next morning. As usual, Geoffrey created the most excitement. Mary Grace and I were talking and not paying any attention to him, so he ate her rubber tree plant. He was sick all night, but I decided to let him be, no matter how pitiful he looked.

In the morning I took a taxi to the station, got there just in time and had to run and jump onto the train (which, with a howling pussycat and a suitcase borders on gymnastics—some good Samaritan had volunteered to carry my typewriter, and thrust it into my arms when I leaped on board!).

When the train let us off in East Lansing, the search began to find a motel that would put us up for one or two nights. It became quite a trek through the city. No one wanted to cooperate; no cats allowed. Exhausted, at the third place I bamboozled the night clerk into letting us in; I even promised that Geoffrey would be quiet when I knew damn well he wouldn't. We were given a spacious room with a great bed on which I promptly crashed, clothes and all, after shredding papers for Geoffrey and slopping him catfood that was rapidly thinning my wallet.

The next day I assessed my fiscal health. I still owed my parents, so I didn't want to ask them for any more. However, I needed something to tide me over the next three weeks until my first paycheck. I decided to borrow some from my aunt Fran, who had plenty anyway, and was a little more understanding of my situation than my parents. I sent a telegram to her at La Quinta, requesting a loan of $125 which I promised to pay back with my first check from Mason. While waiting for an answer, I holed up in my room and got drunk (I could afford that!) The answer came in two days, with the money. Fran was paid back on schedule, and years later she told me that I was the only one of her relatives who ever paid her back. As far as I know, that was still true when she died in 1992.

When I sobered up, I took Geoffrey to a vet for boarding. I could not look for an apartment carrying him. From the vet I took a taxi to Mason. The only realtor in town did not feel it would be easy to find a place that would accept a cat. However, he did know of an old lady who might rent out a room in her attic, especially since I seemed reasonably respectable and was going to be one of the town librarians. With little hope, he sent me to see the widow Douglass a few blocks away.

She had one room, a small one upstairs which shared a half bath with the tenant across the hall. "The cat will be OK," she said, "if you promise he'll be quiet (ha!) and that you'll clean up after him."

"Oh, I will," I said, "and bless you."

The house was pure gingerbread and had two rooms at the top of the stairs which had been added on. They were very clean and well lit. The larger of them was occupied by a would-be artist of twenty or so named Jim Sporkia. I gratefully paid my first $8-a-week rent and went to get Geoffrey. He loved it; there was a crawl space connecting the two rooms where he could have his box and privacy—provided Mr. Sporkia didn't object.

Jim didn't object. In fact, he and I became good friends. Jim worked for a framery in Lansing, and on the weekends he would paint or do woodblock printing in his room. I got in the habit of reading to him as he worked: T.S. Eliot, Melville, Kerouac, Hemingway. We also shared a spiritual interest in the works of Paramahansa Yogananda. What a pleasure it was to discover this farm boy who had read all he could of the Master! An aura of peace permeated these days spent in Douglass' clean, well lighted attic. I think we were both sad when they ceased. Jim left after some months to get married and live in Jackson, Michigan. As his room was the larger of the two, I moved into it—leaving the small one open for a host of incredible midwest characters. Later, I spent many gourmet, booze-filled evenings with Jim and his wife. Although we have not spoken or written for years, I believe a spiritual connection remains. One of his woodcuts still hangs in my kitchen.

After settling in at Douglass', I went on a walking tour of Mason which was a unique experience for me. From what I had read, it seemed typically midwestern: friendly people, an ambience of trust, one courthouse with a clock that didn't work, the obligatory cannon on the lawn, and one of every kind of business from distinguished bank to red light district. I stopped in Morse's Cafe for a drink on this hot afternoon, hoping to find "Mr. Garypie" (I pronounced it so until I met him). I was in Mason a week before reporting for work, when our paths finally crossed. I knew right away that I had found a fine boss who would influence my style in librarianship forever.

I reveled in being given the authority to buy books for nine or so branch libraries—a Jupiterian fantasy for a librarian and bookman in the lineage of Lawrence Clark Powell! I felt like a big fish in a small pond—and I certainly didn't mind! The people I was to work with were eminently comfortable to work with and competent. Renwick Garypie's secretary, Kitty, was right away gracious and welcoming, inviting me to her home for coffee. "The back door is always open," she would say. Our cataloger, Caroline, was a wiry little farm lady straight from Dogpatch, bright and full of energy. Gladys at the circulation desk managed her records and the kids who used the library with dignified grace. The other reference person who worked with me handling the public was Gladys Heipel. Her sense of humor lightened many a dreary day at the service desk when I was besieged with additional duties in the Children's Room. Florence Miller, the children's librarian, was a bright but slightly dour matron who was absent a lot. At the time I was hired, another man, named Clancy Phillips, was added to the staff to be branch coordinator. As I got to know him, I came to like and respect him more and more. Joyce, a young woman I soon acquired a crush on, was the bookmobile librarian. I spent a lot of time buying books for this county service. There was one other staff member, our custodian Ferris, who lived in the basement of the library. It is inexplicable to me, but I have always gotten along with custodians everyplace I've worked, and Ferris and I were always joking with each other. This staff liked one another, and most of them knew each other socially in that clannish midwestern way; this was not a drawback; perhaps it even helped us work together and accomplish more.

Several notable things happened during my two years in Mason, but two in particular stand out because of the influence they had on my future.

The first was my defense of a book in an intellectual freedom squabble with the city attorney, John O'Brien. Several months before I was hired, a title had been purchased for Mason and several other branches called *One Hundred Dollar Misunderstanding*, by Robert Gover. The book had been in circulation as part of the general fiction collection; in accordance with our policy of stamping certain titles "adult" and limiting their circulation to patrons over eighteen, all copies of this one were so marked. We were in the habit of using high school students at the circulation desk in the evenings, as part of a work-study program. In his confession, the pimple-faced page, who allowed this salacious reading to fall into the virginal hands of a teenage female patron, stated that he had slipped it (the book) to her under the desk, where the usually watchful eyes of Mrs. Heipel or myself could not penetrate. However, Mary Ann O'Brien got it, it was Daddy who discovered it—under her pillow a few days later. Don't ask me how he came to be looking under her pillow.

Naturally, Daddy read the book and promptly registered moral outrage and parental indignation. This staunch father of a thirteen year old threatened to have our book budget cut severely if we did not remove all copies of the offending tome from our shelves immediately. Of course, we would not, as the title had been added to our collection legally. O'Brien wanted to sue, so we insisted on an intellectual freedom hearing before the city fathers and citizenry. This was before the Intellectual Freedom Committee of the American Library Association actively participated in such proceedings.

The investigation revealed that we had added one other "dirty" book to our shame: *Tanya*, by Pappy Boyington.

Ren asked me to defend the books because I knew fiction better than anyone else on the staff. So I zealously prepared my brief. The fact that I was pissed off by O'Brien's idiotic holier-than-thou attitude only fueled my resolve. I have forgotten exactly what took place on the evening of the hearing, except that the books retained the right to be on our shelves so long as they were in the hands of adult patrons, not pubescent children.

One sidelight to this escapade: later Mary Ann invited me to lecture to her high school literature class on Henry Miller and the Playboy Philosophy!

The second outstanding event was that I learned to be a bibliographer and lecturer, and became certified by the Michigan State Library in Lansing. I also attained an entry in "Who's Who in Librarianship." As a result of my lectures at the Michigan Library Association conference in Detroit and at Ren's recommendation, I was selected, along with Florence Miller, to author a book selection bibliography for the use of libraries throughout Michigan. Florence was to write the children's book section. As far as I know, this list is still used retrospectively for purchasing books in Michigan libraries—filling gaps in collections.

My work was largely confined to Mason and, aside from being ejected from one of the only two restaurants in town by a drunken proprietor, I got to feel pretty comfortable in this small midwestern town.

When I did work out of town, the experience was always positive. At times I'd be sent to branch libraries to look at their collections; this was especially rewarding at larger branches such as Okemos or Williamston, but there were branches like Onandaga that were so small their only reference tools were a world atlas and a copy of the Lincoln Library. With increasing frequency, I was asked to lecture on book topics by these libraries and other local organizations. I really enjoyed most of these and learned a great deal about people during question and answer periods. Once, Ren and I both talked at Williamston—he on library administration and myself on the Bible as literature. We anticipated some flack from a predominantly conservative community, especially since my usual lecture topics were much more secular. Contrary to our expectations, the crowd was very receptive and asked good questions afterward. However, as we climbed in my car to drive back to Mason, Ren said, as he puffed on his pipe, "One of those ladies gave me a dirty look as I lit up."

Shortly after I arrived, I had initiated a book column in the local paper, and I think some of them were picked up by the Detroit Free Press. The column was entitled

"On the Bookshelf" and ran weekly. Most readers appreciated what I said, although some were irate because I expressed what seemed to them to be outrageously liberal ideas. However, I got along with old man Haydn, who edited the paper. He even printed one gem written five minutes before a deadline in which I lambasted everything from Mailer to marijuana to our sick American society!

I walked to and from work almost every day except in the winter when it was snowing. Even then I often walked because the cold air was invigorating, and it was a joy to make a path through the blanket of white. Sometimes the entire town would freeze over, and the paper boys would make their rounds on ice skates. Just for fun I often drove across the state of Michigan on the weekends and sometimes crossed the Upper Peninsula into Canada where the countryside was new and exhilarating.

Occasionally I'd go to a movie in Lansing or Jackson, or to a museum in Detroit. Spork and I read to each other and played pool (he was very good, and I got a kick out of watching him hustle suckers). I remember one night when, bored, we climbed trees and threw walnuts at passing cars. I also got a kick out of watching Mrs. Douglass play Canasta like a shark. Several times I was invited to have dinner with Ren and his wife, Barbara, an interesting woman who worked for World Book Encyclopedias.

After Spork married and left the Douglass rooms, I had many stirring and dramatic experiences with the old lady's constant string of renters. First, she decided to beef up her winnings at Canasta by renting her spare bedroom downstairs to, Hernan, a part-time student at Olivet College. Now she had every unused room in the house rented out, including the basement, which was occupied by a recluse named Ryder, whom I never saw. Hernan, though, became a friend and would ascend the stairs to my lair every other evening or so after dinner. Being from Costa Rica, he liked to talk with someone who knew Spanish and could teach him how to communicate in American. Also, just after he moved in, I embarked on a bibliographic history of Mason's only industry—a branch laboratory of SMA, the baby formula. Hernan worked there part-time and gave me a lot of details no one else would reveal, such as that SMA was full of copper sulfate and literally tasted like shit; I guess he knew, for the poor man could only work there as a taster, a situation which I thought was very unfair. He often complained about ruining his taste buds.

My old room across the hall was occupied by two entities in rapid succession. The first was a Paul Bunyan type who worked at the Oldsmobile plant in Lansing. He was Polish, and in our brief, blessedly brief, friendship, I called him Little Joe. He would come home at all hours, usually with a girlfriend in tow when it was late enough for old lady Douglass to be in bed. I often heard him, clomping up the steps and leaving dirt, motor oil and other debris behind him. In his more lucid moments, he told Polack jokes about himself and talked to me about his career choices—which were not many, unless he could land a job sleeping. Each morning he slept later. A doctor had told him that the fumes at the plant were killing him and that he should leave and find work outdoors. For whatever reason, he did not do this until we found him one morning almost dead from chlorine gas poisoning.

Following Little Joe, a truly pathetic cook moved in. He was fat, so fat that when he had a heart attack early one snowy morning and pounded on my door, I couldn't get him in my old VW to drive to the emergency room. Desperately, he gave me the keys to his car, a Pontiac GTO. I prayed he wouldn't die while I figured out how to drive this monster; eventually we flew down the highway careening from side to side. I got him there just in time. He had cardiac edema, and it often took him a long time just to get up the stairs at home. He was in the hospital a week, during which time I had custody of his gas-guzzler. He went somewhere after being discharged and left his car with me. I was relieved to see him in fair shape when he came to get it, although I was irked at having been left holding the bag so long without having heard from him. He then moved to a relative's home.

In the evenings after my neighbors left, I usually read, avidly—for my column, for library book selection or for pleasure. The room was small but cozy and comfortable with electric heat in the winter, and I had learned to jerryrig a variety of one-course meals on my hotplate. Geoffrey usually slept all day on top of the highboy and would jump down from it onto the bed and then onto the floor when I came home; after getting fed, he would climb back up again and resume his nap. Then, when he saw me start to read, he would again descend onto the bed and, with incomparable innocence and grace, drape himself over my open book. The ritual demanded that I push him out of the way, at which point he settled at my feet and slept. He usually didn't move again until morning.

This more or less idyllic state of affairs went on for about a year. During this time, work continued to be eminently satisfactory and one of the best learning experiences of my life. Then at home changes began, precipitated by the fat cook's hospital stay and subsequent departure. Mrs. Douglass decided that she had had enough of roomers, at age 90; what with Little Joe having tracked dirt and snow into her house, the old man barely able to get up the steps, the demanding recluse in the basement, and that librarian whose cat makes like an atom bomb whenever he jumps from the highboy to the bed to the floor. So, with the others gone, I was asked to move.

I found a temporary apartment in Mason after shipping Geoffrey off to my mother in the desert. It hurt me to give him away. I loved that cat dearly, but I knew I'd be better off without him now. I needed to be assured that he'd get a good home, and I knew my mother would give him that. He would also be company for her, as my dad was in a rest home by then. I made arrangements for him to travel to her by air, first class as it turned out. I believe I never would have survived those first few months in

A display I had arranged at the Ingham County Library.

Mason without him—having just been rejected by a wife! He was housed in an $18 steel cage, and I found out later that he rode with the stewardesses on the plane, express from Lansing to Palm Springs. For a pet, that's a lot of frequent flier miles. With this experience and his various journeys by train, he was now a sophisticated traveler.

The apartment I found in Mason was again near the library but on the other side of town. The place was new, and Ren and Barbara had also just moved in. I wanted to be near friends. My divorce was now final, as I had procured papers from a milktoast lawyer in Lansing. I felt the need to start dating again, and there was one woman in particular I was interested in. So after I had fixed up my apartment a bit, I invited her over for dinner with Spork and his wife.

My unfurnished apartment was on the ground floor, and that is where I slept. It was light and airy, with one bedroom. I missed Geoffrey, but not his box; he had arrived safely at Riverside and was welcomed by my mother's big lab, Tux. At least he had a friend now, but I did not. The apartment was quiet and, although I did have visitors and dinner with Ren and Barbara once in a while, it was occupied mostly by older tenants with small dogs but no cats, who surprised me every morning by leaving a gift on my doormat. But work was going too well for me to let this potentially boring state of domestic affairs get me down.

I now spent some weekends reading and writing in the library at Michigan State University in East Lansing and, since it was only twelve miles from Mason, I began looking for a place there which would offer a bit more social activity. After some search I found one, a two-room basement studio apartment with bunk beds and electric heat. Next door in a similar apartment were two girls with whom I developed a friendship of sorts—I think I took them to dinner only once, as they had boyfriends who were football players. Above me, however, lived Sarah, a lovely woman who looked great in a sari. We dated a number of times, and I remember necking during a drive-in showing of *What's New, Pussycat?* Geoffrey had been replaced. Mostly Sarah and I sat around one of our apartments discussing literature (which she was studying in college) or about what we wanted to do with our lives. After a couple of months, I broke it off because her father's influence dominated her conversations.

On snowy nights this apartment house was wonderful, with the big Christmas tree on the front lawn clearly visible through my high windows. I got some significant reading and writing done in this creative atmosphere, principally Tolkien's *Lord of the Rings* whose structure and rich mythology were to have great impact on my creative life ever after, and Henry Miller's *Air Conditioned Nightmare* ,which set me to shaking with anger at the stupidity and crassness of our society. I also started writing a book of poems which I continued in New York and finished many years later in California.

I found great pleasure and comfort walking through Michigan woods on the weekends, and the twelve-mile drive to work every day through peaceful farm country always calmed and regenerated me. I believe this meditative time enabled me to deal with books and people, and the O'Briens of this world. I also joined a health club to help with the shaking and to improve my overall well-being. For several months I had a thorough workout after work, and then walks in the snowy and invigorating cold. This went on three nights a week for several months. Unbelievably, I usually went into the bar next door for a beer or two after my session!

I had many friends among my patrons at the library, and some of them invited me to their homes for dinner and conversation. I remember the Grinnells and the refined and cultured atmosphere of their large snow-bound country farm, the ample meals after which Mr. Grinnell would play their organ.

Although the shaking was getting to be less of a problem, I was beginning to feel that I might do even better if I went back into therapy. Now that things were going so well, I felt it might be even more effective; Dr. Card had written me from San Francisco and said that he felt I should try to ride the first year out by myself. I had, and felt very good about myself now that I had achieved some measure of success without help. However, there were times when I still shook a bit, and my thought was that I could eliminate it by seeing a psychologist again. Finding a therapist in Lansing was not easy. One, a Dr. Tien, wanted to give me shock treatments to stop the tremor (after having asked me a lot of rude questions about my sex life). Everything told me to ditch this guy fast. I finally found Dr. Asselin, who guided me with understanding and compassion through my remaining months in Michigan.

In the summer of 1965, I decided to take two weeks of my vacation and drive to New York City and see Charlie, who had dropped in on me at the Mason library the year before. While there, I took in some theatre. Although I had developed mixed feelings about even seeing movies, live theatre remained a passion.

I stayed with Charlie in Far Rockaway, and was constantly busy. For the time, he had paired up with another library school friend of ours, Marge Benson, who was now working as a readers' advisor at the New York Public Library on 42nd. After Mary left me, I had dated Marge once or twice in Denver, but I was glad to see them together. The three of us saw shows together, and had dinner several times at restaurants in Greenwich Village where Marge lived; I remember that we saw Mose Allison at the Village Vanguard after dining at a French bistro where I had Tripe a la Mode de Caen for the first and last time. Another memorable evening for us was the comedy review at Upstairs at the Downstairs. I treated them to a Joan Baez-Bikel-Seeger concert at Carnegie Hall, and Charlie (Marge had to work this day) to a matinee of Eartha Kitt in *The Owl and the Pussycat.*

Most of the other shows I saw alone: *Funny Girl* with Barbra Streisand at the Winter Garden (after this one I got a real taste of what it was like to take the subway and walk the streets of Manhattan after midnite); *Golden Boy* with Sammy Davis, Jr.; *Roar of the Greasepaint*; *Smell of the Crowd* with Leslie Bricusse and Cyril Ritchard; *The Glass Menagerie* with Rock Hudson; and *Oliver* with Ron Moody. These were the Broadway shows, and uniformly great. Off-Broadway I saw *Zoo Story*; *Krapp's Last Tape*; *The Trojan Women*; and a real classy piece in a urine-smelling dive called *Live Like Pigs*. There were others, but that's all I can remember.

During my free time, I visited the Guggenheim and the Metropolitan Museums, toured Central Park and one night even got propositioned downtown by a fat black hooker. On one memorable Sunday, Charlie, Marge and I were joined by a gaggle of New York librarians for an outing on Fire Island. I walked the entire length of the island before we took the ferry back to Manhattan. Charlie and Marge were great to me, and I had by chance hit New York during one of the best theatrical seasons (even now people tell me it was one of the last great ones).

Driving back, I went through upstate New York and marvelled at the graceful landscape, especially the Catskills, that were slowly being destroyed by progress. I was glad to get home to my library and patrons in Michigan, a work-filled and productive fall.

Christmas of 1965 was coming, and Ren convinced

me to visit my folks in California. I took a plane from Lansing to Riverside where my mother was living at the Clifford Street house, with Geoffrey and Tux; my father was then in a convalescent hospital near Indio. Mom and I then drove to the desert to spend Christmas with him and stay at the ranch house in La Quinta.

The ranch itself had fallen into a state of mediocrity and neglect, partly due to my father's illness and the burdens that imposed on my mother. For one thing, she had had to sell off seventeen acres to pay the bills; for another, every available space on the property was rented, including two or three old trailers on the acreage out back. She had even rented out the main ranch house and retained the apartment she and my grandparents had built onto it for her trips to the desert. She had taken a second mortgage on the remaining properties, and with that money bought a triplex on Desert Club Dr. which she then rented out. Before he got sick, my father had sold the Navarro house for much less than it was worth, merely because he was tired of the monthly payments. When I saw this, I knew I needed to pay them what I owed them soon, and I did—but I still wish he had consulted me about the Navarro house as my work in films had made it possible for them to buy it originally in 1947.

My parents were surprised and pleased to hear of the new, successful direction my life had taken. I truly believe that neither one of them had thought I was capable of achieving anything of more than passing value, and that they were truly elated at being proved wrong. I was saddened to see my father's deteriorating condition, but pleased to be able to show him that I had made something of myself. For the first time, he related to me as if I were his equal. Although I felt some kind of breakthrough, I was aware of the irony. He was an invalid in a wheelchair and near the end, whereas I was just beginning.

I spent a long time with him on Christmas day, wheeling him about the grounds and talking about what I was doing and how he was able to conduct business from the hospital. When I asked him if I should leave because I feared I might tire him, he looked me right in the eye and said, "Please stay. I never did talk to you much, did I?" I felt this rush of feeling for him and with watery eyes I kissed him on the forehead as I said, "No Dad, you didn't." I did stay until the nurse said it was time for me to go. That was the last time I saw him, and I cherish the memory.

The balance of my visit was spent with my mother, Aunt Fran, Les Shockley and the ranch house tenant, a lively but vaguely dim-witted and manipulative woman about my age named Merrill. She flirted with me, and seemed to admire the fact that I slept outside on the lawn, drank a lot of beer, and damn near crushed my chest in the swimming pool at the Desert Club—a result of braggadocio and breast beating as I slammed down a water slide into the pool without looking.

I survived.

Overall this was a valuable visit in terms of my coming to understand my parents. This certainly helped when I got back home and found a bill in my mailbox from a doctor in Riverside for the X-Rays I'd had with the epididymytis three years previously. My father had promised to pay this, so I had just forgotten the debt. Instead of getting angry and upset, I just paid it. Before this last visit, I don't think I would have had the maturity to do that.

I stayed at the Mason library for about another year, because I truly enjoyed the job. I was somewhat lonely after breaking up with Sarah, so I worked harder than ever, writing my column, compiling bibliographies, giving book talks and defending banned literature. Near the end of the year, I decided to move out of East Lansing to temporary, more affordable quarters.

At work I had befriended a local eighteen-year-old boy who wanted to become a librarian, Russell Johnson, and had helped him get a job as a page at the State Library in Lansing. Russ wanted to get away from Mason, and his parents said he could if he moved in with me. Although I told them I would probably be leaving Michigan soon; they felt this would give him a chance to try being on his own.

I found a rundown room in an old house near the State Library. The landlord and his wife lived downstairs. Russ and I took one upstairs room, and in the room at the other end of the hall was an East Indian student named Jagit—pronounced Geet. He wasn't too communicative at first, and wore a Turban at all times. Russ asked me if he wore it to keep the cooties in!

Our time there was not entirely unpleasant, and it gave me a central address from which to send out resumes and take exams for library jobs in other states. Russ and I got along well, watching TV at night or listening to Geet's wild stories about his home in India. Russ even helped us paint the Mason library, and, as I coached him, he became very efficient in his job at the library, so much so that he rapidly secured a better post with them, and moved in with friends he made there. I was alone again, but I was about ready to make a move back to California.

When I talked to Ren about leaving, he said that although he hated to lose me, perhaps it was good, not only for me, but because after two years or so a book collection in a public library can become lopsided—reflecting primarily the taste of the person selecting materials. I was very flattered that, when Michigan State University heard I was leaving, I got an offer from them. However, I wanted to try my luck with libraries back home.

I had purchased a new car in preparation for my drive to California. It was a sea-sand colored VW bug—my first new car. Although I had no firm offers, I decided to just leave and wait there. My years in Mason had been more than satisfying, but I knew if I wanted to move up in the profession I should leave now.

On the Saturday morning that I left, it was with a heartfelt tear in my eye and a little choke that I left my key on the circulation desk in the empty library. I drove hastily toward Route 66, regretting that I had reduced the population of that little town of 5,000 by one.

Chapter 13

COMING OF AGE IN FRESNO

We begin on a cold, blustery day in Lansing, Michigan, a month before I left there. I was Head of Reference & Book Selection in the Ingham County Library System at Mason. It was five o'clock and I had just left work. Things had never gone so well for me, I thought, as I drove my new Volkswagen along the highway between Mason and Lansing. In two years I had attained some prominence in Michigan librarianship, but I was lonely for my native California and the life I had known in San Francisco. So I had applied for several jobs on the West Coast: at Daly City, San Leandro and Fresno. The civil service test for the latter had been administered at the Lansing Court-house.

I parked my bug in a snowdrift and skated up the walk to the house where I shared a room with Russ. Russ had gotten home ahead of me, and as I waltzed through the front door he shouted down the stairs, "Bob, you got a letter from Daly City; but be careful coming up the steps 'cause the damn blizzard blew the windows open this morning and there's ice all over."

The steps were nearly impassable and I grabbed the banister to keep from falling. When I made it, I saw that the entire room was frozen, right down to my cigars, toothpaste and bedsheets! The radiator and stove valves were frozen tight; there were stalactites hanging from the ceiling, and every circuit in the TV crackled before coming alive.

The letter asked me to come to California for an examination. I was not about to go there just for that; things would have to be a mite firmer before I would give up this post. But a month later when Russ moved out I decided to go anyway. I was sure that between Daly City and San Leandro I wouldn't be without a position for long. Even if they didn't pan out, I knew I could always go back to work in San Francisco selling camping equipment and awnings at Sullivan Co. until something opened up.

It was not easy leaving the wonderful staff of the Ingham County Library, especially Ren; nor was it without some misgiving that I said goodbye to the friends I had made in Mason. However, after giving a month's notice, I shoveled the snow off the bug and headed west. I figured I'd go first to Riverside, California, to see my dear old mother (a phrase I picked up from Charlie), and then north to San Francisco. I had friends in the City whom I could stay with and, as I hadn't taken a vacation in two and a half years, we planned to spend our time together on the town.

Later, when the couple I was staying with, Bill and Roberta Evans, left for Denver, I moved down to Daly City because I had taken the exam for that library. They still were going to make me wait before putting me on the payroll, so I rented a cheap room there and went back to Sullivan Co. to sell camping equipment, only now I was given a desk and made assistant to the boss.

One afternoon two weeks later, as I was working at my desk, the phone rang. It was a call from Fresno for Mr. Scott. I had no idea what it could be, as I had never been there. I had forgotten all about the test I had taken in Lansing. The call was from the director of the Fresno County Free Library. She asked if I could come down for a personal interview.

That weekend I drove to Fresno and was interviewed by the pleasant gray-haired lady of fifty or so who was the head of the library. I was offered and accepted a job in the Readers' Advisor section, and after returning to San Francisco for two weeks, long enough to thank and say goodbye to my friends and benefactors there, drove back to Fresno to settle for several years.

I liked Fresno right away, although it was a bit too inland after San Francisco, and dry and hot like the Southern California desert. The people of Fresno seemed generally friendly and intelligent. My impression was that they were a good, library-using public and that this would be a rewarding place to be a bookman. This was what I thought as I viewed the place through the doorway of a downtown bar late on the afternoon I arrived. The sunset that evening was inspiring, and besides, Fresno was the home town of William Saroyan, whom I eventually got to know.

I reported for work at the Central Library on Mariposa Street the next morning, to an affable mound of flesh in Personnel named Mable Walling. My first assignment was to Readers' Advisor, and it is there that I stayed for the next four years.

My boss was to be Robert Conover, a pleasant and well spoken man about my age. He was fairly efficient as head of RA, but not a born leader. His boss, with whom I was to get along very well, was a very bright and efficient Estonian lady named Maimu Franosh. My co-workers in RA were the people who served patrons on the floor and in the stacks of the library. Upstairs was: Adult Services, run by a wonderful and precious lady named Margaret Estrada and her sensitive, learned assistant, Barbara Adams; Children's Services, run by the ample Mary Farrel and her assistant, Cynthia King; Cataloging, run by the spectral and emaciated Tom Brooks and an assortment of servants; and the Head Librarian's offices, occupied by the deceptive woman who had hired me, Alice Reilly, and her feral assistant, Nell Minnick. In the Reference Department downstairs, where I worked occasionally when its boss would tolerate my cigars (a popular myth, because I never smoked while on duty; there was some reason other than that which I never discovered), there was a surprising amount of bibliographic efficiency. It was headed by the very aptly named Marie Borum, ably supported by Dr. Sam Suhler (who became a good friend), Edward Plummer, and later John Jewell.

I worked hard during the first six months, reading a lot and learning to match readers and books in ways I had not had to in Mason. I made a number of friends, both staff and patrons. Florine was about my age, and we started going out fairly regularly after I caught her adjusting her girdle on the way from the ladies' room.

After work and often on the weekends we would take in a movie, drive to Yosemite, or attend one of Fresno's rare stage plays. We worked very well together on the job, and we certainly shared interests and tastes in almost every respect. I jokingly and affectionately began calling her "Fraulein," although she was not German at all but pure Italian on both sides, with black hair and warm, laughing eyes. She loved books, as any good librarian must, and we had long discussions and sometimes arguments, especially over Hemingway and what wine goes with what food. She was a delight during those first months and for two years after that. I don't think I'd have made it without her or the movies, drives, hikes, books and food that we experienced together.

As I look back on our relationship now, I feel it was very sad that I dropped her because I started seeing someone else; at the time I did not realize that I cared for her so deeply. Hindsight is always 20/20. I eventually lost Florine for good to an incoming librarian whom, some said, she marrried on the rebound. Knowing her strength of mind and heart, I am sure there was more to it than that, but it was entirely my fault that she had to look elsewhere for the love and comfort I witheld from her. I missed the meaning of our relationship, totally unaware of my own feelings.

After I passed the probationary period of six months, Fraulein and I celebrated. Like her, I was now a bona fide civil servant. I began to love the security and the regular paycheck. I devoted myself to the work, and everyone liked me (well, almost everyone). In addition to RA, I worked in Reference sometimes, made bibliographies, lectured on library science, gave book talks throughout the county (a talent I had begun to exploit in Michigan), and ran discussion groups at the central library.

With Fraulein, Ramona, Jeanette, Joy, Carol, Karen, Brenda and Susie, I was expanding my social life over the next two years. One year I even participated in community theatre and joined the Sierra Club. The trouble was that all of the girls I dated worked at the library! This may have created a jealous mess behind the scenes I knew nothing about.

Eventually, Mrs. Reilly (or Tiny Alice as I had dubbed her) called me to her office. I went with some confusion, for I was fairly certain I had done nothing to incur a reprimand. To my surprise, she informed me that Mr. Conover was leaving at the end of the year and she would like me to become the new head of RA! Since this would entail promoting me to Librarian III, it would be necessary for me to take the county exam. I said I would, and I did and passed, but I heard nothing from her. I got antsy, because I knew how she had treated others on her staff, holding out carrots and then withdrawing them. I had seen employees in tears due to her duplicity and manipulation, especially Maimu, and Elizabeth Majors of my department. So I held my peace and did my work.

Then one afternoon the affable mound of flesh from Personnel came waddling down the stairs and informed me that she hoped I wouldn't be mad, but she had been appointed head of RA.

I slammed a book into the shelf where I was working, feeling outrageously cheated and used by shifty Tiny Alice. Over the years, I had heard no one speak well of her, and now I really knew why. It was my turn for tears which welled up and spilled over. I would like to say that, in true Scorpio fashion, I vowed vengeance; but I did nothing at the time. I would just go on as if nothing had happened, and know that somewhere along the way I would get even.

I knew it was not Mable's fault—it's unlikely she knew that Reilly had firmly promised the job to me. She had been there longer and was Reilly's friend. I liked Mable and her husband, Clay, and over the years had been to their home for dinner several times, so I didn't feel that continuing to work under her in RA would be a hardship. Thankfully, I didn't have to see Reilly, for she usually didn't concern herself with the staff or the actual running of the library; her strength as an administrator was that she had the knowledge to hire exceptional librarians who could run the place. But as time went on, I came to realize that I had to reclaim the power that I had let her take from me.

For two more years I quietly did my job. But I also began to publish bibliographies, give book talks and lectures, and lead discussion groups. These successes served to irritate Tiny Alice a great deal. I got her goat further by reviewing for *Library Journal* (which lasted five years, and gained me a great collection of books).

I dated every eligible woman in the joint, not too swift a thing to do. I was taken with three of them. Whereas I was unaware of the depth of my feelings for Florine at the time, my feelings were self-evident regarding the two relationships that followed my Fraulein.

Ramona was our bookmobile librarian, a puppeteer with a keen interest in many of my interests, especially science fiction. Although we had great times together, we never became intimate with one another because I didn't allow our relationship to deepen. Instead I nurtured a full-blown infatuation and eventually love for our Adult Services Librarian, Margaret Estrada.

My relationship with Tiny Alice Reilly did not improve. She demonstrated her lack of understanding and respect again when she discovered that I had applied for a post elsewhere through the National Placement Service for Librarians at an American Library Association convention we both attended in San Francisco.

At this meeting I was not scheduled to speak, but she was. I could not resist the temptation to disrupt her performance, which was putting everyone in the room to sleep anyway. I thought I'd wake them up. Most of the audience was a little drunk, including myself. I aimed an unopened champagne bottle at a crevice in the vaulted ceiling and released the cork into this with a loud pop and foamy shower. Everyone woke up and laughed, and she soon concluded her exhaustive drivel about the library system. Back in Fresno after the convention dust had settled a bit, she expressed surprise that I would apply for a job elsewhere. This was an attempt to instill guilt and confusion in me. She did not mention the champagne incident.

During this period I had little trouble writing and could easily perform the tasks required by my job. Verbal, bibliographic, and PR skills were the bulk of my duties anyway. The more I did of these, the less I shook or cramped up while trying to write. I will say this for Tiny Alice: she never questioned my abilities, motor skills or otherwise. In fact, at one point she offered me the librarianship at Clovis—a great gesture on her part, but one which I did not feel secure enough to accept. I could handle any patron verbally and bookwise, and I was fully confident enough to eject the rude or drunk ones from the building, often forcibly (I almost killed one pervert when he tried to have intercourse with the card catalog!). About the only time I did have trouble and my entire body shook was when we rearranged the library; the physical work did not agree with me evidently. After dropping several loads of books while shelving them, I sat in the basement and cried in frustration and discouragement.

I had hoped I had finally conquered this plague on my life. As in the past, I felt something was not right or complete in my body, but "the experts" said it was psychological in origin. This diagnosis offered the hope that I could cure myself through therapy and spiritual work. I didn't argue with them, which I see now was wishful thinking. At this point in time, no one, including my doctors, could fathom the truth. The advanced technology of the MRI, which would later reveal a developmentally small cerebellum, was years away.

Shortly after coming to Fresno, I had found a wonderful therapist named Dr. Sylvia Sonder, and I remained in her care for several years. Such treatment helped cure my insecurity and neuroses carried over from childhood, but unfortunately it had nothing to do with the etiology of my neurological disorder.

The last year or so at the Fresno library was spent on my love affair with Margaret Estrada. She was an alluring and ethereal blonde with lots of book knowledge and a love of theatre. She was forty-four and I was 29 when we started dating, but the age difference wasn't an issue. It was a time of comfort and domesticity for me and, for the first time in my life, I learned how to truly love a woman.

I also learned what it was like to be a parent to her teenage daughter, Rebecca, and her younger son, Marc. I think I managed to be a good influence on her son, who was eight. Mostly I remember busting my ass teaching him to fly a kite! I learned not take her daughter's hostility toward me personally—Rebecca would have actively resented any man in her mother's life. However, her anger was so extreme that I suggested and finally convinced Margaret that what her fourteen year old kid needed was psychotherapy. I paid for the initial sessions. After Margaret saw that they were doing the girl some good and healing their relationship, she insisted on paying for them herself. They went on for years. As far as I know, Rebecca is a happy woman today.

Margaret and I never married. When it came down to it, I just couldn't imagine marrying a woman fourteen years older than myself. This was, perhaps, a mistake.

The truth is that, without her wonderful love and attention, I could never have stayed so long in Fresno as a reader's advisor, nor would I have achieved what I did.

In the department, Maimu and Mable tried to make up for what Reilly did by giving me more responsibility, like buying for the record collection and acting as supervisor when Maimu took a vacation. Although these "gifts" of professional friendship and belief were appreciated and helped make my work tolerable, I could not ultimately find satisfaction there—so long as Tiny Alice retained her power over my position.

Chapter 14

IS THERE LIFE AFTER FRESNO?

Men are merriest when they are home . . .
—Henry V

A great deal of will was required to leave the Fresno library without damaging my career. To make matters worse, I really didn't want to leave a job I was good at and very comfortable in most of the time; nor did I feel right abandoning the many friends I had made in the San Joaquin Valley. I did know that I would never be allowed to advance in my career as long as I worked for Alice Reilly. I updated my personnel file at the University of Denver and applied for every appropriate job I could find in the nationwide listings. Thankfully, I had accrued a lot of vacation time, so I was available, when asked, to go on interviews all over the country—even one pleasant, first-class sojourn to St. Johns, Newfoundland for the American University there. I didn't get the job, but the fresh codfish dinner the librarian treated me to made it almost worth the trip!

I knew that leaving Margaret behind would not be easy for me, but I also knew that I couldn't remain in a stagnant position. Margaret also realized this and supported my search. If we had decided to marry, I certainly would have sent for her later. But my lack of self-worth and insecurity subverted our future together. I was offered a post as Field Librarian for the State in Caspar, Wyoming, and Margaret was excited about my buying a home there for us. But I got cold feet and turned the job down. Casper was just too rural, and I couldn't imagine married life there; eventually, another job did present itself, but by that time my relationship with Margaret had ended.

So while quietly working, I applied for other jobs, including library director. I did not believe I was ready for administrative work, but Maimu assured me that I was. Like Ren at Mason, she hated to lose me, but supported my need to extricate myself from Reilly's orbit. I spent several weekends interviewing, and finally two offers came in—one from Pendleton, Oregon, for library director, and one from Middletown, New Jersey for assistant librarian. Maimu, knowing me, advised me to take the Jersey post. But, with all the encouragement, I had gotten over-confident in my judgment—so I accepted the Oregon post. I had been there for an interview and liked the challenge the small library presented. I suppose I felt I would really get Reilly's goat by getting a job equivalent to hers. After all my successes, this was to be my first big professional mistake. After spending two days in Pendleton, I should have known that it was very unlikely that I would ever be comfortable living in such an unsophisticated cowtown, let alone trying to conform to its ideas of how a public library should be run. Revenge is not always sweet.

After a few false starts, though, I got the hang of working with budgets, scheduling work hours, hiring and firing, and dealing with a conservative city council and the innumerable book salesmen who descended like locusts on my office. But where were the books? I bought them, but the only time I got to handle any of them was when I had to weed the collection! Our sweet reference librarian gave me dirty looks if I invaded her territory by helping a patron, even though I was the boss.

I was able to control her territorial vigor after discovering a bottle of Vodka in her desk drawer. I wouldn't fire her — unless she had been guilty of mayhem. I merely warned her not to drink on the job. Besides, the rest of the staff would have gone on strike had I let her go.

Gradually, I improved the library through actions like putting the library on the Canadian Film Circuit, which was logical, and changing all the touch-tone phones in the building back to rotary to save a few bucks, which was not logical. After a few months of travelogues, which everybody liked and which accounted for the rise in circulation of travel books, the circuit sent a movie on wine making in the Napa Valley. There was an immediate outcry that the library was a sinful place, encouraging the use of alcohol. The film was returned, unscreened. Surprisingly, my staff liked me—or I got along with them despite their possible resentment of my "California ways."

I didn't move from the Temple Hotel where I stayed when I arrived in town; I planned to wait until I had earned enough to buy a car and could afford rent on an apartment. The hotel was four blocks from the library (this distance seemed to be a pattern of mine). I had sold my '66 VW before leaving Fresno, and needed a car in northeast Oregon. As it turned out, the library supplied the director with a car which I could use at any time. I drove many times to the Blue Mountains and the Wallowas, especially since the library had stations there; I took a load of books to these outposts every month or so, when their shelves of Zane Grey or Jean Stratton Porter needed replenishing. The people in whose homes these stations were located were polite but distant, so after exchanging loads of books, I would take my leave and drive around among the pines before descending once again into Pendleton.

Within a month I had settled into a fairly comfortable routine and, despite the pointed but dull differences between being a librarian and being an administrator, was beginning to find the job more than tolerable. At some point, I moved out of the hotel and into a partially furnished one-bedroom apartment; this didn't work out, so after a month or two I returned to the hotel.

A number of people entered my life at this time, but I found that I couldn't relate satisfactorily to most of them. I made a few friends outside the library. Two, Robert Hoeft and his wife Marjorie, I still correspond with and we exchange poems we have written and other ideas. I spent a lot of time with them and their fiftyish friend, Dorothy Baskins. We had a number of things in common including writing, librarianship and teaching. But people in northeast Oregon were generally more conservative and unsophisticated than I had found Oregonians during my graduate school days in Eugene; living in Pendleton demanded an understanding and tolerance I needed to cultivate.

Despite this, after a few months, I began to enjoy the job, walking every morning the few blocks to the 1916 Carnegie Library on the hill above the Umatilla River. I was usually asked to dinner one or two nights every week or so, and the local Kiwanis invited me to join and speak on library science—which, with some reluctance, I did.

Although there was some public resistance to a few of my policies, the library board stood behind me, and we did see a little progress in the quality of library services in Pendleton. At least the board approved of my innovations to a point — until I ordered two books for the collection which outraged them: *The Sexually Responsive Woman* by Phyllis and Eberhard Kronhausen, and a collection of erotica. To make matters worse, I did not order a book that was a favorite of one of the members: *The Confessions of Aleistair Crowley*—a work of dubious merit and dispensable to a small library with a limited budget. This was clearly an Intellectual Freedom issue.

In July of 1970, I made a formal complaint to the Intellectual Freedom Committee of ALA about the library at Pendleton. During the week or so of our disagreement, I had told the board I would resign over this, but I retracted my complaint and decided not to fire myself. I came to realize I wanted to keep the job. I withdrew the two "questionable" titles, but remained adamant about the Crowley. The board seemed to accept my action, and I breathed a sigh of relief and went on with budgeting, scheduling and making personnel decisions.

One morning in August, after I had settled back into a comfortable routine, I received two phone calls in my office. The first was from the Drama Department at Blue Mountain Community College, asking me to direct two comedies for their new play season. I was thrilled to be acknowledged by the community, and accepted the offer, resolving to do the best job I could on my weekends off! The second call was from the chairman of the library board, saying that they had decided it would be best if I left. I was devastated by this news. I had pulled in my egocentric horns and decided to learn something by staying and serving this community. I told the man I wanted to stay, but he said no. So, I addressed my staff, making up some cock and bull story about why I was leaving. I believe a few of them were sorry to see me go.

At that point I had no choice but to leave Oregon; I could think of nothing to do but call my mother in the desert, for although I had some money saved, I didn't feel like squandering it, returning defeated and humiliated to somewhere like Fresno. I could not bring myself to tell my mother that I had been fired, so I simply said that I was uncomfortable in such a podunk town and that I had decided to quit; she begged me not to, but said that if I did, I could always come to the ranch—one of the rental units would be available for me. My decision was to head for the ranch in La Quinta until I could sort things out. My mother and the rest of my family didn't seem too happy with me when I arrived at the desert.

Surprisingly, I did feel sad about leaving. Only after I had been back at the desert for a few weeks did I realize I had not been a complete failure. I had accomplished something, even if it was not particularly memorable. I mailed a silly complaint about Umatilla County Library to the ALA Intellectual Freedom Committee, an action which I came to regret. This was my second big professional mistake. It was wrongheaded, totally unnecessary, and ultimately caused me much more trouble than it did anyone else. I took over the management of the apartments my mother owned on Desert Club Drive, and spent a lot of time dealing with difficult renters and chasing leaks in the ceilings with pots and pans. Professionally, I did not know what to do; I applied in writing to many libraries, and went on a few interviews. I even toyed with the notion of creating a vineyard on the seventeen acres adjacent to the ranch, but finally rejected viticulture and oenology because of the tremendous amount of labor involved. In short, I was extremely distraught over the mess I'd created for myself.

The one thing I did during this period that bore fruit later was to immerse myself in the study of tarot. I began to give some tarot readings and continued reviewing for the *Library Journal*, which kept me from feeling that I had burned all my bridges before I crossed them!

From there I traveled to several places seeking professional employment: Modesto, San Bernardino, Las Vegas, Riverside.

Finally, I got a call from a distraught librarian who had also been the victim of an Intellectual Freedom battle, Homer Fletcher. He offered me a post as reference librarian in the new public library in Vallejo, Calif. With relief, I packed my things and took a Greyhound bus to Vallejo to begin the job when school opened in September of 1970. After a hectic month, I could leave the desert and start all over again.

I could not yet foretell that the next year would probably be the worst year of my life.

When the bus let me off in the middle of downtown, my first impulse was to escape from this urban blight by getting back on the bus. Instead, I registered at a hotel in town, a mausoleum of quasi old Spanish architecture. As in most cheap hotels, the room I got was dismal; the few items of furniture were tacky and dilapidated. I sighed, washed up and decided to introduce myself to Mr. Fletcher. As I approached the new library building on Santa Clara Street, I had an inkling that working in this new facility would be a treat.

Homer's office was off the balcony on the spacious second floor, and we hit it off right away. A tall, affable ex-navy man, he seemed to be a competent administrator—certainly without the warmth and personality of Ren Garypie but very unlike Alice Reilly. I knew we'd get along, especially when he said that he was most impressed by the fact that my resume stated that I had picked pole beans. In fact, I never had; Bill Evans and I had picked strawberries for a few days one summer, and we had intended to do the beans, but we never did. In a burst of Neptunian creativity, I had put this in my vitae—and it did just what it was meant to do, impress. So, Homer and I were off to a lying, but creative start.

My job was to be one of the professionals in the new Reference Department, not the head of it as I felt I deserved. The nature of the Vallejo library patron proved to be quite different from any I had ever encountered. We were not only asked to find information for these people, but they expected the librarian to interpret it for them. This was especially true of the wealthy retirees, of which there were many, and of these, it was the most true of Vallejo's "old money" scions. They felt they owned the library, and those who worked there.

Needless to say, this was not a fun job; I was being paid only $4.12 an hour (not good for a professional), and it soon became apparent that we were not working as librarians only, but also as under-paid baby-sitters. Here I learned not only additional professional skills and how to handle the most difficult and demanding patron, but also incorrigible squads of undisciplined school children.

Opening night was a nightmare: one teenage boy threw another down the stairwell and cracked his skull open. There was blood all over. I caught two guys necking in the stalled elevator. Kids broke lights, destroyed books, microfilms, emptied sand-filled ash canisters onto the floor, smoked marijuana in the seminar rooms, poured ink from copy machines on tables, asked rude questions and were generally despicable. Despite our efforts, this behavior went on all year, even in the presence of undercover cops. One night they blew up a copy of *Moby Dick* with homemade firecrackers they had learned about by asking at the Reference Desk. One librarian was badly beaten in the audio-visual room downstairs; another had her purse snatched as she left the building. I was mugged in the stacks by a kid whom I'd thrown out earlier, only to be saved from real physical harm by one of my pages.

On top of all this, I contracted bronchial pneumonia; Vallejo's damp and smoky climate, coupled with my transient-like living conditions at the Vallejo Hotel, created a miserable environment from which I had to escape in order to get well. It had been hanging on during January of 1971 and I worked every day, but finally got permission from my boss to leave for a week to dry out. I went back to the desert and did get well in a week; I was tempted not to go back. I did, and worked very hard in the next months to become an effective bookman-policeman.

I stayed in Vallejo until June of 1971. On the one hand, it had been a good working relationship, and I hated to go, but on the other, I detested Vallejo as a place to live and could hardly wait to get out. I was overjoyed to be gainfully employed by a library again, but living in that colorless city (and, at a hotel) was not exactly my idea of improving one's life! Some weekends I spent with my sisters in Berkeley and Oakland; others I spent writing short stories, reviewing books for the *Library Journal*, and continuing my study of the tarot. Every other week, I took the bus to Fresno for a therapy session with Dr. Sonder, to visit friends and generally to aerate my brain and legs. The stewardesses on Continental Trailways made the bus trips passable.

By about March of 1971, I was getting so desperate for companionship that I agreed to a blind date through a computer dating service in San Francisco, where I was going to attend some tarot classes at the Metaphysical Bookstore on Sutter Street She turned out to be a fairly pleasant lady, but no cigar! We had dinner a couple of times in her home town of Turlock, and that was it.

In June, I received a notice from the city that they could no longer fund my position. To be honest, I was not the least bit broken-hearted. I saw it as an opportunity to return to Fresno and mend some fences professionally, and as a chance to continue therapy with Dr. Sonder. Leaving Vallejo was like what I imagine being released from prison feels like— it remains one of the best days of my life.

In the Middle Way

My middle years were really a continuation of the life I had begun at age twenty-six—a period of growth and personal achievement. Middle age is indeed a second flowering.

One of the biggest regrets of my life is that I never had children. True, I might not have been a very effective parent, but the desire to have offspring is natural, and the longing I have felt to be a parent has eclipsed all else. In my marriage with Mary, I knew that parenting would undoubtedly have been a disaster. However, the notion that I might have fathered someone who could have contributed to "the world's pleasure and the increase of laughter" will follow me to the grave.

Chapter 15

COMING OF AGE IN FRESNO II

Presume not that I am the thing I was,
For God doth know, so shall the world
Perceive, that I have turn'd away my
Former self . . .
  —Henry IV

By July of 1971, I was thirty-six years old, and on the road again. I refused to return to the desert, nor did I want to mark time with my sisters in the Bay Area. So, the bus automatically headed for Fresno. I hit the streets of Fresno after midnight, and immediately got a room at my old weekend stop, the Blackstone Motel. Now, this joint was several shades of class less than Motel 6, but the people were nice and the roaches generally minded their own business. And it was cheap ($240 a month for a kitchenette, with daily maid service).

I wasn't there but a few days when a letter came from Hays, Kansas, asking me to come out for an interview for the post of director at their public library. Needless to say, I went; the evening interview passed smoothly (once I got to the appointment, for I had forgotten about the time change) and I took to both the people and the library. I returned to Fresno, and before the end of July, I had a firm offer from them.

But by this time, my shaking symptoms had increased and I was more concerned with getting well than with advancing in the library profession. And I believed I was healing, even since my interview in Hays. I was with a good doctor who assured me I was making progress; not only that, but I was facing a number of those people, and also neuroses within myself, that I felt were the root of the shaking. My study of metaphysics was also healing, and my study of tarot was occupying much of my time. I had even begun coloring my own cards.

I was almost thirty-six in 1972 when my father died. I had just gotten out of the shower one morning when sister Pat called from Oakland with the news. He died in Indio, and neither my sisters nor I were asked to attend the funeral service. For a few days I mourned his passing, and that our relationship had not been more intimate. But then turned back to concerns about my own life and health.

Because of the shaking, I had come to fear dealing with the realities of being an adult. I retreated into my studies and therapy sessions and declined the post in Kansas. It did not occur to me that I could have continued to heal and do metaphysics out there—and have been gainfully employed in my profession to boot! It saddens me to note that I now know that neuroses and imagined fears had absolutely nothing to do with my shaking, at least in the beginning. Rather, neuroses and fears were a product of the shaking and made my condition worse by creating overwhelming anxieties out of the routines of daily living. I like to think that if I had known then what I know now about my cerebellar condition, nothing would have stopped me from taking the job in Hays. It is true that the decades of therapy had helped me immeasureably, but it went on far too long, and it certainly couldn't treat the cause of the shaking. Therapy was invaluable in treating my anxieties and fears, but they, as we know, were caused in large part by my condition.

I was to stay in Fresno for the next two years, working part of the time as a security guard at K-Mart and later as a camping equipment salesman at Tent City on the road to Yosemite. I also continued my studies of astrology and tarot, taking classes and teaching some myself on the "History of Metaphysics." I also began to give tarot readings and I was soon asked to give lectures. As a result, publication in magazines came for the first time, possibly because I felt creatively freed up. Two articles appeared in journals of literary criticism a year apart, one on *King Lear* and one on T.S. Eliot and the tarot.

These activities were energizing. I was getting around so well and feeling so good that I was sure I was going to be completely cured of the shaking. Any lack of coordination I always thought to be nothing more than mere clumsiness, and this was never bad enough to interfere significantly with what I needed to do in life. I continued therapy with Dr. Sonder, writing, and reviewing books for *Library Journal* and the *Fresno Bee*.

By September of 1973, I was hired by the Fresno County Economic Opportunities Commission to create an in-house library. It proved to be quite successful; after a year we were written up in the National Directory of Special Libraries. With a secretary, who had the clerical skills I did not, the basic collection was created in a room no bigger than a large closet. When we moved downstairs in the Rowell Building on Tulare Street, the library was given a room surrounded by glass three times the original size. Fresno's business community soon discovered that what they could not find at the County Library, we could probably supply.

I administered this library happily until the summer of 1975, and even badgered the boss into giving me a raise in 1974. This was after my first book appeared, a how-to manual for creating a CAP (Community Action Program) Library. The book sold internationally and went through two small printings. I was quite pleased with it, although I got no royalties, as it was written as part of my job.

Without the typing and drawing skills of my secretary, Margie Wong, I never could have published this book, which one reviewer said "demystified the library profession." A lot of the credit goes to Margie, who typed the chapters immediately after I wrote them and made diagrams where necessary.

When the book came out and started selling to public libraries, schools, and community action programs, we celebrated by taking our vacation time that year in Ashland, Oregon, for a round of playgoing at the Oregon Shakespeare Festival. Margie was a very intelligent microbiology major and had never seen much theatre, if any. My taking her was purely in appreciation; there was nothing romantic between us. She enjoyed the long weekend tremendously, reading, for the first time, every Shakespeare play we saw. When we came back to the Fresno airport, she told me she'd remember this time and the plays for the rest of her life. That was royalty enough for me.

The long weekend over in that summer of 1974, I returned to find that the library had survived without me and to a stack of book orders. Aside from these, I was getting pretty bored with the job. Lecturing and astrology work were fully occupying the off hours, but I did not look to that for making a living as yet. So, the interview procedure started again, and after one in San Francisco for the public library in Lorain, Ohio, I was hired to be reader's advisor there, starting in September of 1975. As always, that "still small voice within" told me not to take this job, but I did. After all, the position was a good one.

Chapter 16

ANOTHER BEGINNING

Why then the world's my oyster,
Which I with sword will open.
　　　　　—The Merry Wives of Windsor

The position was a good one in many ways. I was the head of the Reader's Advisor Department and had my own parking space, but I was uncomfortable there. While disenchanted with librarianship and feeling frustrated in general, I was also experiencing a certain degree of culture shock. At that time, Cleveland had one of the highest crime rates of all American cities. One could get mugged just walking to the corner. I was afraid, depressed by the crowded and ugly surroundings, and unsure of myself. So after several months of ups and downs, including a personality conflict between the boss and myself, I decided to leave Ohio and return to the West Coast.

I flew back to California to stay with my sister, Pat, in Oakland. We had always had a good relationship, so I felt comfortable to come and go as I pleased. We saw each other for dinner and spent evenings talking about Freud, Jung, Adler, and Rogers. We also discussed literature and metaphysics and watched PBS. It was an enlightening and enjoyable time.

During the four or five months that I was in Oakland, I did a lot of research on Shakespeare and the tarot. These apparently dichotomous interests would someday prove symbiotic. Shakespeare would prove to be an excellent diviner and interpreter of both tarot and astrology. I have since used his understanding of the human psyche in countless readings. At this time, I felt like I was beginning to realize the desires of my heart. I knew that I wanted to continue exploring metaphysical work, and so, I became involved with the Metaphysical Center on Sutter Street in San Francisco. The building housed a large bookstore with a variety of new age material. I took classes there in astrology and tarot and learned to give in-depth readings.

Pat was teaching Women's Studies at Laney College and also practicing clinical psychology. She began to refer a number of her clients to me for astrological work, sometimes asking me to do the charts of difficult patients. As a therapist, she believed it was a valuable tool in the treatment process. It also eliminated a lot of couch time. I was grateful for the experience and eager to learn more.

I asked Lynn Palmer, a world famous astrologer and friend, who was living in New York at the time, and other astrologers at the Metaphysical Center whether or not I should continue this practice and eventually go into business with it. The answer was always a resounding yes. They said it would give me the opportunity to fulfill the part of myself I had never dealt with and that turned out to be quite true. It seemed everything I did at this time conspired to lead me to my life's work.

So I moved back to Fresno and rented a place to set up shop. My office was an upstairs room in my house. It was a good way to start out since finances were thin. I was living off money I had saved and rental checks from the desert properties which my mother sent once a month.

It was during this time that I became acquainted with the Church of Religious Science (a minister who also lived in the housing complex introduced me). It was to be one of the crystallizing spiritual experiences of my life. I started attending Sunday services on a regular basis, something I had not done since childhood. The fellowship provided a sense of brotherhood for me, a communion of like-minded souls. It was the first time I had ever been to a church where I actually enjoyed the company and felt enlivened by the people. We shared meals together quite often and organized meetings to discuss relevant issues. The teachings were very affirming for me and opened me up to essential truths like the idea that we create our own reality, including to a certain extent our physical conditions. I still believe this is true, but to a limited degree—certain things we cannot direct, such as being born with a cerebellum that is too small. Perhaps it is how we use what we are given that is, in the end, important.

Around this time I crossed paths with an old friend who took me aside and wanted me to become a Mason. I never did, but the philosophy that he introduced me to was extremely important to the development of my work as an astrologer. You see, the tarot was, at one time, an integral part of Masonry. It seemed more like a spiritual order to me rather than a formal religion, kind of liberalized Christianity. They taught that there is magic in creation, and that we have the ability to use it for the good of ourselves and others, and, above all, that life is a miracle.

I also began to study Hatha Yoga. The class, taught by a woman who was a disciple of the famous teacher, Charles Shalom, met in a room at the Church of Religious Science. This practice improved my physical condition tremendously and calmed my mind. I continued doing Yoga for a couple of years and this, along with my exploration of metaphysics, contributed to a sort of spiritual awakening. But I still felt I needed to shed a lot of emotional baggage in order to move forward.

It's important to remember that the 1970s were the flagship of the human potential movement. As if in answer to my need Pat called me, and she said I ought to look into taking the Fischer-Hoffman process. They were having a weekend retreat in San Francisco. Bob Hoffman was the director and Fischer was a dead psychiatrist whom Bob channeled. He received instruction from Fischer for conducting the process. Today, twenty-five years later, at the end of the millennium, the idea of channeling is still a maverick idea at best. So, although a bit skeptical, I said I'd look into it. After a week went by, it dawned on me that I'd damned well better try it. I felt there was something to be found that I really needed. I got on a plane from Fresno to San Francisco.

Most of the productive sessions of the Fischer-Hoffman process were conducted upstairs in a large office building. I remember it was a very warm and beautiful summer, the spring of 1976. There were about twenty of us taking that session. One was a professor of psychology at Fresno State, Harrison Madden. It happened that we knew each other and could ride from Fresno to San Francisco together. We rode back and forth from Fresno several times to the sessions. We'd talk about the process, its potential and our goals. However, after the first four sessions I elected to remain in San Francisco rather than travel back and forth. For three grueling, heart wrenching months the Geary Hotel was to be my home.

Bob Hoffman was the teacher as well as the director. He pointed out that during the Process we would go through four distinct processes. It was a complex procedure and involved a total reorganization of the self. First you had to get divorced from your mother and father. Only then could you come to a full realization of who you are as an individual and as a soul; only then could you begin to reintegrate body, mind, and spirit. The theory was that through this divorce you first learn how you truly feel about your mother—often a vast array of negative and positive emotions—hate, love, betrayal, abandonment, yearning, etc. After the divorce, you then go through a process of learning to unconditionally love your mother. You then do the same thing with your father. And then with yourself. The final process was to integrate the results of all three in order to realize the total potential of one's self. This process resonated with me. My secret hope was that maybe this would help me stop shaking. Of course it couldn't have had anything to do with the shaking, except for my ability to cope with it and to live productively in spite of it.

At one point, Bob got me out in the middle of the floor. Holding a cushion in his hand, he said, "Well, this cushion is your father. Start talking to him." I ended up in tears, beating the shit out of the cushion. "You fucking bastard; you son of a bitch," I screamed, tears streaming down my face. I'd never shaken so much. This was a true emotional upheaval, and I felt so much relief. I had no idea I was harboring such depths of hate and love for the old man. The task afterward, Bob said, is to integrate these feelings, because that's part of our conflict.

I wrote a journal which was four inches thick. Our job was to examine every angle of our feelings about mom and dad, ourselves, and the important people in our lives. Both the writing and the sessions were very intense. We usually met at seven o'clock in the evening in an office building on North Van Ness. We'd go through the different steps of learning to love and hate, and what they actually meant. We wrote out everything. We had assignments to rail at mother, at father, at ourselves. Sometimes my rantings became very physical. I'd scream, pound the bed, the walls, jump around till the floor shook. Several times I got thrown out of my room in the hotel.

For some of the sessions I went to Lake Merritt in Oakland and was able to carry on as needed outside. I left my negative father on Point Reyes, a beautiful and wild jetty overlooking the Pacific. I was up there walking and yelling my heart out. Walking back to my car crying, I felt as if I'd left pounds of shit behind. That negative father didn't follow me back; he was gone. Perhaps he's still there, hoping I'll come back to claim him, hoist him on my back and carry him with me to the grave. I advise him to wait no more.

I remember I had my last beer up there and never

drank again. Some of the ranting sessions I carried out in a secluded part of Golden Gate Park, where I beat the tar out of a tree with my feet and some stray branches to exorcise my rage. Then I drove into the mountains to work out how I felt about myself.

One night toward the end of three months, we all took any unresolved feelings we still had and just talked and screamed, acting our feelings out. Anything went. You could hit people, objects, anything. That room, filled with ejected pain, was a big mess at the end because one young woman brought a big cabbage and pretended it was her father's head. She threw it at the wall.

I stood in the center and declaimed against my father with Shakespeare, reciting the speech from Henry V, "Once more into the breach dear friends...for Harry, England, and St. George," all the while pounding the floor and furniture in anger. At the time I felt that while it was partially an act, it was also a great release. But when I went out into the lobby and bought coffee, Bob said, "Why can't you learn to love your father?" And I said, "You goddamned son of a bitch, I'm tired of you, too." Then we both let our mutual frustration go. Finally, he threw his arms around me and said, "That's what I wanted!" I realized then that this was a cathartic experience, although it did not do much for my shaking condition.

I rarely thought about the shaking for those three months, except once, when the group challenged me to change a lightbulb. I was shaking too much to do it. I couldn't screw the bulb in. My fellow students and teachers still thought there was something neurotic about me that caused me to shake, so they weren't exactly cooperative or sympathetic when it happened. I imagine they thought, "Oh, it'll be good for you. Work through it." Little did they know that their demand was torture. I look back on much of my life and see my own and others reaction to my shaking—it rankles me that I was defined by something that I couldn't control. Still, I sometimes wonder if it would have changed my life positively had I known the cause. Perhaps my motivation to understand myself and others would not have been as strong. Perhaps I would not have undergone therapy or the Fischer-Hoffman process. Perhaps my seeking would have been limited to finding a good woman and a satisfying job. There often seems to be a hidden process directing where we go. As Theodore Roethke wrote, "We go by going where we have to go."

The morning of the last day I woke up in my hotel room to the phone ringing. It was my mother. How she knew where I was, I'll never know—she hadn't known where I was for the past three months. No one had told her. But she tracked me down. The fact that she called me on the phone the day of the closure ceremony caused the strangest sensation; there was something almost metaphysical about it. I believe she got the message that it was all right to talk to me and that I loved her more than ever.

After closure, I checked out of the hotel and went back to Fresno, feeling like a new man. I thought, well, now I'll really be able to open my business, to do it with self-confidence and self-esteem, and I will be a better astrologer for it. I will be able to help people all the more because I have now helped myself. The Fischer-Hoffman process was one of the most important things I ever did. Much of my success as an astrologer, and as a vice president of the Shakespearian Festival in Visalia, was due to that process of unraveling my history, my self-image, my neuroses for I've never had a feeling of self-doubt since that time.

If you don't internalize the process, it's not going to work for you. And there were a couple of people in our class, which was about twenty-five, who had taken the process twice because it didn't get to them the first time. One of the things you had to do was to go through all these negative feelings. Then there was something you had to throw out and up—into the toilet. I had a rough time with that. I induced vomiting with Ipecac at first. But on the final night, all the negative stuff came up about my mother and father and myself, and my role in our relationships. I was literally so angry that my stomach churned. I went into the head and just vomited in the toilet. Afterwards, I felt a lot of weight slide off my back, leaving me clean and clear.

It was one of the peak experiences of my life, and I think after college, it was the most important thing I did. UCR took care of the mind; Fischer-Hoffman took care of the emotions. Later, the Temple Beautiful program and the Edgar Cayce Institute in Arizona served to alter my physical and spiritual lifestyle in new ways.

Now I felt free to go on and continue building my life.

Both before and after Fischer-Hoffman, I worked with Dr. Sonder. Our primary goal was the issue of shaking. I wanted to eliminate it entirely, and she seemed to think it was possible. I recall her saying, "I think when you get older, you'll get over this." Her aim was to give me effective coping mechanisms to deal with the day-to-day pattern of my life, to increase my ability to function in society. She kept up my self-esteem and gave me a renewed sense of faith in myself. She was always there encouraging me and saying, "Hey, *yes* you can." With her help, I made it through a lot of physically trying times.

So between the support of Dr. Sonder, Fischer-Hoffman, and my immersion in metaphysical work, my understanding of myself and my role in building a fulfilling life became clear. I finally decided to move from the townhouse to a little apartment on Shields Avenue in Fresno It was a humble dwelling, just room enough for an office, a bedroom and a kitchen. It was to be my home for the next four years. I set up my business and continued to do astrological work for people.

Obtaining permission to see clients there was no small feat. At the time, Fresno had an ordinance on the books against the black arts. And astrology was seen as the blackest of the black! There was really only one way to get around the ordinance—to become a minister. I had never put up a false front before, but after talking to enough people in the business I knew I had to do it if I wanted to successfully continue.

So I found my way to a psychic fair in Fresno. The whole scene was pretty disreputable. I came across the head of the Universal Life Church led by a guy who could have been straight out of skid row. He was granting ministers' licenses for the munificent sum of two dollars. With an offer like that, I couldn't refuse. In the lobby of the Fresno Municipal Auditorium, he placed his tobacco-stained hands on my head and pronounced me a minister and sent me on my way with a scrap of paper declaring my credentials. I had the authority to perform marriages and a number of other ministerial duties—all for two bucks. Years later, a client of mine asked me to officiate at her marriage and I said, "Honey, no way! That certificate was nothing more than a legal buffer between the jailhouse and me."

But I was able to continue the practice of astrology without fear of being shut down. My business expanded. I built it up to the point where I was getting word-of-mouth referrals, and I had a pretty good clientele. Then a very important thing happened. A wonderful bookstore/cafe called the Upstart Crow opened up in downtown Fresno. It was a classy place with a huge selection of books, and they served gourmet coffee. I started spending all of my free time there, and eventually got to know the owners. They allowed me to give tarot readings in the back room. It wasn't exactly legal at the time, so if a client wanted to pay me, we had to go out in the street to exchange money. The store wanted to be clear of any liability. It worked out that way for three years. The Crow became my home away from home. I met a lot of people I could talk to there— philosophers, metaphysicians, poets, and the like. It was a time of great intellectual stimulation.

I met one man there who became very influential in my life, George (aka Brother Paul), who was a previous doctor of divinity. We had tremendous conversations about comparative religion and philosophy. I talked to him about astrology, and he taught me more about meditation and new age philosophy. He helped me in innumerable ways—body, mind, and spirit, which I was ripe for after the Fischer-Hoffman process and my own journey through tarot and astrology.

These various things went on through 1979. It was a good time, profitable both monetarily and spiritually. I'd met George. I had The Crow. Life was fulfilling. I continued therapy with Dr. Sonder, which helped keep my hope alive in other ways. I was beginning to feel that I had finally found my place in life; I felt at home in Fresno for these four years. At the time I thought I would never leave.

In the midst of this nurturing environment, I believe it was about 1977, an actor from Stratford, Ontario decided to come down to California and start a Shakespeare Festival in Visalia. At the time I could not have known the frustrations his vision would wreak on my life. Somehow the word got around The Crow that someone was developing plans for a festival. Ever since I'd been going to the Shakespeare Festival in Ashland, I'd wanted to start something similar in Fresno. And here was someone who was interested in doing it. I thought, "Hot damn, let's hit the wagon, head for the stars."

I went to the organizational meeting, and was elected vice president of the Fresno Guild, the largest in the area. One of my responsibilities was to give presentations at fundraising events. I loved lecturing and writing about Shakespeare.

During the period of my vice presidency, I wrote my second book. It was a biblioportrait of William Shakespeare. In actuality, it was an extended narrative bibliography, a list of books divided into subject categories with brief annotations. It was widely sold and distributed, for a pittance, of course. The four-hundred or so delegates to the founding convention in Visalia each received a copy of the book. It went through two printings and is still used today at the Shakespeare Festival in

Ashland. The books listed are somewhat outdated now, but the volume still contains important information about Shakespeare. I now had two books under my belt—and I wanted to use the success as a motivation for writing more, which I did, but not at the rate I would have liked.

The California Shakespearian Festival and Performing Arts Center paid for the printing. The success was very encouraging, and I knew that something would come of it.

I did a lot of things in connection with that guild, mostly in terms of promoting the idea of having a theatre around Fresno County, hopefully a permanent theatre at College of the Sequoias in Visalia. Just the idea of Shakespeare was kind of new to the farming communities of that area. Educating them was not easy; how to impress on them that the goal was not esoteric, but rather entertainment of the highest quality? To this end, I organized fund raisers, sold T-shirts, and staged functions like wine tastings and celebrity balls. I became friends with people like Bill Shatner and Theodore Bikel who helped us get started. One keynote speaker at a celebrity ball was Richard Chamberlain.

Most of the festival events had good turnouts. The biggest event I planned and coordinated was to be a *Twelfth Night* program at the Ahwanee Hotel in Yosemite. It never came off. I had actors and musicians arranged to do a number on the balcony during the feast. It was to be a dinner, like the Ahwanee's *Bracebridge* dinner which celebrates the Washington Irving sketchbook. They do this on Christmas or New Year's Eve, complete with sleigh rides and bonfire. We were going to do our version of it on Epiphany, January 6 of 1978 or 1979.

While working with the festival, my childhood acting career revisited me. Dr. Sonder and I had quite a few discussions about my feelings about the stage versus films. And they're as strong now as they were then. I have a passion for the stage. But that's acting. Films are not really about acting in the same way. It's a different art form, really. Films are an illusion; what we watch are images on film in contrast to the dynamic a live interchange with an audience creates.

So I think of stage and film as wholly different. I felt involvement with the festival was a way to satisfy my having been bitten by the theatre bug when I was a kid without all the negative claptrap of the films.

We had three good years of promotion of the festival, '77 to '79. Then we finally got started with productions at the College of the Sequoias in Visalia. For several years it looked like the festival would take off, but it folded for monetary reasons. Shatner was scheduled to open with *Richard III*, and I think he was quite disappointed when it didn't come off.

Although pleased with my efforts, I did feel thwarted. Looking back on my life, I see this event as one in a series of frustrations, yet while living it, the frustration is merely an aspect of the life lived. Within this pattern is another, a thread of consistency that served to hold my life together: literature, librarianship, astrology, and the theatre.

In fact, as luck would have it, during this time my literary and dramatic life seemed to be pushing through me for fulfillment in other ways. For three years I did a Christmas Eve program for the Festival at a savings and loan bank near Fresno, reading Dylan Thomas' *A Child's Christmas in Wales*. I also read Dickens and others. We gave poetry readings at The Crow. I helped many budding poets find their way to the stage.

But luck has a way of moving people around. I was hired in 1979 by the University of California at Santa Cruz to teach the plays of each season at the college. They fingerprinted me. The class was advertised. And nobody showed up. So I had been feeling very good about myself and very successful in what I was doing, and thought teaching would fulfill my literary and intellectual needs. When the class fell through, disappointment hit me like the wind of change.

As has often been the case with me, I said the hell with it, I'm going to get out of here, even though it's going very well with my clients and life at The Crow. My sister, Harriet, called and said, "Come on down to the desert and do your business. I'm going to take a real estate course. Why don't you do the same?" My aunt was a very successful real estate broker in the desert. She owned Coachella Valley Realty. We could work for her. I hadn't seen Harriet in several years. My mother was getting up in years; she was about 85 at that time, and was losing her eyesight. She had a detached retina. It seemed the stars had placed all the elements to make a successful and purposeful change.

So, at the end of 1979 I prepared to leave my clients, my friends, my life—and begin another.

With my friend Charles (Monty) Montgomery.

Chapter 17

THE DESERT YEARS

One man in his time plays many parts . . .
—As You Like It

I took a real estate course in Fresno at Anthony Schools in preparation for the move. I was excited about the change. My family and I could be together again, and I'd develop astrological clientele at the desert. The real estate would be good to do while I was building up the business, and I could take care of my mom. I left my West Coast clients with my address, so they could get in touch with me. I still have clients call me now and then from Fresno and from Palm Springs. Sometimes they want updates or simply to talk about their problems. So, although in some sense it was a risky move, I never really lost anything. Although perhaps peripatetic in nature, my moves have, including this one, always been positive.

I got down to the desert in late 1979, and Harriet and I started working for my aunt in her real estate office; she also owned an apartment house on Desert Club Drive. She turned over the management of the apartment house to me; in return, I got a free beautiful three-bedroom apartment. I used the back bedroom for an office. Naturally, the tenants weren't always responsible. But it was a job and my aunt was very gracious, allowing me to work minimally in real estate. I had little to do with real estate except to sit at open houses and put up signs. This left me a lot of free time to manage the apartment house and to get my business started.

And start it did. With a bang. But one that wasn't too loud. I had clients right off. Not too many, but enough to satisfy me.

Although astrology was now the focus of my life, I also wanted, if possible, to retain something of my former library life. I knew a lot of librarians down in Indio and Cathedral City, Palm Desert and Palm Springs—so I applied to libraries at all three locations. I was hoping for a little part-time work, maybe five hours a week, just to keep my hand in. I was offered a job as a reference librarian in the Audio-Visual Department at the Palm Springs Public Library, but the boss, Nancy Watt, wanted me full-time. Despite some misgivings, I took it.

Thankfully, work at the library didn't take much effort, leaving me energy to concentrate on astrology. Harriet also lived in that apartment complex in a separate unit, so between the two of us we could take care of it. My mother didn't require too much care at this time either. She lived on the ranch separately. It was a good time for about a year and a half.

For a while, Harriet and I spent a good amount of time together. After several years of being apart, we began to learn to relate as siblings again. It is not something that ever dies, but it does lie dormant. It was fun for us to be together. We did a lot of swimming at the Desert Club, talking, and generally getting to know each other. We were creating a feeling of family in the midst of a family that didn't really show much feeling. Unfortunately, she left several months later, being perhaps even more peripatetic than I. This left me at the desert with the entire responsibility for my mother and the apartments—and now my aunt, who was getting up toward ninety.

After about a year, the astrology business got to the point where I couldn't comfortably manage the hours required by the library. So I was not too broken-hearted when the City of Palm Springs had some personnel upheaval, and my position was scrapped. I had built the business up to the point where I felt leaving the library in Palm Springs was not going to be financially detrimental. In fact, I welcomed it in a way because I was tired of showing films to the wealthy of Palm Springs. In addition to astrology, library and apartment house, I had taken on the responsibility of managing rental units on my mother's ranch. There were three or four renters. Mother had an incomparable ability to get lousy tenants at that ranch. One gentleman threw his wife through the wall. A beauty of a man.

At this time, something fairly dramatic and fateful occurred. My aunt sold the apartment house, sweet-talked out of it by some old man. He took her out, wined her and dined her until she capitulated. Although shocked by this change, I still had a good apartment and a good business going in the back room. This was fine until the new owner told us he was going to boost the rent. One of the apartments at my mother's place had recently been vacated, so I moved into a unit at the back of the ranch house, which was entirely separate from the main house. I moved my office to another building owned by my aunt. The transition was difficult at first, but it worked out just fine.

Reflecting on these twelve years of my life, from 1980 to 1992, I see how fruitful they were, although I did not realize it at the time. I had about 250 good, solid clients. I saw numerous others at several psychic fairs where I read tarot. And, of course, there were numerous walk-ins or people who just wanted a chart calculated, without any counseling, which was the emphasis of my business.

The difference between my professional tarot readings and what I would do at the psychic fairs would be the depth to which I would allow the glyphs or images of the tarot to go in my consciousness, or my spirit. At fairs I didn't say too much, just stuck to the basic interpretation and meaning of the cards.

I always refused to read astrological charts at fairs because a chart demands much more attention than tarot does. A chart takes a long time to set up, even with the computer. And you must be one hundred percent accurate. You don't have to do any calculation with the tarot. It is straightforward and psychic. This may seem like a contradiction, but as with something like physical evidence, a psychic reading runs in straight lines from client to card to reader. A chart involves complex rules and regulations and arithmetic which can't be done spontaneously.

Early on, one experience served to raise my consciousness and the direction of my work to another level. One afternoon the phone rang; it was a woman named Renée, with whom I felt an instant and intimate connection. We talked for two hours—about metaphysics, astrology, life goals, and we ended up making a date to go to the Church of Religious Science in Palm Desert the following Sunday. And that was the beginning of something very important. The affiliation with the church would help me direct my business toward a spiritual connection with my clients. My relationship with Renée Hatfield would prove to be volatile and enduring.

Renée was an astrologer herself, and a Scorpio as am I. She had just returned from Spain and, not knowing anyone, had looked in the phone book and found my ad. This was a truly serendipitous event. Our rapport was marvelous from the moment we heard each other's voice, but it wasn't based on a physical attraction. When I meet someone I don't focus on the sexual element of the connection. If a relationship comes my way, I have always poured myself whole-heartedly into it. But when it comes down to it, there were times when I felt I just couldn't be bothered. There have been too many things that are more important to me in this life. Our relationship has been profound spiritually from the very beginning; it has operated all these years on the transcendental plane. We never seemed to get along on the mundane issues of "day to day life." She was born in Detroit, but I sometimes wonder if she's not from some other planet!

During this period, I continued to attend the Church of Religious Science with Renée. Someone in the congregation started a prayer table which lasted, on and off, for four years. We met weekly for meditation and to pray for others, as well as for ourselves. The group energy was healing, spiritually and emotionally. It helped keep my focus on what I really wanted to do. Between the prayer table and Edgar Cayce group I had a lot of spiritual support in the desert.

So, Renée and I became involved in the church, and all the avenues of my life seemed to coalesce. Many members of the congregation became my clients. They seemed drawn to me, although there were other astrologers in the Coachella Valley. Because of our close affiliation with the church, I had the benefit of seeing a number of clients outside of my office; I had the opportunity to see them pick themselves up by their bootstraps and improve their lives.

During the early 1980s, Renée and I both gave lectures on astrology. Tom, our minister in Religious Science, seemed open to every "cockamamie" thing but astrology. He couldn't accept that those rocks up in the sky might influence what we do. He believed we are the sole creators of our destiny, that what happens to us is a direct result of mental work. I agreed with him for the most part then, as I do now. However, it is also true that the quality of a person's mental work is reflected in those rocks, and once the astrologer can read those rocks, he is able to discern tendencies and possibilities. Despite Tom's misgivings, Reneé gave a lecture on astrology at the church, and it was very well received by the congregation. But her words didn't make much of an impression on Tom at that time. Years later, however, I did.

It is interesting how it happened. I was resident astrologer on a breakfast radio show that was broadcast daily throughout the desert during most of the '80s. I had been doing this show nearly every Friday for two years when the Red Baron, the program manager, asked, "Bob, how would you like to have your own show?" And I said, "Hell yes! When do I start?"

There was a free hour on Wednesday nights.

I had some fairly famous guests on the show, which was called "Cosmic Connection," with a bow to Carl Sagan, who at that time was very much anti-astrology, but a good astronomer and a good thinker.

I decided to ask Tom, the minister at the Church of Religious Science, to be a guest sometime to get his views on metaphysical and psychic matters. He accepted. I was hoping for an open debate on the air for the sake of broadening the base of discussion. We began the show talking about religious science, affirmations and positive thinking, and taking responsibility for one's own actions. Out of the clear blue sky, he said, "Well, the work you've done on my chart has certainly convinced me there's something to astrology. And you know, it seems to me that a chart is nothing but a series of affirmations." We started on that one and took up the whole hour talking about it, except for an occasional call-in.

I had metaphysicians of all sorts on the show. Damian Simpson, founder of the Universal Mind Church in Long Beach, California, was on a couple of times. We discussed metaphysics and fielded phone calls from the radio audience. I had guests such as spiritual authors and speakers from the human potential movement, motivational speakers, and also other astrologers. I invited people from San Pedro and San Diego, where many famous astrologers resided. Most of them came up free of charge. They had a good time and loved the exposure.

I remember that the Red Baron was there operating the controls one night because the regular operator was ill, and the Lakers and the Celtics were playing for the world championship. I had this woman up from San Diego, and we were doing astro dice (dice you throw that immediately give the signs, planets, and houses). And we were answering a lot of questions from people on the phone. The general response ws that "this is really right-on, good information." The Red Baron came in from the control room and asked the dice, "Hey, who's gonna win the NBA playoffs?" He threw the dice and I read them—I said there was too much dissension in the Laker locker room, that they weren't emotionally up enough to win. And they didn't. Predictions like this always pleased people and seemed to validate astrology to the skeptics. To me, of course, the show was just a lot of fun and didn't reflect the true purpose of my work. But I did get a lot of clients from the shows.

The radio shows were a step above the fairs. I used astrology, but there is a definite way that you do this on the air, at least the way I developed it—someone would call in, tell me what sign they were, and tell me their problem. And I would go from there, with the disclaimer at the end that we could only give so much information on the air, but that my office was always open. Working speedily and intuitively became a habit. I got to the point where I could just take the Ephemeris, which is the catalogue of the stars for any given year, look up the planetary positions in the particular signs, and go from there. It takes a long time to develop that talent.

When I did this on the radio, just like the tarot readings in the psychic fairs, I would never go too far. I'd sometimes say to myself, I'm getting this message but I can't trust my own intuition at this point. And I would tell them something totally innocuous, like "You will find love in your life," something that would be very to come true in some form. The point of this is that radio is an area where astrology or tarot, the psychic and entertainment, are crossed. But it's like a salesman's pitch, or a lead-in. I'll give you so much, but come to my office where you can get the real straight poop. It worked and I wasn't ashamed to acquire new clients by this means. If people were happy and could be helped toward being original and living their lives in a unique, productive way, that's what I cared about. As I look back on it now, I am just amazed at how much good I was doing, even though I didn't realize it at the time.

In 1980, prior to the radio show, I had a public television show, "Today's Astrologer." It only ran for seven weeks, but it was good exposure and brought clients in. I was surprised that they gave it to me in the first place, because astrology was just beginning to be accepted at this time. It wasn't legal yet in California, so we were all treading on thin ice. I was given *carte blanche* to write the format and the scripts as I wanted.

In the media you have to make a hit right off the bat with something spectacular, so I decided to do Ronald Reagan's chart on the air. It took up parts of my show for several weeks. Each week I'd take different aspects of his chart. I delineated the president fairly well, which kept the show going. I remember that Reagan has Pluto opposite Mars. I concluded from this that there would be a big shakeup in the economic arena, although I couldn't see the details. It's important to remember that this was before Reaganomics. I also saw a lot of unusual events in the White House, but I had no idea that Nancy was using an astrologer. That came out later when her astrologer wrote a book.

After the TV show ended I started doing the breakfast shows more often, which is when the Red Baron offered me "The Cosmic Connection." We had two good seasons before getting bumped by a sports program—the Lakers or some baseball team.

After the radio shows, I had a lot of success, and was beginning to be known around the valley as *the* astrologer. I acquired more clients and had to move to a larger office. I was tired of my current office anyway. As it happened, the building right next to my aunt's had a large office available. It was huge (16x20) in comparison to my previous space. There had been a flower shop there before. I thought, "I'll have clients in here. If Reneé comes back, I'll even have Reneé in the office with a desk, doing her own thing." (And she did return to Indio for a few months. Since she was fluent in Spanish, she did charts in Spanish.) I had a huge library at the time which consisted of over 3,000 books. I had my computer set up at a desk, and plenty of extra room for clients.

I thought this was the time to get into teaching. I had had a few students before, but many people were now asking if I would teach them astrology. I had plenty of space, so I set up a blackboard, an easel, and classroom chairs. I gave several classes in beginning and intermediate astrology. It never went beyond that, because most people start studying and then quit after only a few lessons. They discover it's not that easy. Some would learn how to set up a chart, and then they'd leave and go out to practice astrology. They did considerable damage by telling clients things that just weren't true. Despite some frustration with students, this was, overall, a wonderful time for me; I enjoyed teaching and had my own apartment on the ranch, so I could be at the house in case my mother needed me.

There were two architects in the office next to me, and a novelty salesman in the office on the other side. So I had this big room in between with clients coming in regularly. I don't think I ever had more than two clients a day. I didn't want more than two, because I would usually give clients two or three hours of my time. You couldn't shut me up once I got started. They sat there enraptured. They couldn't get up from their chair. But I soon had to learn to curtail that. Although I wasn't necessarily losing money (I had income from the rental units and my library work, which I had saved), I was draining myself, especially when it came to tarot readings. I used to give three-hour tarot readings. I couldn't do anything until the next day, and sometimes felt spent into the next week. Thankfully, I learned that people wanted readings, but in smaller doses. Long readings were really a bit self-indulgent. I found that when I had two clients in succession, I would have to go into deep meditation just to get myself to the physical point where I could stand it, let alone bear up mentally.

Since the 1970s, I've done all my readings at the same table. During the period which I taught the history of metaphysics, there was a young man who couldn't afford the class, although I only asked him for a five-dollar donation. He said he wanted to do something for me. He said he would build me a table on which to read tarot. The top of this table was made from an old church door, and the cross that's inlaid in the center was made from a couple of slats out of an old fig crate that had been in the sun for years. The table turned out to be a rare beauty and a conversation piece. It has been with me ever since that first day, lending its own grace to hundreds of readings.

During this period, astrology was not illegal technically in most of the United States; it was just illegal to do it for money, although in some communities it was forbidden to practice it at all. I had the minister's license, which protected me. I could have set up my own church in the desert with that big room. But, of course, I didn't want to pretend to be a Man of the Cloth. In the late '70s, a five-member board of professional astrologers tried to get it legalized in California. Their proposal went to the State Legislature. After some contentious debate, it lost.There was also a big bill that went to the U.S. Senate after passing in the House. But it, too, was finally tabled. I'd been going to American Federation of Astrologers conventions from time to time, and I became interrerested in the legal problem through several workshops and seminars on the ins and outs of what we could do to get our profession on the same basis with lawyers and doctors.

In states like Georgia, and even in Nevada, it was legal and indeed there were even psychic communities in

Georgia. California was behind the times, and I got tired of saying I was a minister when I was not, so I thought I'd do what I could to help legalize my profession. The main thing that any of us could do was to be honest and ethical in our practice and to do what we could to be as professional as possible, which is why I didn't do parties. Clients would want you to put a turban on and be a mystic, gimmicky and all that. I'd say, "Well, lady, I'd be happy to entertain them, but I'm not going to use my profession to do it. What you want could be easily handled by the Comedy Store in Palm Springs. Just call them and rent a psychic."

Most of the astrologers I knew were respectable and fair; they charged decent fees. Most of my colleagues were professional, especially at the conventions, because we really saw how much knowledge and professionalism were in the astrology business.

The legal status of astrology at this time was indeed terrible. California and Oregon were two of the most resistant states. I got in touch with dozens of people, mostly by mail. We'd talk about the situation. We were going to lobby for our rights in Sacramento. Finally, the professionalism of our psychic trades and the weight of public opinion influenced the right people. What actually precipitated this response to our lobbying was a court case. A self-styled witch in Azusa, California, was raided for practicing astrology. The initial court decision went against her, but she later appealed and won. Public visibility of issues can take a cause a long way fast.

One by one the ordinances at the desert began to fall—in Indio, Palm Desert, Rancho Mirage, Indian Wells, Cathedral City. Only one—Palm Springs—held out. The cities could no longer dip into our pockets for the psychic fee they'd been charging. I remember one special morning in this period. I received a phone call from a colleague in Washington, D.C. He said, "Bob, the ordinance in Cathedral City just fell." So that's how it went. We all felt free. No longer would we humiliate ourselves with bogus ministers licenses.

Once astrology was legalized, interest in the art heightened and we acquired clients. I noticed more of an interest after legalization. The connection between Nancy Reagan and her personal astrologer, Joan Quigley, broke into the media at this time, and astrology quickly became newsworthy. My contribution to all this had been through the TV and radio shows, always trying to keep the work on a professional level, answering questions in a logical and non-threatening manner and believing that what I was doing was really helpful to people and not just a game. I was always careful to make clients feel they were not consulting some mystic or "woo-woo" from the other side. I was not practicing hocus-pocus, mumbo-jumbo. It was always important for me to put up a very professional front, a nice office without a lot of symbols or the usual old trappings of the palm readers.

I had clients from every community in the desert, even Yucca Valley, and some from as far away as Albuquerque. I had one client from Washington, D.C., who was with me for years, and she had politics all over her chart. She was an aide to some local congressman at the time. And she ended up in Washington, D.C., marrying a senator and being responsible for all the scheduling of Air Force One during the Republican era. She had consulted me every step of the way. I was very proud of the work she did. She was a prime example of the client who would take what astrology said seriously, and then get some sense of direction from it. Some people would just go home and put the chart in a drawer and say, "My, my, that was interesting."

Her self-doubt was stifling her when she first came to me. So part of the function of the astrologer is to encourage the client in the direction of their real strengths and talents. I remember asking her, "Wouldn't you be more comfortable pursuing politics rather than trying to sell hairdos in a salon?", which is what she had been doing.

The individual who takes the trends or the potentials in the chart and works with them will achieve a much more comfortable and successful life. I am a hundred percent convinced of this. And I've seen this through hundreds of charts. I think it's also very important to observe the failures as well as the successes and to know why they occur so it won't happen again. The astrologer, being human, can't spot all of the mistakes, but certainly most of them can be caught. If something is done wrong one time with regard to a certain planetary position or aspect, the astrologer learns not to ever make that mistake again. This is a major reason why I believe proper training and being licensed is very important for the astrologer. A competent professional cannot mimic Madame Lasagne down the street who reads a few books and thinks she can set up a chart. I read every book I could lay my eyes on when I was starting, but I still didn't feel I could do the work professionally. I took additional courses in Fresno. I knew more than the teacher did. But she gave me the chance to actually work in a kind of laboratory situation. I went on to take a correspondence course with the London School of Astrology. I was taught to be professional and had the opportunity to study with excellent astrologers and teachers. Good training not only helps your credibility, but it helps your self-image and your actual ability to deliver.

The experience of teaching and counseling was joyous for me. There is no greater reward than service and the fulfillment that comes from seeing a soul rise up and take responsibility for its own joy. During this period of metaphysical exploration, I turned to meditation and Edgar Cayce's materials as another source of knowledge and inspiration.

It was late 1979 that I became associated with the Edgar Cayce Search For God study group. I didn't know such a group existed before I got to the desert. I'd wanted to get more involved with Edgar Cayce previously, but thought I'd have to go to Virginia Beach to do so. And then, like so many other things, here it was in my own backyard.

I had been reading his books for years. When Renée discovered the local group we decided to look into it. For some reason she dropped out after one meeting. But then, that's Renée. I'm sure she simply had other metaphysical fish to fry at that time in her life. But I was a steady member of the group, and we did readings for at least three or four years. These readings were based on excerpts from Cayce's writings on past lives and reincarnation, as well as on portions of the Bible.

I also acquired several clients who were members of the Search for God group. This was particularly satisfying to me because as members of the group they were spiritually inclined, whereas most of my clients in the desert were more, shall we say, practically oriented.

The Edgar Cayce teachings were a seminal experience in my life, a real turning point of sorts. I learned meditation and spiritual aspects of life that I had felt alienated from. Some of the impact had to do with the unveiling of Biblical concepts, but mainly it had to do with the Cayce teachings on healing (the idea that mind is the builder, and that everything is in the mind). This was one of the most important concepts that came out of my studies because it went right along with Religious Science—which is really the science of mind.

In addition, the Religious Science prayer table gave me a religious faith and ability to relate to other human beings on a deeper level. A typical meeting consisted of sharing experiences and praying together. If we missed a couple of weeks, we all seemed to feel our energy drop. We'd have to have a meeting again, and we'd build up the energy, usually by chanting and prayer.

"Oh, Father lift me up, Oh, Father lift me up, " we would chant, in the manner of Yogananda's chants—mantras that were recited over and over, building up one's courage, energy and positive thoughts.

All of my activities and interests at that time fit into my astrology practice. I am convinced that my metaphysical and religious background made me a much better astrologer.

An Instrument of Transformation

I have been asked why the stars have meaning. In all honesty, I don't know *why*. I do believe that the entirety of God's creation is within each of us, which means we're all connected. When you see a segment of the universe, the rocks in the sky, brought down to a horoscope map, if you know how to read it and you're sensitive to it, you can tell something about the other parts of that creation. It is simply a tool for establishing some sense of order amidst chaos. This has always been my philosophy.

The horoscope, or more specifically, the natal chart, does not mean a thing in itself. It's merely a map of rocks hanging up there in the sky until the astrologer attaches it to the individual; then it becomes meaningful. Every person on earth is composed of all twelve signs. When someone tells me that their sun is in Taurus, that only means that their sun is in Taurus; the other planets, Saturn, Jupiter, Mars, etc., may be in Virgo or Pisces or Gemini. All these factors are going to alter the chart. So one thing I would never do, and this is part of my philosophy, too, is try to guess sun signs—they're meaningless in themselves. A complete horoscope is necessary to understand an individual and his or her direction.

The planets, and stars, are rocks in a physical sense, but energetically they're part of the universe, and they move in regular patterns around the sun. We have no idea how many other suns there are, or how many solar systems outside of our own make up the pattern of the universe. But as long as those rocks are part of the universe, they're part of us, too. And they demonstrably have something to do with our personalities.

Look at the moon's effect on the tides. Look at the moon's effect on criminal behavior. These are things that are statistically proven. The reason why they're part of our behavior, one could say, is that they're part of the universe, and we're also part of the universe. So it becomes kind of a tautology to explore it too far. But it's also a matter of intuitive assurance. In other words, I feel intuitively that this is correct. I've seen it in the lives of hundreds of people. Those rocks in the sky are symbolical—they're God's symbols for what can be going on inside an individual. Now, why they're God's symbols, I can't answer; but that they are, I'm sure.

The ancient Sumerian, Egyptian and Greek astronomers, ascribed symbolism to the planets, for at one time astronomy and astrology were considered to be the same thing. Only in the last several hundred years have the two been differentiated. Until then humankind used the stars to guide all its activities in the ancient world, planting, harvesting, etc. Rulers didn't do anything without consulting the court astrologer. And if he was wrong, he got his head lopped off. So they were very careful, believe me. A lot of the old stuff is quite accurate; the new astrology is based on the same principles.

New techniques were enabled through telescopic observation and computers. We have a myriad of statistics to prove a lot of the relationships between various ports of the universe. When I cast a chart, what I'm doing nothing more than mapping a particular moment in time and the way it's configured in the heavens. It doesn't mean anything except in a mundane sense; if an astronomer wants to get angles and parallax, and measure light and all the light between the various planets, then the map is sufficient. But when I take your birth date and the time you were born and apply a map to you, then it begins to mean something astrologically. Now that is not a difference between the old and new astrology, but it's one of the things that I would say characterizes modern astrology because astrology, when it first sprang up in Sumeria, Egypt, and the Fertile Crescent, was not person-centered at all. Men consulted the stars to determine when they should or should not do something. Am I going to become a ruler? Will I get along with the king or is he going to cut my head off? When is the best time to plant?

From top left, my good friends Charlie and Marilyn Amick, Pete Zelles (Christmas at La Quinta, 1986), Renée Hatfield, and Doris and I during a 1987 visit to Ashland.

My great friend in La Quinta Monty (as a monk), the Round Table in Ashland in 1985 (I'm at the far right), my mother at 90, and me showing my brawn during the 1986 Christmas party in La Quinta.

Person-centered astrology began in Greece with the advent of democratic ideals. This was ancient Greece, about 400 BC.People realized that not only did the ruler of the state have a chart, but everybody else also had a chart. That's when they began to see the relationship between the rocks and what's going on inside of the individual. I think this new understanding or relationship became an important point in the development of modern metaphysical thinking, new age philosophy, and other modalities of thought.

Of course that technique has been refined greatly today and is the basis of all astrology. Although it was an accurate discipline, we do not generally use astrology as the ancients did, except in a special branch called Horary astrology (Horary is the art of finding lost objects through astrology). Today we use a more psychologically-centered astrology. The ancient person-centered astrology was mainly used for a specific purpose or event, such as should two people get married, when was the best time to begin promoting oneself, when was the best time to plant, or when should one go to the dentist. And astrology does work for these questions. It's an ancient discipline which I've used successfully for clients.

But my aim as an astrologer has always been to help the client live a better life. Some astrologers read all sorts of complications into a chart to demonstrate how expert they are. My approach to reading a chart is rather simple: there are signs, and there are houses; there are aspects, and there are planets. In those four areas lie the basics of astrology. Cosmodynes or asteroids are unnecessary; they may have meaning to certain astrologers, but they essentially duplicate the material in the basic chart. Once you realize that the basic chart has seventeen hundred factors that have to be considered by the astrologer, nothing else is really needed.

When I practiced, I would sit with clients and do their charts in detail, asking them thorough questions about where they were with regard to the area of life they were asking about, whether it was health, financial, love affairs, and what the chart said about that particular area and what they might do to incorporate the chart into their lifestyle to make it better. I tried to give every client tools to improve their life.

Of course, the individual astrologer can be wrong, as I've probably been at times. If you become disconnected from the rest of the universe, and consequently from yourself, you can't be an effective astrologer. And there are a lot of charlatans who are just out to show how proficient they can be. I assiduously tried to avoid that ego trap.

Perhaps one of the most important things to learn is what to say and how to say it in a way that will be useful to the client. If the astrologer sees devastation, he doesn't want to say, "You're going to die tomorrow" or some damn fool thing like that. One of the primary parts of the astrologer's code, which every professional has to sign, is that you never, never, under any circumstances, predict death. But if you're saying "You're liable to be in danger," you could say, "Just be careful about such-and-such a date. I know you're careful anyway, but be especially so—if you're using machinery or sharp objects, or something." There's always a way to get around it without shocking yourself and the client.

I've seen death in a chart only once. It was so blatant and strong that I faked illness. "I just don't feel like going on any more," I said and asked him to leave. I refused to tell him what I saw. He committed suicide six months later. And *that* is what I had seen—self-destruction. At the time, it deeply affected and frightened me. The reality hit home hard—I fully understood this was not a game I was playing. What I said or didn't say could directly impact someone's life.

There was one other very troublesome client whom I told to be very careful in his actions. He had a prison record. I said, "Just watch what you're doing or you're going to end up in jail." And so he did, locked up in the Oakland City Jail.

These instances point to the verity of all these "psychic" modalities—tarot, Runes, the I Ching, and even tea leaf reading, and I suppose even standard playing cards. I believe there is something to all of it. It depends on the operator who's using any particular method.

I, for one, cannot read ordinary playing cards; they are simply silent to me. But the glyphs of the tarot just scream out loud, as does the I Ching. Both are marvelous literary devices if you are open to them.

The bottom line is that nobody can tell you why it works. But you can approach the theory that all parts of the universe work in unison, and that, spiritually, we're all parts of a single and quite beautiful picture.

Reflecting back, the years between 1979 and 1992 were a period of immense personal growth for me. I add it to my college years and the Fischer-Hoffman experience, as one of the three most significant periods in my life. During this time, I was offered many challenges and opportunities for self-renewal.

I was busy, but it was a beautiful, productive time.

On the one hand there was the convergence of my various spiritual studies and quests. On the other was a personal life that might seem to have little connection to my spiritual and professional life. Yet I was fulfilled and strengthened by this side of my existence as well.

I was living on the ranch in an apartment which was attached to the main house. I could easily take care of my mother or answer her calls. At the time, a woman named Doris rented a room at the ranch. We didn't fall in love, but we certainly fell in lust, and after a time she moved into the apartment with me. At first, Doris helped me take care of my mother, and, eventually, she became her principal caregiver. We had a very satisfying and sustaining relationship and having her with me certainly added stability to this period of my life.

But Doris and I were very different. She had little interest in my metaphysical or intellectual pursuits. Still, we shared a love of theatre and film, among other things. I even brought her up to Ashland, Oregon several times to attend the Shakespeare Festival. She was important to me, so I made time to share these passions with her. Although we were different, she was a truly wonderful, caring woman with common sense—a very down-to-earth type, and an anchor for me. If I got too wild or too Uranian in my desires or things I wanted to do, she could sit me down and talk some sense into me.

Doris' common sense made her a very attractive person. She was very petite, with mousy blonde hair, very comely, but not beautiful. She was six months older than I. We always joked about that, about her seniority.

When Doris came into my life, she relieved a lot of my duties in caring for my mother. I continued to keep my mother's financial affairs straight, run the ranch, and take care of repairs and maintenance. Doris took on the burden of clothing, feeding, shopping, washing, cleaning, and other household necessities.

At times, it is difficult to believe how integral Doris was to my life. That time seems so distant and she so different in so many ways. Does anyone understand what draws two people together and then pulls them apart? Perhaps it is more a matter of need at the time, what each can do or give to the other. I sometimes wonder if this is what love is?

My mother was rational up until she was about ninety or ninety-one, and then she got pretty senile. It was difficult to carry on a conversation with her. She got along with Doris just fine, until it became physically impossible for Doris to handle her, for, while Doris was petite, my mother was not. At a certain point, she could no longer lift or bathe her because my mother, who was quite large, became easily upset and refused to cooperate. She was a very manipulative woman and did a lot of things that Doris couldn't understand. For instance, she wouldn't tell her when she needed to go to the bathroom, and then she'd soil herself. Some might say it was typical old lady antics. Doris certainly believed it was done to make her life more difficult.

Doris left me in 1988. For two years, I had full responsibility for my mother again. Then Doris returned. Not to me, but to my mother. Despite their difficulties, Doris was attached to her and wanted to help. But I didn't see much of her. In 1991, I finally put my mother in a nursing home; she wasn't safe at the ranch without constant care, and she was just becoming incorrigible. Doris could no longer take care of her at home, and neither could I. It was an excellent home and she came to like it very much.

I was devastated when Doris left, but I understood her position. Possibly we could have done something with my mother at the time, so Doris wouldn't have had to leave, but I'm fairly certain she wanted to try something else anyway.

During the first several years of life with Doris, I decided I wanted to study psychology as an additional qualification for being an astrologer. This was in the early 1980s, a time when freedom coursed through my veins and I had the energy to explore new interests. Still, classes had to be worked around my various responsibilities. When I had time, I took evening courses at Chapman College, which had a branch in Palm Desert. I worked toward a master's degree in psychology, which I almost completed. Even without the degree, I could now offer a little expertise as a counselor in my astrology practice. My deepened understanding of behavior and motivation helped my business tremendously.

People liked what I did, but there were very few people on the desert whom I could really relate to other than my clients and Doris, and with Doris there was no intellectual stimulation. I guess you could say I was in the midst of an intellectual drought at the time. It wasn't exactly a brain trust out there in the desert. I missed being able to discuss Shakespeare. But I became close to some members of the prayer group.

The year Doris left, I finished a book of poetry. Poetry had been part of my life since college. My love of poetry was heightened by the readings at the Upstart Crow Coffee House in Fresno, and I had begun to write earnestly during my time back east. I put the book together in 1988, produced it on my computer, and published it. It is called *The Lions' Tears*, after the two lions flanking the entrance to the New York Public Library. Although most of the poems were written while in New York, I wrote some new ones too. I wrote to satisfy myself. But then the poems became something of a project, and filled some time between clients.

While living in the desert, I met one of the most influential persons in my life. His name was Charles Montgomery (Monty), and we became fast friends. We bonded over our profound interest in astrology. He was a lawyer and past president of the Burbank Bar Association. He was approaching eighty when I met him. He became a member of the Desert Astrological Association, which I founded, and taught me more about astrology than almost anyone. He wrote articles for *American Astrology* magazine for forty years, while he was on the bench. Monty was a popular guest lecturer for a lecture series I organized and was also a guest on my radio show.

We had wonderful conversations about metaphysics and even legal points. We talked about Greek philosophers like Socrates and Plato. These conversations were a lifeline for me in the desert where the intellectual terrain was as dry as the landscape. Monty and his wife, Dodi, became very good friends. They were also good friends to Doris, even though they were well aware of the intellectual void between us. Their acceptance of us as a couple helped to bind the relationship during our seven years together. I assume that he has made his transition because he was around ninety years old when I left the desert in 1992. I've always remembered him for the light, wisdom and truth he provided.

Monty was more spiritual than he cared to admit. He went to the prayer table with me several times, and seemed very attracted and intrigued by the discussions, although he didn't talk about them very much. We had an intuitive rapport regarding these experiences, and when I worked with a psychic in Palm Springs, Monty also became good friends with him. There was a circle of people from different places with similar interests, goals and accomplishments. All this was very rich and life-supporting.

During this period, Monty encouraged me to write for *American Astrology* magazine. So in 1984, I wrote two articles, both of which were accepted. One was on Freud and astrology and the other, written several years later, was on Shakespeare and astrology.

There was one other friend, Pete Zelles, an Ohio-born Greek who was extremely smart. Our friendship was based on a love of the theatre, particularly Shakespeare. He had done a lot of directing when he was in college in Ohio. Our relationship was another key aspect of my intellectual development.

So, as the intellectual and spiritual aspects of my life were fulfilled by Monty and Pete, the physical and emotional were nurtured by Doris. When she left, I missed what she had provided.

All in all, I was very satisfied with my desert life. I probably could have accomplished more if I had just settled into my life and acknowledged how good it was. At least that's the way I feel in retrospect; this is one of the nagging regrets I am trying to dispense with, knowing that all of my experiences have led me to the present.

I tell myself that if I had persevered at my business more energetically and if I had followed the spiritual journeys of the various groups more seriously, I probably would have carried them to a much higher level. However, there must be a reason I didn't, as there's a reason for everything. Perhaps I needed to get involved in many different things rather than one thing in depth.

I still suffered from tremors, especially if I was under an unusual amount of stress. So I learned to avoid stressful situations, and of course all of the metaphysical and spiritual work I was involved in—church, the prayer table and the Edgar Cayce group, all the inner work—helped. My therapeutic and spiritual activities had dispelled my neuroticisms, and for the first time in my life I truly felt psychologically healthy. If I did get into a stressful situation, I learned that by meditating I could alleviate the stress and sometimes the shaking along with it.

My health was good. Of course, I had the Cerebellar Ataxia during this time, but it was in a kind of remission, as I had very little shaking. I was able to write and could do almost anything I chose to do. I wasn't running foot races and I wasn't as coordinated as some, but my activities were not curtailed as they later became.

What is fascinating is that I was feeling fulfilled for the most part and yet I was still hampered by physical ailments. This fact would soon shatter the notion of disease as a manifestation of mental and emotional distress. I continued with therapy, but the purpose wasn't to expunge physical symptoms as it had been in the past. I no longer believed that my physical health stemmed from neurotic impulses.

I didn't have any significant health problems during 1992, the year I left the desert. But I suspected there was an underlying physical problem, no matter how slight or controllable the shaking had become. I decided to have an MRI done because I wanted to find out if there was something organically wrong somewhere. And it turned out that I was right. The MRI in Palm Springs revealed the deficiency to be a small cerebellum and led to the diagnosis of Cerebellar Ataxia. After thirty some years of therapy, I was finally diagnosed!

I wasn't terribly distraught by the diagnosis because I had, of course, suspected something was seriously wrong. I had prepared myself for the inevitable. I'd never heard that term "Cerebellar Ataxia" before. A few doctors had used the word in the past, and said "You have an ataxic reaction," but they never referred to it as a serious medical disorder.

They proceeded to explain the whole thing to me. The reason it didn't manifest until I was eighteen years old is because my cerebellum was perfectly adequate for a boy. It was when I reached physiological maturity that it became too small to process all that was coming in. Basically, I don't have the central processing unit required to handle normal adult motor functions. When my body gets overwhelmed, it simply shakes to compensate.

After the results of the MRI, I did a lot of soul searching. I had been seriously considering a move to Ashland, but when I found out that I had an actual disease, I spent some time reevaluating. In the end, I just had to trust my feeling that the time was right.

I had liked living in the desert for those twelve years. I had spent half of my childhood there, so it retained a certain familiarity for me. I was drawn to the landscape — the mountains, the sand, the dunes, the whole panorama. And I liked the weather, but it was the peace and quiet that I truly loved.

But the physical terrain could no longer hold me. I had twelve years to observe the people of this land, and they were not, in general, a mix that I would choose to live with. Because of the circles I moved in, I was blessed to meet some very fine people. I don't know why, but I met more Scorpios (my own sign) down there than I've ever met in my life. They were, for the most part, intellectual and very intuitive, colorful types who had similar interests to my own. The majority of the population was big on pastimes like golf, tennis, swimming or night club hopping, none of which really interested me at all. There certainly was no theatre, Shakespeare or literature. I knew that if I stayed on the desert I would be doing myself a disservice.

I had felt for years that the desert was no longer where I wanted to be, but that I couldn't get out of the desert until I had things settled. I could have stayed there and continued my business, but that would have entailed a lot of changes because my office building had been condemned due to the threat of earthquake damage.

Certain familial ties had also changed during this period. I no longer had primary responsibility for the care of my mother. She had moved into a home in 1991, and my Aunt Fran had died in 1992. My mother pined away for her sister for more than a year before she, too, left this world. I had recently been diagnosed with a disease I would live with for the rest of my life. My good friend Monty was getting on in years, and other friendships lacked the depth I needed. I had been visiting the Shakespeare Festival in Ashland since 1985, and had become an integral member of the Shakespeare Round Table group. I was no longer willing to settle for my life as it was, particularly since I had a clear idea that I could be more fulfilled in Ashland, a place where my passion for Shakespeare would have a clear outlet and the people were more spiritually oriented. And so, I made the decision to move.

At this time my sisters were out of the picture. They were both living in Santa Fe. So I thought, well, there's nobody to keep me here—no Reneé, no Doris, nothing of my former life. My mother was safely ensconced in the home. The prayer table and the Edgar Cayce group had gone the way of all flesh a couple of years before, and there was no hope of reviving that. The energy was just not right. It had all dissipated.

We all had come together for a very specific spiritual reason, I'm sure of that. And that reason was over. I felt very strongly motivated to get out of there.

I saw a more exciting life ahead of me.

Chapter 18

THIS SIDE OF THE STAGE

They thought it good you hear a play,
And frame your mind with mirth and merriment,
Which bars a thousand harms and
Lengthens life.
　　　　　　　—The Taming of the Shrew

I've made a lot of moves that some might call courageous, and others, foolhardy. I have a history of establishing myself and then moving on because there is something on the horizon that interests me more. Perhaps it comes down to following what you need for your own growth.

For this reason I left the life and security I had established in the desert. I started making plans to move to Ashland, Oregon in 1988. It took me several more years to make the move, but I believe it was the right time. It was the summer of 1992, and I got to my new home in time for the Shakespeare Festival Round Table. I rented a lovely place on Nevada Street with a spectacular view of the mountains that shape the narrow valley of southern Oregon. I lived in this house for a little over a year before buying a condo.

Transitions are rarely smooth, and this one soon proved to be fraught with emotional strain. When I left the desert, my mother was in a nursing facility in Palm Desert. I flew down about six months later when she took a turn for the worse. I visited her every day—to feed her, to take her the things she wanted, and to simply spend time with her. After a month she seemed to be doing fine, so I decided to return home.

Not long after, around three in the morning, I got a call. The voice on the other end said, "Your mom died in her sleep of pulmonary cardiac arrest." And so with her only son far away, my mother departed from this life.

I took a plane to the desert later that morning, in time to make all the memorial service arrangements. My minister at the Church of Religious Science conducted the service. It was very nice, and I felt at peace about her. The absence of my sisters was another story. They had opted to stay in Santa Fe after receiving the news. Although she had raised them from the ages of five and eight, they still didn't think of her as their mother. They had good reason, but it was still painful that they elected not to come.

I had done all I could for my mother in terms of encouraging her spiritual path. The month I was there, I read Yogananda to her and various spiritual works I felt she needed to hear before her departure. We communicated largely without words. I could actually see her ego falling away. I could feel it. There was an unmistakeable radiance to her, and she looked almost young again and peaceful. The game playing, manipulation and frivolity that she used to engage in vanished.

In front of me was a different woman from the one who had raised me—a woman with less weight to bear. I recalled that, in the 1940's, Yogananda had asked her to be a disciple. And I saw her in that moment the way that he must have seen her so many years before, her face full of light. The masks that I could not penetrate during her life dissolved at the time of death. And I returned to Ashland at peace with the death of my mother.

During my first year in Ashland, I really didn't feel ill. I was beginning to slow down a bit, but I was determined not to let the diagnosis of cerebellar ataxia influence my every move. I went on with living, refusing to let physical difficulties overshadow my life. I had used this approach to combat my symptoms from the time I was eighteen. I was not about to let the diagnosis of physical disease change that. And so I was able to fully enter into my life in Ashland. There's a book about the Tudor Guild entitled, *We Didn't Know It Couldn't Be Done*. Well, I refused to acknowledge that I couldn't do certain things, so without that mental constraint I was free to attempt them.

I dove into my astrology practice right away. It was a bit slow at first, but I built up a fair number of clients and was able to pursue my theatrical interests.

I first advertised under the astrology section in the Yellow Pages. People would give me a call and come to the office in my home. I also gained visibility for my business through lectures at the Discovery Center, a kind of new age, metaphysical hub situated in the Mark Antony Hotel in downtown Ashland. I lectured on astrology and related subjects, and attended their brown bag sessions every week. It was at one of these meetings that I met a therapist who got me involved with an intimacy group in Talent. The support this group provided enabled me to explore my feelings about the diagnosis I had received in Palm Springs. This group was a sort of flashback to the group experiences I had had in the desert. We all became very good friends. The group is no longer in existence, but for those two or three years it was a success.

I also did a bit of astrology work through the mail. I was still in touch with clients from the desert—the postal system was a way for us to avoid losing contact.

I've noted a definite difference in the clientele from one place to another. There is a certain spiritual orientation alive in Ashland which seemed to be missing, for the most part, among the people in the Palm Springs desert area. People in Ashland are much more concerned about the condition of their spirits, rather than "Am I going to make money, am I going to succeed, does so-and-so like me, how's my love life?, etc." They're much more concerned with questions like "Am I on the right path? Am I fulfilling my needs?" Not that people in the desert don't have those concerns; they do, but they seem to be more on the back burner. In Ashland, they're in the forefront. I identify with this type of consciousness. It has given me more of a chance to work with people who are very serious in coming to astrology. Many of the clients I've had seem to have intuitively followed their charts in the course of their lives. Also I've found much less ego involvement, which is infinitely more enjoyable to be around. I guess one could say that Ashland is an emblem of the marriage of intellectual and spiritual development.

The clientele has been much more satisfying in terms of their input during the sessions. Their level of intellect and education has astounded me. They're people I can actually engage in intelligent conversations about many subjects, and they have a fairly good grasp of astrology as well. This ultimately made my counseling much easier because I was able to use the proper terminology and still be understood.

Surprisingly, I have met very few other astrologers and psychics in this area. I believe one reason is that I'm a professional, and there are a lot of amateur astrologers around, some of whom are very good, but they seem to have some reticence about associating with a professional. I'm not exactly sure why that is and I wish it were not the case. Maybe they're afraid of showing their lack of formal education. Many of them are exceptional, even brilliant readers but, as I've emphasized before, formal training is extremely important to the integrity of this work.

While the business aspect of my life in Oregon has been rewarding in more ways than I expected, my purpose in moving to the area was to foster a greater connection with the theatre.

The Ashland Connection

I first became aware of Ashland in 1958 while house-sitting for a professor and his wife from the University of California at Riverside. For several summers, they traveled to Oregon. When they returned from their second sojourn north, I asked the professor, "What do you do there, where do you go?" He said, "We go to the Oregon Shakespeare Festival in Ashland. You and Mary ought to go sometime." I was majoring in Shakespeare and Renaissance Studies at the time, so I promised myself that we would go one day.

It didn't re-enter my consciousness until about three years later when I was in graduate school at the University of Oregon in Eugene and working part-time in a bookstore near the campus. The bookstore owner had extra tickets for the Shakespeare Festival and offered them to me. When I got home, I told Mary, and she expressed an interest in going. So acting the role of what I considered a dutiful husband, I said, "Well, honey, why don't you and Vernette (the bookstore owner) go and I'll stay and mind the shop." The practical side of me spoke louder than personal desire, and I knew I would earn extra money for taking care of the store. And Mary, who was almost as much a Shakespeareophile as I was, wanted to go very much—with Vernette. I was disappointed that Mary agreed to go without me, but I realized I had created this domestic scene of self-sacrifice.

Stacey Keach played Henry V that year. They had a great time, and I had a great time too—cleaning up after Vernette's little dashschund. But on the bright side I did earn a few extra bucks. After they returned, the Festival once again slipped to the back shelf of my mind. Then when the time came for me to take a vacation in 1968, I finally came up to Ashland. By this time I was divorced, a librarian and soon to become an astrologer.

I hopped in my VW bug and drove up to Ashland in the summer of 1968. I came for the usual "Stay four days, see four plays" type of thing which was standard at the time. And it was really a wonderful experience. Having made a distinction between film and stage acting very early in life, I acquired a profound respect for those who have genuine talent. I truly enjoy seeing those actors at work. That feeling has never left me.

At the time I was graduated from University of California at Riverside, a man named Jerry Turner from Humboldt State College took over the UCR Drama Department. He was there for about two years before Angus Bowmer hired him as artistic director for the Oregon Shakespeare Festival. Jerry had been coming to Ashland during the summers to act when Angus appointed him. He brought many of the styles he had developed at UCR to Ashland.

When I made it up to Ashland in 1968, I well remember experiencing a kind of shock. I thought, my God, these people approach the plays with the same integrity as I'm used to. The style involves a very clear presentation, an

With Doris at Crater Lake during her 1994 visit to southern Oregon.

insistence that the words and the text be eminently clear. (I was also impressed by the costuming, which we were very aware of in Riverside. Costuming and set design remain very important in Ashland.) A Festival director may take liberties with the interpretation of the text, but they rarely change the words.

In 1968, I was astounded by the production of *Hamlet*, with Richard Risso playing the lead. Although I'd cut my teeth on Olivier, Gielgud and others of their ilk, the 1968 production was full text and brilliantly executed. At this time, the Festival still retained Angus' tradition of doing the plays without a break, as they were written, one scene following another. This meant five hours of sitting out in the old amphitheater. You could have heard a pin drop. The audience was mesmerized. Risso later became one of the deans of the drama department at UCR, thus continuing the long line of connections between my alma mater and the Festival.

At the time, I noticed a clarity of projection in Risso's style that would have been highly regarded at UCR. There was a distinct effort to avoid flowering the text with distracting and unclear speech patterns and movement, relying on the words to convey the meaning of the play. I was so emotionally charged after that production that it took me an hour to return to a functional state. That was truly a memorable season!

Even then, the Festival was noted for a tradition of excellence. I felt very comfortable with the theatrical scene because it reflected many of my own ideas about acting. I also felt more intimately involved with the process because of the connection with Jerry Turner, whose influence on both UCR and the Festival was pervasive then and continues today. Several people currently on the staff and in the acting company are UCR graduates. None is old enough to remember the things I remember, but they are some of the best people there, like Pat O'Scannell, co-director of the Green Show, who received her music training at UCR, and actors like Marco Baricelli, whose father taught at UCR. In discussions with them I could relate to their ideas and concepts of acting.

An interesting sidelight was that, prior to graduation, I had played a secondary role in developing the Drama Department at UCR by encouraging the staff and helping actors rehearse their parts. Our first production had been *Heracles* by Euripides, which was not very popular. But we did the *Second Shepherd's Play* and *Yes is For a Very Young Man* by Gertrude Stein. And we did Machiavelli's *Mandragola*. Also *The Good Woman of Szechuan*. It was *The Good Woman* then, and the Festival produced it in the 1999 season as *The Good Person*, which is much closer to the German.

As I've mentioned, the style of acting that we developed at UCR had a lot to do with the way the style was refined and developed in Ashland. The plays we did were often offbeat. We had a very fine head of the Drama Department at that time named William Sharp, who engineered a lot of this. I remember especially *Juno and the Paycock* by Sean O'Casey. Sharp's assistant was Harold Gould, who is known for his work on *The Golden Girls* and other TV shows. He opted for TV and the money, but he was a fine actor. In *The Duchess of Malfie* he played the best Bosola I've ever seen. Although I loved drama, I didn't major in theatre for the simple reason that I knew I didn't have the desire to devote myself to acting. Being in the English Department and being an advisor to the Drama Department was really the best of both worlds for me.

After that season, I became too busy to return to Ashland until 1974. I was thrilled to be able to introduce that quality of the Shakespeare Festival to my library secretary, Margie. I think it was the first production she had ever seen, and she was absolutely riveted by it to the point of emotional exhaustion.

That season we saw William Saroyan's play, *The Time of Your Life*. This marked my first introduction to the great Mark Murphy, who played Kit Carson, a drunk at a bar.

In the play Carson gives a lengthy monologue, for which Murphy is now quite famous. He reprised the monologue in 1998, at the tribute to Bill Patton in the Elizabethan theatre. It was terrific—the funniest thing I had ever seen. Mark still maintains to this day that it is his favorite role.

When I returned to Fresno that year I was determined to meet the playwright, Bill Saroyan. I had heard that it was impossible to move in library circles in Fresno without running into him. So I waited for him to come into the library where I worked and then one day, lo and behold, on one of his junkets back from Paris, it happened. It was a very stormy day. He went upstairs to look at the used books, which was his usual routine, and right then a bolt of lightning blew out all of the lights. One of the ladies from upstairs called me on the phone and said "Bob, would you please come up here! There's a strange man in a trenchcoat reading all the titles to himself in the used book section, and I'm scared!"

I had a hunch that this man was harmless, but I charged up the stairs anyway and confronted him. I asked him if he would feel better going downstairs until the lights came on and he could see better.

And he said, "No, goddamnit, I'm fine—get the hell out of here." He really said that.

I responded, "Well, I'm afraid I'm going to have to insist that you go downstairs." He got mad as a hornet.

Right at that moment old Mrs. Reilly came around the corner and said, "Well, Mr. Saroyan, how can I help you?" I, of course, did a doubletake as I was about to throw him out the door. Finally, she calmed him down.

For three years after that he wouldn't speak to me, though he'd come in from time to time. Then one day he shook my hand and said, "I hear you're a writer, trying to write. Would you like to talk about it sometime?" And, by God, we went down to my desk in the basement, and he sat there for an hour and talked to me about writing and a writer's life and what he had accomplished. And, of course, it was all centered around William Saroyan, who had a magnificent ego, but the conversation was very interesting and, at times, even awe inspiring.

He felt it necessary to come back to Fresno every once in a while to stimulate his creative juices. He obviously still felt a strong connection to his hometown, and yet he seemed to consider himself superior to everyone in it. But he tried to appear humble. I told him, "I saw your play last summer, and I must say I think it was brilliant, one of the best comedies of its type that I've ever seen." And he said, "Yeah, it was, wasn't it?" However, I felt privileged to meet the man and to have him take the time to talk to me. I also developed a deeper appreciation of comedy and of his particular process in writing. I believe he felt that he had to experience something before he could really write about it. He talked about *The Man On The Flying Trapeze* and writing *The Human Comedy* and *My Name is Aram* and *My Heart Is in the Highlands*. He was a very flamboyant man who threw money around. He talked about losing $5,000 in one night in Las Vegas. It became obvious that he thought the world revolved around him. Maybe that was the key to his success, as with many artists.

He was, in a sense, paving the way for artists of his type who were into the short story and plays. He has also written some very fine essays. He seemed to move easily between different literary forms. I wish that he had written more plays. I definitely think *The Time of Your Life* deserved to win a Pulitzer Prize. At least it was included in The Best Plays series. He must have only had a few plays in him because the vast majority of his published work was in the form of novels and short stories. In any case, it whet my appetite to get more plays like *The Time of Your Life* produced in Ashland.

I made suggestions, and I probably talked to Jerry Turner about doing more of that type of comedy, which they did. In 1974, the Ashland productions were spectacular, especially *Two Gentlemen of Verona* in the Bowmer Theater, which is still remembered. Pictures of that production are in almost every book about Ashland. This first *Two Gents* was beautiful, and, as any actor will tell you, it's a very difficult play to do. It was stupendous; the 1998 production of *Two Gents* paled by comparison. Although the latter was great cabaret theater, it certainly wasn't *Two Gentlemen of Verona*.

My love of drama was shaped in large part by my experiences at UCR and in 1968 and 1974 at the Shakespeare Festival in Ashland. I went through a long period of feeling that the novel was my favorite literary art form; later I felt the short story was, and now I feel that drama is, and tomorrow it may be the essay or... who knows?

In 1975, I decided to come back to Ashland and drove up again from Fresno. That year was also an outstanding season, but in a different way. In the early 1970s, around 1975, the Festival was just beginning to get into the practice of having equity actors as guest players. OSF was still an amateur house, so they brought in an actor for *Hamlet* who was just horrible. The poor chemistry between him and the rest of the cast was evident. I knew several actors in the show, and they told me he'd come into the green room and change the TV without asking, rarely showed up for rehearsals and that finally they had to get a stand-in. That same season they also brought in an equity married couple to play Orlando and Rosalind in *As You Like It*. And the same thing happened. They were prima donnas; backstage they disrupted the cast, and when they got onstage nothing worked—there was no magic. In the 1980s, Pat Patton again brought in an equity person to play *Richard III*, and once again the chemistry was off. There may have been some resentment that these equity actors were getting paid equity rates. And all the amateurs, who were in most cases better actors, were getting paid less. It didn't make for good feelings. Unfortunately, this often came out on the stage, and that was hard to watch.

The most memorable experience in 1975 was *A*

Winter's Tale directed by Audrey Stanley from Stanford and starring James Edmondson. Brilliant, simply brilliant. And le Clanche du Rand as Hermione. She was a startlingly beautiful actress. The perfect Hermione. I had tears in my eyes at the end of that production. Edmondson was also magnificent. I was sitting in the audience next to Bill Patton— crying. He patted me on the back and said, "That's okay, Bob, you can cry. You know, it's okay."

The whole Ashland experience was very sustaining to my life during my years in Fresno, while building the library for EOC and getting on my feet in my astrology business. The struggles of life were made more tolerable by the intellectual and creative stimulation generated, in large, by the theatre. I also reflected on acting as a career. Since my early career in movies, I'd retained a very poor opinion of acting. I now saw that it was indeed an honorable profession. It also affirmed what I already knew—that I had no desire to be an actor myself. Being jobless a great deal of the time is certainly no fun, and most actors have to endure that. In contrast, I was secure in my work, but could find inspiration by going to the theatre and participating in the Round Table.

My state of mind allowed my artistic side to blossom. I felt encouraged to write and to begin several projects during those years. I understood that the creative process could really help people in the end, and what one did with one's imagination could really be of benefit to people. When I came for visits, I observed the changes that theatre had the power to elicit. There were throngs of happy people enjoying themselves, doing something that was ultimately fulfilling. It definitely enabled me to work better. When I went back to Fresno in 1975, I started my astrology business. Then we started the California Shakespearean Festival and Performing Arts Center. In 1978, I was vice president of the Fresno Guild, and we were planning summer productions in Visalia. I said, "Well, I know these men up at the Oregon Festival who will probably be very glad to give us a hand as play advisors, Bill Patton, Jerry Turner

The Round Table in Ashland, 1997. I'm the gentle-
man at the back to the far right with the dapper cap.

and Pat Patton." I called them and asked if they would come down, and all three of them did.

The California Shakespearean Festival had a good start with the help of Bill Patton and Jerry Turner. When they came down, they altered a lot of my suggestions. Homer Swander also came from UC Santa Barbara. At that time he was Director of the Renaissance Institute in Ashland. He was quite an intellect, quite a character, and a very popular educator, a good teacher. We had a lot of fun together. The plays were a way for the average person to escape from the humdrum and enter the realm of imagination.

For me, it was the 1968 experience of *Hamlet* that influenced me to study Shakespeare in more depth. I wanted the intensity of my involvement in theatre to deepen. I wanted to fully understand this literary form — which I believe to be the strongest statement of human values there is. Good theatre brings wonderful things to the surface of the viewer. A great production of a great play illuminates areas of consciousness which had been dormant.

Seeing that brilliant performance by Richard Risso inspired my future path. It took years to fully manifest, but I believe that that point was the seed of my decision to pursue the study of drama. It took a long time for me to throw off the shackles, so to speak, of having to make a living, as a librarian, and even as a counselor, but I knew I wanted to explore human nature through the plays.

The profoundness of the theatre was brewing inside of me. I was beginning to understand what it meant to the progress of my soul and psyche. The California Shakespearean Festival had fallen through, and by 1983 I felt I had to get back up to Ashland—I couldn't stand the desert any longer without a break. It was a very lonely time, and I was beginning to realize that the plays were of great value to me. On one of my previous visits, I had told Angus Bowmer how much the Festival meant to me, so I had some contact with him, too. I realized then that these men of the theatre were actually creative artists, and that they were doing with their lives what they wanted to do. I believe the theatre had freed them to be themselves and to fulfill their creative spirits. And so my visit in 1983 was to be one of my most important experiences in Ashland. As for the season itself, my memory is cloudy, except I recall that Mark Murphy played Hamlet.

It was the best year from a social standpoint, also. I met Mark Murphy, and we became friends. I was beginning to get to know people within and outside the Festival, and I liked the scene. I felt comfortable and alive. I finally realized how different the world of theatre is from the world of film. I found myself relating to people much more personally; I was able to talk to people one-on-one with much more ease and to get the response and reaction that I felt I needed. This, in turn, served to stimulate me to create better relationships with clients.

Due to health reasons, I was unable to return in 1984. I was very disappointed because they did *Troilus and Cressida*, which is my favorite satirical Shakespeare play. But in 1985, I came back for the fiftieth anniversary of the Festival. This was the year I first became involved with the Festival Round Table. I discovered that by paying one flat fee and joining the Round Table, I could get tickets and get all the paperwork done in one fell swoop. This made the mechanics of coming to Ashland and seeing nine plays in two weeks much simpler. Most importantly I now had a format in which to discuss the plays with others, something I sorely missed living in the desert. There were usually about thirty people at the Round Table, all avid playgoers. We would see a play at night, discuss it the next morning for a couple of hours, and then we would see one or two more plays that afternoon or evening, and so it continued for two weeks. A very heavy and tiring routine, but pleasurable because we were getting in and using our creative energies. The process nurtured and stimulated the imagination.

Since 1985, I haven't missed a year. Some of the outstanding productions I've seen include the 1992 *Othello* with Mark Murphy as Iago and Lewan Alexander as Othello. This was a marvelous production, which I at first thought was very poor. But in the Round Table process one's understanding of a particular play had a chance to breathe and the opportunity to evolve because at that time you could see plays more than once, and in this case, since I lived in Ashland, I was able to see *Othello* many times.

When I saw it with the Round Table in June of 1992, I thought Jerry had certainly not directed this according to what I would do, or what UCR would have done. There was a departure here that at first I did not understand. When I saw it on closing night in October, I had come to see it as the definitive *Othello*.

Not only had the direction of the play been unique;

the quality of the production improved over the course of the season. This is a consistent feature of this company. The actors have a wonderful ability to grow and evolve in their roles over the several months of production. To me, this demonstrates the wonderful plasticity of man's imagination, that he can be immersed in something creative and enduring and still have the ability to enhance his skills or, in this case, to evolve in a role.

There are so many things live theatre offers that are not found anywhere else. Although my experience has been limited elsewhere, except for that season in New York in the 1960s, I've had enough people tell me who have seen theatre all over the world that they can't find anything better than what they can get in Ashland.

The theatre sustained me from 1985 until 1998. It enabled me to build my business with a freer mind, knowing I had something to look forward to the following year. I could bear doing what I had to do to survive while I was in the desert, because the next year I could go to Ashland for two weeks,—travel all over the world, and experience different types of people, without ever leaving my theatre seat.

After sitting for three hours or more watching a play, you feel you've had a workout when you get up. It's like playing a game of chess, a total involvement and relaxation of the mind. You're totally focused on the chess board. For good plays, you're totally focused on that stage. In a sense, it's a form of meditation, because your mind is totally focused on that one point, and there's no room for random thoughts—if the production is good. That's what the value was to me. I felt I could really get out of myself and at the same time develop my own creative imagination. When I began to write articles back home in the desert, I'd get ideas from the plays that I'd seen. I felt more value in the creative process. I thought, if these actors can put on a play and use their art form and their creative process to enlighten and improve the people who view it, can I not do a similar thing by presenting articles and materials that will educate and entertain people in the same way?

They are different art forms, but both bring some kind of surcease or relaxation or refinement to the people who read the articles or those who view the plays. If I hadn't felt stimulated by the artistic community in Ashland, I don't believe I'd have accomplished as much as I have.

I was involved with the Round Table for thirteen years. The quality of people who attended the Round Table and the variety of opinions expressed about the plays kept playgoers coming back year after year. Some particpants have been very intelligent critics. Even those who made absolute fools out of themselves in discussions, completely missing the point of the plays, have kept coming back. I saw that the plays did them good. Over the years, I came to realize that no matter what a person's makeup or level of critical sophistication might be, the theatre is an art form that speaks to them in some meaningful way. We do not need to know or understand what that is.

This observation convinced me that theatre is transformative and that I, too, am deepened by the experience. I saw that the plays made something happen to me that I don't fully understand or am not aware of. There is some unconscious aspect to the experience that makes it more meaningful to me. I can't say what would have happened if I had continued living in the desert, but I know the landscape of my imagination would have unfolded differently without the Ashland experience.

When I moved to Ashland in 1992, I was determined to deepen my experience with the Round Table and increase my involvement with the plays. I was not disappointed. I feared living in Ashland might taint my previous experience. I wondered, "Will the magic of this creative alchemy be lost?"

Instead my relationship to theatre actually deepened as I became more connected with the Festival behind the scenes. I wasn't able to expand my involvement as much as I would have liked because I was busy building the astrology business. Still I got acquainted with the staff, stage managers, production crews, even custodians. I became closer to many of the actors and began to volunteer as an usher. The more I did, the more the magic of theatre became real and meaningful. I didn't lose my sense of perspective; the perspective deepened, and I came to understand even more that this process of writing and producing plays can really be quite significant to one's own world.

I gave informal lectures in the lounge, and people would often ask my opinion of the plays. I took people around and gave them tours, although I wasn't an official tour guide. I had hoped to become more involved in the creative mechanism of the theatre, perhaps through play selection. Instead, I got involved with the Ashland New Plays Festival, making selections for the 1999 season. It involved reading and discussing many plays with like-minded people—the kind of in-depth challenge I really enjoy. It was a perfect outgrowth of the Round Table for me. Although they are unrelated events and two different groups, they have in common the idea of people getting together to discuss the plays, and what they mean to our lives.

Theatre has given me a foundation on which to build my life. I've come to understand that in looking for answers to life's dilemmas, which each one of us faces one way or another, if you look closely enough at the plays—I don't mean just Shakespeare but the plays of O'Neill and Pinter, Arthur Miller, and Ibsen, and other good, classical dramatists—answers can be found right there on the stage. It's unlikely that one's situation will mirror the exact context of a fictional play, but the incidents in the plays will contain solutions that can be applied to one's life. That's why I've often used them in counseling clients, because I would see incidents that related to what they were experiencing. Playgoers who approach the plays with an attitude that encourages self-discovery find their experience much richer, more rewarding, and enduring.

These various involvements and uses of the theatre

have been marvelous for me. After so many years, the Festival has truly become part of me and my work.

As I've said, the plays opened me up to being able to practice astrological counseling more effectively. Although my main interest in Ashland has always been the Festival, when I relocated I knew I had to generate some income. I wasn't interested in making a lot of money and didn't need to. I had investments and proceeds from the sale of property in the desert, so I cut my prices from $95 to $45 per chart. And I think it was a good move, because it certainly brought people in. I soon bought a condominium on Hersey Street, a beautiful piece of property, with flowering dogwood and a creek that flows through the backyard. I had clients in my home office on a fairly steady basis. There were slow periods, but I had enough to do with writing, trying to keep my library current, and the Festival (ushering and other volunteer work), and other involvments in the community. These activities took up most of my time. Stepping back for a moment to regard all my various activities, I see that I have been quite happy, fulfilled and busy the past seven years.

The most rewarding part of my practice has been watching people be helped by what I could offer them through astrological counseling. I'd gotten into the healthcare network in Ashland, so when people came to me with very serious problems, I could easily refer them to a psychologist or psychiatrist. Those who came to me with smaller problems I could handle myself. There were many who came in disturbed or upset. One or two sessions would often give them enough insight and fortitude to take steps to dramatically change their lives. That has been as rewarding to me in Ashland as it was in the desert.

Being more intellectually fulfilled than in the desert, or even in Fresno, enabled me to give more to my clients. I often used situations from the plays to relate to problems that would appear in my clients lives, for instance, referring to the role of jealousy in a play like *Othello*.

A client might get suspicious of someone close, as

Othello was suspicious of Cassio. I would caution them not to listen to the Iago voice, but rather to listen to the voice of spirit and common sense. One fellow was insanely suspicious of his girlfriend; he didn't want to be away from her at all because he was afraid she was going to sleep with everyone in town if he turned his back. His jealousy subsided—for a little while anyway. Even so, eventually the woman left him. She'd become a client also, by his referral (one satisfied client leads to another!). She was annoyed because he followed her around, and once came to her apartment at three in the morning to check up on her. It was truly a kind of madness, as the "green eyed monster" of jealousy always is.

Individually they were both quite appealing, but very young. I like to think that he was helped by our sessions, which pointed out his fear of abandonment. When he left the last time, he was going with another girl, and had realized that he had to trust in order to have a satisfactory relationship. I illustrated this idea with planetary configurations—these always convince a client. The only way to deal with such problems is to go through the situation with the clients and deal with the causes as best as you can. His first girl had a lot more sense than he did. She was older, too. But I think he matured through the work we did. So astrology can do those little things, and that's also how I used the plots of the plays.

To encourage most people is easier than one might imagine. Show them their planetary relationships and their untapped potential. Tell them to get rid of their fear and use some of their potential to manifest their many talents. Such work has helped many overcome the fear of taking on additional responsibilities. I've counseled some actors who have gotten sick during the run of a play and others who came to realize they needed to leave the Festival to advance their art. They wonder how can they survive and get a job. And I would just talk to them, go over the chart and show them their potentials and what kinds of roles they should pursue—whether they're a leading man or lady or a character actor or supporting actor. I've seen several of them who are not here anymore, and they've gone off to do Berkeley or South Coast Repertory, or somewhere else. They're working and they're succeeding at what they want to do. Now, it's very likely that they may be back here one day, but it's very important for them to leave in order to grow. Then, if and when they come back, they can utilize the potential that they have perfected. Several of them still keep in contact with me every few months, or maybe once a year they call to get an update on their chart.

Such a procedure takes little effort on my part. I put all the data into the computer and run it off. I know that several of the actors follow the daily affirmations I give them to govern their lives. Once an actor became a client, the word-of-mouth got around, and others would call. It really has been very gratifying to me.

I have had a few Horary clients up here (Horary is the art of finding lost objects through astrology). Once somebody wanted me to find their pussycat. After much searching, they found it. I told them if they didn't go out and search for the cat in the ways that were delineated in the chart, they would lose the energy and the moment, and the cat would be gone. I found one woman's granddaughter who had run off. The woman didn't know where she was, and she was frantic. She called me and asked me if I could do a chart and tell her where the girl was. It turned out she was in Spain.

I didn't even have the girl's birth date and other relevant information. The Horary works on a whole different set of principles. All I had to do was take the time that the question was asked by the woman and do a chart of that time. It gets very complex, but that's a good lead-in to explain the union between all parts of the universe and the person, because our thoughts are also in tune with the cosmos. When the woman was prompted to ask the question, the answer existed. It is God's symbols, the signs and planets of the zodiac, and the knowledge of how to read them that are going to lead to the answer. That's what happened.

Another time I found a lost article. The client looked in the closet under all the shoes as I had instructed, and there was the lost article. This type of astrology occasionally misses because it's so complicated. Each step has to be followed precisely. This is another reason I personally prefer working with natal astrology, the psychology of human beings—it isn't so fixed. There are more variables and more room for intuition, making it more an art than a science.

Mainstream or natal astrology is concerned with helping people and finding out what's going on in their lives. Doing this work has been a very rewarding trip for me. Throughout my career clients have liked my work, and I've had good relationships with them, which has been very pleasing. I've had no fly-by-night clients in my last six years, either. They must go to somebody else, and God knows there are plenty of astrologers to go to. I've been blessed to have really enjoyed the people I've worked with. I would like to have done more, and I regret not being able

My sisters, Harriet, left, with a young friend, and Pat (Nereyani Ma), right, after becoming a Hindu monk.

to continue my practice. It seems ironic that I can't do it any more, as business was picking up when I got sick.

My sister, Harriet, is now a primary person in my life. For years I had tried to get her to move to Ashland from San Diego. She finally took the challenge in 1997 and seems very content in Ashland, having herself become involved with the Festival. I'm glad for her sake. For my own part, having her nearby has been extremely good for me. She has offered me a wellspring of friendship and has helped me deal with the ravages of my illness.

My relationship with Harriet has changed over the last few years. I think this has a lot to do with our connection on the spiritual plane. Harriet is a Zen Buddhist (my other sister is a Hindu monk—we're an eccentric bunch, I guess!) and I have truly witnessed an opening in her as a result of her practice. Harriet and I have also developed an extremely fine intellectual relationship based on mutual caring and love for each other. We're closer now than we have ever been, having developed a deep respect for each other as individuals. Although we're very different in many ways, we do think a lot alike. We don't always feel

alike though. I tend to be much more emotional than she.

We often agree in our evaluation of a play, except if it's something that's extremely emotional, such as a many Shakespearean tragedies. She tends to define things intellectually. I've learned from this example, that we learn our individual tendencies through our reactions to theatre. Of course, there are some plays that bring the emotional and the intellectual together which she relates to. The emotional needs an intellectual couch or prod. But generally, if it's emotional, like *King Lear*, she does not appreciate it as much. Whereas if a play is highly intellectual, like Simenon or P.D. James, a mystery or something that appeals mostly to the mind, I'm not that enthralled, but she is. I think she related to *School for Scandal* more than I did. I appreciated the exquisite writing and the wit. But, for me, it's just not on a par with *King Lear* or *A Midsummer Night's Dream*.

So, in contrast to Fresno, where a dearth of theatre prevented me from in depth development of my interests, in Ashland I have been able to fulfill intellectual and emotional needs by intense participation in the play process. In Ashland, I have been involved with the stories of the plays, the plots, seeing them several times, and getting to know the actors. I have spoken with numerous actors about what it is like being in the company and mounting the plays. Actors also often participate in the Round Table. They give a talk and answer questions, which is often very stimulating. They make participants feel like they are part of the production. This process has been immensely fulfilling for me and has put a cap on lots of my questions about my life and being a librarian, building a library, and being involved in the creative process through writing. The plays pulled a great many unexplainable feelings and events together, and pointed out similarities in things apparently unlike. I've been able to see all these threads come together in the creative process of theatre, which I really would like to have done a long time ago, but that wasn't my karma or destiny.

I do believe I was led to Ashland seven years ago. This town of dogwood and rolling hills, of theatre and like-minded souls has been the final coda of my education. It's sorrowful that my business had to come to a halt just at the time when it was really flowering. My involvement, too, with the Festival has to come to an end.

I cherish the memory of being involved in the production of *Magic Fire* which now would not be a possibility. If I were physically able I would devote myself even more to the Festival as I've devoted myself to the study of Shakespeare over the years. I believe I have a lot of depth and background to offer. In 1999, I could have helped with *The Three Musketeers* because Dumas was a major influence on me as a teenager.

While I did lecture informally on Shakespeare, I never did so in an academic setting. In a town like this everyone has Shakespeare on the brain, so I may have felt a bit intimidated. I shouldn't have because I've successfully published and lectured on the Bard before. I took all of Michael Girard's classes in Shakespeare that were offered at Southern Oregon University beginning in 1994. I met a lot of people in those groups and they have all been my teachers, as I have been theirs. Some have become clients. We have had dinner and discussions at their homes. We have talked about Shakespeare, plays and philosophy and other intellectual concepts.

I also enjoyed a social life and friendships outside of the Festival. From 1993 to 1994, there was an intimacy group that met in Talent, just North of Ashland. Being involved with that group was a real turning point for me. It was a tremendous source of emotional support and encouraged me to use my potential and to continue to do the work I needed to do. There were about fifteen people in the group, and many of us became friends. I learned a number of things about myself which is always the case with friendship—we become a mirror for each other. I had one friend in particular, Joan Lavelle, who was a great source of inspiration. She was in her late 60s. We had a very close relationship—she gave me rides to the group; I did her chart and took her to social events. We shared our hearts and minds, and our conversations were a celebration of the metaphysical.

I also attended the Unity Church (not to be confused with the Unitarians) in town for awhile. At that time they were still meeting at the Mark Antony, I think until 1994. Then, in 1995, they moved down to Main Street. It was good at first because, like the church in the desert, it kept me going spiritually. I could go there and get my charge for the week. It was also another source of clients and social contacts. The Unity Church and Church of Religious Science are closely related. They are very similar philosophically.

There are at least two good friends from the intimacy group that continue today. We'd attend lectures and readings, concerts, etc., together. One place was at the Old Siskiyou Barn. A lot of the same people are involved with the Festival, so we have a double connection. And there's no end of things to talk about. And I think the church, the intimacy group, and the concerts were probably the three biggest things for me in the last six years, outside the Festival. Through my clients and friends, I have met a wider spectrum of people in Ashland socially, so I feel more at home here than I ever have before. Even at the desert, where I knew a lot of people and had good friends, they weren't always on my wavelength. I always had to make adjustments when I was in their presence. I didn't want to make demands on them that probably neither one of us could really deal with. Somebody would end up being hurt or embarrassed. I never felt the need to compromise in that way in Ashland. It's the first place I've ever lived where I really felt free in that way, and it has been a great experience.

So, Ashland became the fulfillment of my dreams, intellectually and creatively, professionally and personally. These elements were combined through involvement in the theatre—my friends were Round Table participants and actors and others of like interests. Finally I was with people who shared my interests and knowledge. Little did I know that what I found was to be so short lived.

But it is too easy to look at life with regret for what cannot be. I can't look at my participation as being "over." Instead I begin to look at my life as taking a new direction, and who knows what the next year will bring in terms of discovering new things about myself. New surprises will occur and there may be things I never even dreamed of just waiting over the horizon.

Chapter 19

THE FINAL STAGE

Reason thus with life:
If I do lose thee, I do lose a thing
That none but fools would keep.
> —Measure for Measure

My disease hit hard around December of 1996. The Cerebellar Ataxia seemed to be under control fairly well at that time, but then, I believe, the ALS started to kick in. A number of external events occurred at the time which may have had some bearing on the manifestation of my symptoms. For instance the New Year's Flood of '97 might have triggered something. And it was then that Doris told me she had married. Still my symptoms were controllable. Then June of 1998 rolled around, smote my body a heavy blow, crippling my hands and to a degree my ability to communicate verbally. Since then it's been an extremely rapid decline.

I felt good for most of my life, except for the shaking, which I expected to go away as I got older. Of course, it didn't. I was to put it out of my mind for the most part, until after the MRI in 1992, when I knew there was definitely something wrong. There were times when I was a bit dizzy previous to that date. And I was not able to run, because my gait was awkward. But I didn't dwell on my condition. A healthy observer might think to live with such a burden to be a courageous act. But, as history has demonstrated, human beings are very adaptable.

The dizziness started in 1983. My eyes were not working together as well. I didn't think much of it, except when I went to Ashland to see plays. I noticed my peripheral vision was off. I would see four instead of two actors on the stage . It was then that I began to worry. I had vision therapy, which seemed to work for a while, but then in June of 1998 my hands started crippling up, and I started going to doctors and specialists. They discovered the ALS in addition to Ataxia.

For quite a while, my physicians treated my symptoms. This wouldn't have been so bad—but everything, feet, hands, eyes, speech, were beginning to fade. The treatment for specific symptoms seemed useless.

In spite of everything I was feeling relatively very well. And then one night in August of 1997, I fell in my living room. I really scrunched my sacroiliac and my lumbar region. It was very painful, and I thought for sure I'd done some serious damage. They took x-rays, and nothing was broken. They kept me in the hospital a couple of days and then released me. I recovered from that, so I got halfway through the play season, and things were going very well. I was ushering and volunteering and doing many other things just as happily as before. Then it just started one night. I noticed my hands—I couldn't move my index finger. I wondered what the hell was going on. And as the days went by, it got worse. I went to a chiropractor and a hand specialist. They thought it was carpal tunnel disease, which it wasn't. I went to several specialists in Medford. The final ALS diagnosis was made by Dr. Michael Narus, a neurologist.

Not being able to move digits is an ALS symptom. It is very consistent with that particular disease, but not necessarily with Cerebellar Ataxia. Also the muscles in my body were constantly twitching, which is another ALS symptom. My hands didn't start contracting until June of 1998. Before that time they were just fine. I guess the slowness in the gait is also related to ALS. The inability of my eyes to focus or to work together is a part of the

Ataxia and not ALS. I have perfect vision in each eye—they just don't want to work together. It's like a pair of binoculars that is constantly out of focus. You can't bring them into alignment, so I wear a patch when I read. That is a symptom of Ataxia more than ALS.

I don't advocate support groups for someone who might have this disease. I don't recommend them because they tend to be depressing. You begin to compare yourself to others, and that breeds anxiety. One either thinks, "Am I going to get like that?" or "why aren't I as vibrant as that person?" Groups are more important for care givers. I've talked to others with Ataxia; generally they are depressed and unresponsive. I don't want to be around that. It is important to be as independent as you can be for as long as you can.

I've had Ataxia since 1987; at least that's when it was first diagnosed. The diplopia has been gradually getting worse. The specialists in Medford who were diagnosing me said they thought it was ALS. They said that's going to really be unique, because they knew I had Cerebellar Ataxia, and to have ALS on top of it is extremely unusual. They had never seen that combination before. They recommended that I go to Oregon Health Sciences University in Portland for a confirmation of the diagnosis. I did go to Portland in December of 1998, and it was confirmed that I have both disorders. The speech is slurred because of both ALS and Ataxia, which is a characteristic of both. I would describe my speech at this time as slow. I have extreme difficulty articulating. My energy is increasingly diminished, and I get a quavering in my jaw and tongue as the muscles in the face are wasting away. There's nothing I did that caused this—it just happened—and for some unknown reason I was destined to go through it. Maybe for some medical knowledge or something. I don't know, but I can't let it get me down. And it won't. I've been spiritually prepared for dealing with this kind of thing, although I never in the world thought it would progress this fast. But it is, so you just take it one day at a time. I look at the richness of my life and what I've accomplished, and those memories keep me going from day to day because they can't take that away. The mind is not affected. Maybe by Ataxia, but they don't even know that for sure. Doctors look at me kind of blankly because they don't know what to do for me. The doctor in Portland explained to me that I have a slow case of Ataxia, but the ALS is progressing very rapidly. They sort of feed each other. The ALS probably would not proceed as rapidly if I did not also have Ataxia. It's just one of those things, I guess. I look back on my memories and the life that I've lived, and though it's not been a great life, it's been a good life. Like the song says, I have no regrets! At least too few to mention. Who knows what's around the bend? I don't. I'm not afraid of dying; in fact, with this body, I sort of look forward to getting rid of it. Maybe on the astral plane I'll be able to be a lot more than I am now because, at this point, my hands are literally tied! Boy, are they tied! It's getting to the point where life is just not fun. You keep going on from day to day because, quite tritely, hope does spring eternal. I think all this physical and speech therapy that I've had is all well and good if you're going to recover, but as far as we all know, no matter how much therapy I receive, I'm not go-

June 1999, with my sisters and friend, Terttu Harker. Terttu and my sisters have devoted much time to my happiness, including reading to me.

ing to completely recover. I've got a terminal disease.

It is a hard judgment to decide whether you want to go on living with these symptoms. People like Stephen Hawking, the brilliant scientist confined to a wheelchair for thirty years now, go on. Their minds are fine; they still are able to taste life. I believe that I, too, will always have a creative role in life. I hope the diseases never reach a point where I feel life is unbearable. It *is* a temptation at times to let go.

There is a book that just came out that really has inspired me a lot called *Tuesdays with Morrie*. It's about an ALS patient, a professor, whose former student comes and spends every Tuesday with him. Dying is a matter of the body. Death is a matter of the heart. As Morrie approaches the heart, shedding the dying body becomes easier and easier. That's almost the way I feel. Let's get it over with! In a play that the Festival did a few years ago called *The Illusion* at the Bowmer Theater, one of the lines sums up what I feel; "Well, if not in this lifetime, the next." I feel very strongly that that is so. I don't feel that this is my last trip around; I haven't got that much hubris. My soul has a lot more to learn about life. If it didn't, I might not be sitting here with two diseases. Like the doctor in Portland said: "You've been hit by lightning twice." I don't know if I would endorse being hit by lightning, but it's a miracle that I'm still alive. You do the best you can with this life, but I think if you have enough reassurance that there's more than just this life, then it is not quite so hard to take, being struck by lightning twice. It's hard to say how much longer I'll be able to articulate. The loss of speech is an artifact of Ataxia and ALS. But whatever happens, I am determined not to harbor any regrets.

One can have all sorts of fears and imaginings about illness. I expected my body to begin failing me when I was 85 or 90, not at 62. And so at first I found myself in shock to be in this position, my body betraying me at every turn. Of course my physical disintegration is a struggle, but I'm at peace with it now. Actually, I'm surprised I'm taking it with such equanimity.

There remains a certain beauty to my existence. The love given by those who care for me provides an additional spiritual sustenance to my life and hopefully to theirs as well. I share my life with them. My physical and emotional life is in their care. They in turn share a part of themselves.

My health care is somewhat of a challenge for my providers. They know what do with a patient who has ALS but not with one who also has Ataxia. My symptoms don't reflect the usual patterns. Dizziness is one of my main frustrations. I'm not sure when I'm going to lose my balance. It makes things difficult when I have to expend so much energy for trivial things. But as time has gone by, I've let go of my former lifestyle. There is a philosophical benefit to a relatively slow debilitation. I've lost interest in doing certain things I used to do, which makes letting go much easier.

For example, I used to love going out to eat. I would have predicted depression or at least deep regret at the loss of this activity, but as the time approached when it was too difficult to go out I merely said: "Well, I don't want to go—it's lost its flavor, so to speak." I felt this way about going to plays for a while, too. It was just too difficult to maneuver myself there. Now I go in a wheelchair. My experience is just in the play, not in the struggle with the world outside it. Perhaps this is what it is like to live in a play, a la Pirandello's *Six Characters in Search of an Author*. I still hope to see more theatre. I didn't believe I would be able to see plays in the 1999 season, but already I have been blessed to see three. The theatre remains both a connection to the world, but also to the spirit. It helps me connect the lines of my life.

I might ask, "Why did this have to happen to me, a person who lived a decent life and treated the body as a temple?" Science has no answers. The answer lies with God. While my relationships, and my studies help tremendously to lift me up, the inevitable disintegration of

My loving caregiver Jennifer Moon whose spirit and humor keep me on my toes. The love she and my other caregivers have given has truly been a blessing in the latter stages of my life.

the body leads to periods of depression. But this does not deplete the riches I now have in my life. Rather it attests to the fact that my life is still full—the ups and downs of existence still apply.

As far as ordering one's life, I believe one has to take it one day at a time. As Heraclitus said, "You can't step in the same river twice," so don't worry about it. It takes much less energy to live in the moment than it takes to create an elaborate plan which may never come to pass. As Shakespeare wrote, "There is nothing good or bad but thinking makes it so."

I find myself associating with people more involved in the spiritual side of life. I am studying scriptures of all religions, examining the different paths to God, through the teachings of Yogananda, Jesus, and Edgar Cayce. My relationships with these spiritual masters have become more important than the people I might see socially. What

I'm facing is a kind of journey, an adventure, and it's not to be feared. When you let go of fear you realize the love that is life.

There are many things that are becoming apparent to me as I approach the time of my departure. I now see my work as an astrologer as significant in the eyes of God. But as one approaches the end of this life, you want what you do to be as close to God as possible. This makes what you have to endure much easier. I wish that I had gotten to know Yogananda better when I was a child. I feel very close to his Self Realization teachings now. I hear the authentic voice, God's truth, in his teachings. With the help of these and other teachings, I am consciously taking my religious beliefs to a higher level.

I listen to tapes by spiritual masters. I listen to devotional music. My sister Harriet and I read the Bhagavad-Gita together. I have a thirst for commune with the divine. I understand things now that I never did before. I relate to life differently, more purely perhaps. I've re-listened to lectures on human potential from fifteen to twenty-five years ago. I can see now that I was being prepared for this time— my life's work, in a way, can be seen as a preparation for dying.

When I was young and my body full of fire, I opened to life as it was offered to me. I created a world to inhabit. It is a different act of creation now, but no less joyful. We are called upon to change direction many times in life. Indeed, I have had to alter my course along the way. When a plateau is reached, we may rest for a while. Then we go on, for so we must to enter the garden of our spirit's unfolding. Without the challenges of my past, I would not have the strength to face the challenges of the present. I have a great deal of peace with God now. It is not merely resignation—it is acceptance of life in all of its beauty and sorrow. Our days in this world are composed of pleasant and unpleasant events that we have to work through. The journey is learning how to accept both, for it is often through the negative that the positive emerges.

Progressive physical debilitation allows one to let go, to accept things with more grace. Attachment to the physical form gradually falls away and with it the idea of a fixed self. I'm not the same man who worked in libraries and counseled people. But the passing of that time in my life is not a measure of loss. I have no use for regret. What matters is attention to the landscape of my soul. I don't want to leave. I still feel a longing to reach out to the world, to offer a song, perhaps more so than ever before. But to everything there is a season, and finally it is the relationship with the universe and God that matters. W.B.Yeats, the great Irish poet of the twentieth century, wrote "There is but one history and that is the soul's."

Namasté

The Final Reference

When the answer ceases
to intimidate the question,
And no fears of living
Stand in the practised way;
When in a light-filled day
There is no contradiction,
And you welcome evening
with a living, active grace
Of meeting joy in crowning
All your days with new dimension
With life learned turning
As you kneel to pray;

Then will the question be the prayer
Which before was merely answer.

Editor's Afterword

I first met Bob Scott in mid-October 1998 in the upstairs coffeehouse of Bloomsbury Books in Ashland, Oregon.

At first our conversation was a bit stilted as Bob tried to gage how it would be to work with me. He explained his illness, cerebellar ataxia, and how it had progressed to the point where his hands were functionally useless. He could no longer type or handwrite as his fingers had curled up and he could straighten them only through great will.

I found myself tentative. The work with Bob would be a challenge I was not sure I was prepared to undertake for several reasons. It would require several months of interviewing, writing, and rewriting. More significantly, I was not yet convinced he and I spoke the same language. His dress seemed to belie the life experience he'd summarized for me as poet, Shakespeare scholar, astrologer. He wore polyester slacks, a golf shirt, clay-colored shoes. And a stylish hat.

However, I did find it easy to talk with him, outlining my experience, and what I envisioned our working relationship would be. To myself, I thought, if we meet again I can assess the writing he has done so far, and whether I can be responsible to his needs.

Bob called one or two days later, saying he'd like to meet the next week. When the time came he could no longer make it up to the coffehouse, let alone the steep cliff of stairs to my office. I offered to meet him at his home, an offer he profusely thanked me for. I believe he feared I would not be willing to work with him in his home. I decided if he was willing to take a chance on me, I would go ahead with the project. I began to look forward to working with a man whose life seemed so different than mine.

When I entered his home I was hit by a visceral sensation. Although I did not know he was terminally ill at the time, I became a bit overwrought. I recollected the dying of family members. Did I want to undertake such a project, establishing an intimate relationship with a man who might soon die?

Yes. I considered it a grave responsibility and an honor.

I put doubts aside, and began working with Bob on translating his manuscript chapters into a format compatible with my computer system. Within two weeks we began a series of intensive interviews on tape, from which the last third of Bob's life story would be constructed. Bob's memory was and remains prodigious. He knew what he wanted to write but was physically unable to accomplish the task. During these sessions, my job was to draw Bob deeper into his subject matter. As I familiarized myself with the chapters he had already written, we backtracked and reviewed various periods or events and relationships about which I was unclear and wanted to explore further.

After several weeks of interviewing and talking, I became close to Bob-a man whose life history was so contrary to mine and yet bore astonishing resemblances, even down to his first and last experience with hunting: a B.B. gun to the head of a lizard.

Toward the end of November, Bob informed me that a local neurologist had tentatively diagnosed him with ALS (Lou Gehrig's Disease). In December he saw a specialist in Portland who confirmed the diagnosis. At the most Bob had two years to live. The book took on greater urgency. He unflinchingly spoke with me about death and dying and living with a terminal disease.

The disintegration of Bob's body progressed, but the sense I had of encroaching death had all but receded. Still I witnessed his struggle to speak, walk, lift an arm to shake hands; and once the agony I inflicted as I hugged him good-bye and he tried to reciprocate, pushing his atrophying muscles to the limit. His cry tore at me and I remembered my father's pain while dying of cancer several years previously. I began to see my editor's role as both watchkeeper of his life and as the porter who was ushering him toward the unknown. The book became his testament to what he had lived and accomplished as well as the umbilical chord which kept him connected to this life.

Bob's life and his book became a mirror for examining my own life. I saw almost daily how Bob came to terms with his mortality; he admitted to bouts of grief and depression but he was spiritually reconciled to the disposal of his body. I doubt anyone can truly imagine an experience like his: to retain full retention of one's mental faculties and watch, sometimes as a rueful observer, as the muscles of one's body stop working, and then dissolve. In the face of all, his sense of humor and deep belly laugh continue to grace all who come in contact with him. His last months have truly been a "profile in courage."

One can define Bob's life as one of service and the search for the place he might call home. As a librarian, arts organizer, and most importantly as an astrological counselor he has provided hundreds of people with a key to knowledge, inspiration and direction. Despite many hardships and living with disease all of his adult life, Bob has retained a commitment to wrangle meaning out life. Following his story has been truly inspiring.

His example has taught all who have come to know and love him that our time is limited and that we have an obligation not to take for granted the life we are given. These are not new lessons, but they are all the more real by knowing Bob. In the face of death Bob has not become bitter. Instead I have witnessed an unfolding, as he accepts and embraces the confines of his world. His love for art and language have continued to be fulfilled through books and poetry read to him by caregivers and friends.

Still, I know that he was ready to let go months ago, cut the chord that tethered him to the earth. It is difficult to observe the continued disintegration of his body. It is increasingly difficult to understand his speech. He is now on oxygen twenty-four hours a day, and spends his awake hours in a wheelchair. Yet, against all odds, and the urging of his hospice nurses, he still eats solid food, finding pleasure in simple things. He continues to grow and love the life he has, just as he determined he would when he concluded chapter 18 two months ago:

> "I can't look at my participation as being 'over.' Instead I begin to look at my life as taking a new direction, and who knows what the next year will bring in terms of discovering new things about myself. New surprises will occur and there may be things I never even dreamed of just waiting over the horizon."

Jonah Bornstein
July 10, 1999